Praise for *Move, Play, and Learn with Smart Steps*

"A fabulous resource for teachers, parents, and anyone wanting to understand child development and really stimulate children's learning. Combining a career-long interest in brain development research with practical applications, the authors have developed this huge collection of background knowledge and useful teaching ideas. This text should be compulsory reading in all early childhood teacher training courses but is equally valuable to parents and other adults in the lives of young children." **—Janet Channon,** cofounder and director of Kids Music Company

"Very accessible and loads of fun! Placing physicality at the heart of learning, all the principles of strong ECE practice are skillfully harnessed. Superb color images illustrate how movement can be joyfully integrated into daily life with everyday resources, enabling every child to 'follow nature's plan.' The depth of knowledge regarding being physically active from birth matched with a clear explanation of how learning takes place through body-brain develo gives this book a valuable place in the work of those caring about children and their throughout the early years." **—Jan White,** early childhood consultant specializi play and author of *Every Child a Mover*

"A gold mine! This well-thought-out and organized resource explains the stages o. motor development in concise language and clear graphics, making it accessible and er-standable to parents and professionals alike. *Move, Play, and Learn with Smart Steps* offers a multitude of activity ideas and includes fun and creative modifications for kids of all ages and abilities. I recommend this book to parents, teachers, and therapists who are looking for ways to enrich the motor skills of their kids." **—Brenda Richards, OTR/L,** pediatric occupational therapist, author, co-owner of the Center for LifeSkills, and codirector of TimberNook of Greater Cleveland

"A must-have resource for all those engaged and involved in the lives of young children in whatever capacity. A uniquely refreshing combination of practical know-how and underpinning knowledge, bound by a profound belief and understanding of the role movement plays in supporting overall development. Easily accessible for parents—there are wonderful ideas for promoting active play—this book also provides professionals with a clear framework to inform and support their daily practice. Well-written and beautifully produced. A 'smart step' would be to source this book, now!" **—Dr. Lala Manners,** director of activematters

"A wonderfully clear step-by-step activity series providing children with a 'rich diet' of movement and play. The very easy-to-understand-and-do series of everyday activities builds the critical body and brain interrelationship essential for children's optimal learning and transition into school. This outstanding book sets a new benchmark in children's activity programs to develop their bodies and brains. It is the most scientifically advanced program currently available and a must for educators, childcare providers, and parents who want to provide the best possible start for their children!" **—Graham D. Dodd, Ph.D.,** founder and chair of TriSkills Australia and Fellow & Life Member of Australian Council for Health, Physical Education and Recreation

Move, Play, and Learn

with

Smart Steps

Sequenced Activities to Build the Body and the Brain

Gill Connell, Wendy Pirie, and Cheryl McCarthy

free spirit
PUBLISHING®

Library of Congress Cataloging-in-Publication Data
Names: Connell, Gill, author. | Pirie, Wendy, author. | McCarthy, Cheryl, author.
Title: Move, play, and learn with smart steps : sequenced activities to build the body and the brain (birth to age 7) / Gill Connell, Wendy Pirie, M.H.Sc., and Cheryl McCarthy.
Description: Golden Valley, MN : Free Spirit Publishing, 2016. | Includes bibliographical references and index.
Identifiers: LCCN 2015039674 (print) | LCCN 2015051406 (ebook) | ISBN 9781631980244 (paperback) | ISBN 1631980246 () | ISBN 9781631980749 (Web pdf) | ISBN 9781631980756 (epub)
Subjects: LCSH: Movement education. | Physical education for children—Study and teaching—Activity programs. | Learning—Physiological aspects. | Thought and thinking—Physiological aspects. | BISAC: EDUCATION / Preschool & Kindergarten. | EDUCATION / Physical Education.
Classification: LCC GV452 .C659 2016 (print) | LCC GV452 (ebook) | DDC 372.86/8—dc23
LC record available at http://lccn.loc.gov/2015039674

Charts on pages 6, 8, 12–17, 32, and 44–45 are used or adapted from *A Moving Child Is a Learning Child* by Gill Connell and Cheryl McCarthy, copyright © 2014, and are used with permission of Free Spirit Publishing.

Front cover photo credit: © Jun Mu | Dreamstime.com
Back cover photo credit: © Sergey Kolesnikov | Dreamstime.com

Editors: Marjorie Lisovskis and Christine Zuchora-Walske
Cover and interior design: Michelle Lee Lagerroos and Colleen Rollins
Illustrations: Heidi Panelli

10 9 8 7 6 5 4 3 2
Printed in the United States of America

Free Spirit Publishing Inc.
6325 Sandburg Road, Suite 100
Minneapolis, MN 55427-3674
(612) 338-2068
help4kids@freespirit.com
www.freespirit.com

Dedication

Over my many years of teaching I've stood in awe of children's intuitive ability to create what they need through the pure act of play. Each time they play, they learn. Each time I play with them, I learn more than they do.

To my favorite playmates and greatest life teachers: Becky, Milly, Lucy, Caitlin, Jacob, and the twinkles of joy I have yet to meet but hold in my heart for the day we will play together.

G.C.

To my three children, Kaleb, Max, and Carter, who wow me every day with their inspiration, joy in being active kids, and amazing attitude toward life.

To my husband Colin, whose motivation, drive, and energy I could not live without.

W.P.

To my sister Jill, for your unyielding, relentless belief in me. I love you.

To Gill, for showing me that changing the world is simply a matter of choice. Thank you for choosing me. TBIABS.

C.M.

Contents

List of Digital Reproducible Forms

Download these printable forms at **www.freespirit.com/smart-steps-forms**. Use the password **2learn**.

Digital content includes **all the activities in Part 2** as well as the following:

Introduction

//

Welcome to *Move, Play, and Learn with Smart Steps*!

It may not look like it, but every wiggle and every giggle of early childhood is power packed with learning. That's right. *Learning.* That's because movement and play are nature's chosen tools for developing the body *and* the brain. Strengthening and supporting that natural development is what *Move, Play, and Learn with Smart Steps* is all about.

Smart Steps is a developmentally based step-by-step activity series designed to provide young children from birth through age seven with a well-balanced physical "diet" of movement and play—in order to optimize their physical, cognitive, social, and emotional foundations for early learning and school readiness.

Wiring the Brain for Learning

In our companion book, *A Moving Child Is a Learning Child*, we talk in detail about the role movement plays in early brain development. During early physical and sensory experiences, the brain is recording information that builds the child's unique understanding of his* world. Through that very process, movement is literally wiring millions of neural pathways in the brain—pathways it will use for a lifetime to take in, process, and respond to stimulation and information. In other words, physical experiences and play activities in early childhood help lay down the cognitive wiring that will one day help the child learn to read, hold a pencil and write his name, reason through a math problem, paint pictures, play the piano, and all the other things he will accomplish and enjoy throughout his lifetime.

Automaticity

While that wiring is going on, something else is happening at the same time. Through movement, the body and brain are learning to communicate with each other, creating a seamless, instant, "smart" relationship. In fact, that relationship is so important that one of the brain's primary goals in the early years is to *automate* movement—to make movement something the child *doesn't* have to think about. We call this *automaticity*.

Of course, a smart relationship between the body and brain creates efficiencies and harmonies that make most movement patterns effortless. In and of itself, that's worth striving for. But in the natural order of things, automaticity is also the key that unlocks the brain's power for higher-level thinking, reasoning, creativity,

---

* When referring to children in this book, we alternate the use of male and female pronouns section by section. The information applies to girls and boys alike.

> Physical experiences and play activities in early childhood help lay down the cognitive wiring that will one day help the child learn to read, hold a pencil and write his name, reason through a math problem, paint pictures, play the piano, and all the other things he will accomplish and enjoy throughout his lifetime.

and learning. That's because of the way the brain is designed.

The human brain is capable of doing only *one* thinking task at a time. This means that when the brain needs to think about moving, it *can't* think about learning—or anything else, for that matter. So, in order to free up the brain's full attention, automated movement has to come first. In short, without automated movement, a child would not be able to fully focus, think, or learn.

Apple Is for A

When a child is born, the world comes to her: Mommy smiling into the crib, a rattle placed in the child's hand, a ride in the stroller, Grandpa rocking her in his rocking chair. As passive as these experiences may seem, to a young infant they are rich in physical and sensory information about the world she's been launched into. Later, independent movement exponentially increases her information-gathering abilities, even if the quest for knowledge only takes her to the potted plant across the room.

This process of compiling tangible, physical, real-life, in-the-moment experiences one on top of the last is the essential first step in early learning. And the reason is simple. All learning, at any age, stands on the shoulders of prior knowledge—*from the known to the unknown*. We call this the "Apple Is for *A*" principle.

As children build up a bank of experiences with their bodies and through their senses, the brain is busy learning how to store, associate, analyze, and retrieve information. For instance, if a child has lots of varied experiences with apples, she's built a baseline familiarity—something *known*—about apples. She can then use this knowledge when presented with something related to apples, such as the letter *A*. She might not yet fully grasp what that squiggle *A* is all about, but she stands a better chance of grasping and remembering that the apple she *knows* has something to do with this new, *unknown* squiggle.

Smart Steps has been designed to foster and support this natural, experiential, physical-first style of learning—not by providing the apple, but by building the capabilities to successfully reach for the apple.

About This Book

Move, Play, and Learn with Smart Steps is for educators, childcare providers, and parents with young children birth to seven years old. Designed for large- or small-group settings or one-on-one interactions, the Smart Steps activities take children on a sequential journey of physical development structured for optimal learning impact.

The activities are based on a fundamental teaching principle: make the activity fit the child, not the child fit the activity. To that end, Smart Steps is composed of 50 activity sequences, each with 18 steps tailored to children's natural development. That's 900 play-filled, learning-rich activities in total.

Our goal is to provide children with a well-balanced daily diet of physical activity that builds the body *and* the brain. To achieve that, Part 1 of the book gives you a foundational understanding of movement and its role in early learning and development. In addition, we provide guidance for implementing Smart Steps, including observational assessment tools, activity selection tips, and individualization techniques to help children make the most of each wiggle and giggle.

From there, it's on to Part 2, where you'll find an at-a-glance guide to the Smart Steps activities followed by the activities themselves.

At the back of the book you will find "Additional Resources" (which provides song and rhyme lyrics, game rules, ideas and strategies for getting kids moving in a variety of ways, and more) and a glossary of key terms related to early development and movement.

We'd like to hear about your experiences using the Smart Steps activities. Please write to us at in care of our publisher: help4kids@freespirit.com.

It's plain to see: in early childhood, learning never sits still. So let's get moving!

> The activities are based on a fundamental teaching principle: make the activity fit the child, not the child fit the activity.

PART 1

Building the Body and Brain for Learning

CHAPTER 1

The Kinetic Scale: An Overview

In order to understand how movement underpins early childhood development, we need a deeper understanding of movement itself. So let's start by breaking down the basic elements of movement—the raw ingredients. To do that, we've devised a tool to help you visualize those ingredients and the dynamic relationship between them. We call it the Kinetic Scale.

The Kinetic Scale

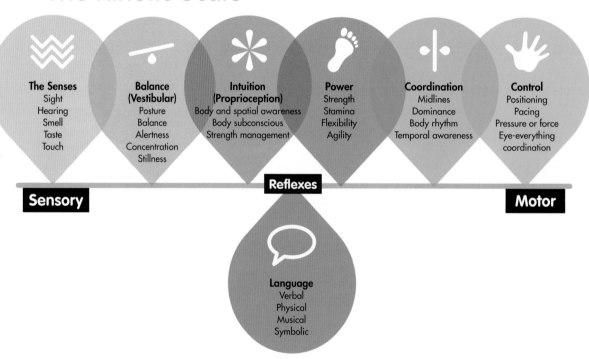

The Senses
Sight
Hearing
Smell
Taste
Touch

Balance (Vestibular)
Posture
Balance
Alertness
Concentration
Stillness

Intuition (Proprioception)
Body and spatial awareness
Body subconscious
Strength management

Power
Strength
Stamina
Flexibility
Agility

Coordination
Midlines
Dominance
Body rhythm
Temporal awareness

Control
Positioning
Pacing
Pressure or force
Eye-everything coordination

Reflexes

Sensory

Motor

Language
Verbal
Physical
Musical
Symbolic

The key components of the Kinetic Scale are reflexes, six physicalities (the senses, balance, intuition, power, coordination, and control), and language.

Reflexes

The reflexes are nature's way of assisting babies at critical junctures in the early years of life and throughout life as needed. First, early reflexes known as the primitive reflexes assist baby in utero and during the birthing process. After birth, they trigger important involuntary movements babies need for their survival, such as grasping or pushing away. This, in turn, begins to build strength in the muscles, tendons, and ligaments for independent movement a little later on. Primitive reflexes eventually integrate and give way to postural reflexes, which assist baby to get himself upright for crawling and walking.

All early movement depends on reflexes, so in the Kinetic Scale diagram, you'll see they serve as the platform for what we call the six physicalities.

The Physicalities

Three sensory tools (the senses, balance, and intuition) and three motor tools (power, coordination, and control) make up the six physicalities of the Kinetic Scale. Together, they ensure a rich, daily movement diet that builds the body *and* fosters the deep and intricate neural wiring in the brain that occurs in the early years.

As you'll see when you look at the Smart Steps activities in Part 2, we've provided an at-a-glance guide to the kinetic value of each activity so that you'll be able to prepare a well-balanced progression of move-to-learn activities for the children in your care. We'll get into more detail on activity planning a little later. But for now, let's briefly take a look at the six physicalities.

The Senses

The senses are how children perceive the sights, sounds, smells, tastes, and textures of our world—the physical, tangible experiences of life. In the early years, sensory stimulation provides the child's brain with the essential information it needs to learn to navigate and interact with the people, places, and things in the child's environment. In other words, the senses are the origins of learning.

Balance

Balance underpins virtually everything we do. It provides us the stability we need for everything from everyday tasks (like staying upright while you're reading this) to extraordinary feats of physical skill and daring. Governed by what's called the vestibular system, it is our internal sense of what feels in and out of balance. It works in conjunction with our sense of intuition (the proprioceptive sense), continually evaluating and calibrating our orientation so we always know which end is up!

Intuition

Intuition (also known as proprioception) is our sense of the external conditions of our environment—the space and the objects in it. Think of it as the body's internal GPS system. It provides us with a sense of our physical selves by answering important questions such as: "How big am I?" "What shape am I?" In turn, this gives us the intuitive sense of how to navigate the space around us: "How tall is that step?" "Will I fit through that tunnel?"

Intuition also gives us the tools we need to interact with our environment: "How hard do I need to push to open the door?" For adults, all of this happens without conscious thought. That's because we've had literally millions and millions of physical interactions over our lifetimes. Children's intuition is still very much in training, so "clumsiness" from time to time is to be fully expected. (After all, we adults still miss a curb occasionally, too!)

Power

To achieve fully automated movement, muscles need strength, stamina, flexibility, and agility. And not just the big muscles we think of as "gross motor." All muscles—big and small—need to be able to carry out whatever the brain asks them to do. But helping children achieve their optimal physical power is more than a matter of fitness. Early on, children begin to adopt attitudes and behaviors about their own power—enthusiasm, willingness, perseverance, resilience, kid-sized courage, and a sense of experimentation and adventure—that will serve them well on the playground, in the classroom, and in life.

Coordination

Putting one foot in front of the other seems easy unless you've never done it before. Coordinated movement—moving two or more parts of the body in synergy—is how we get things accomplished, and it's dependent on the development of the *midlines* in the early years. Imagine the body divided by three lines. One line separates left

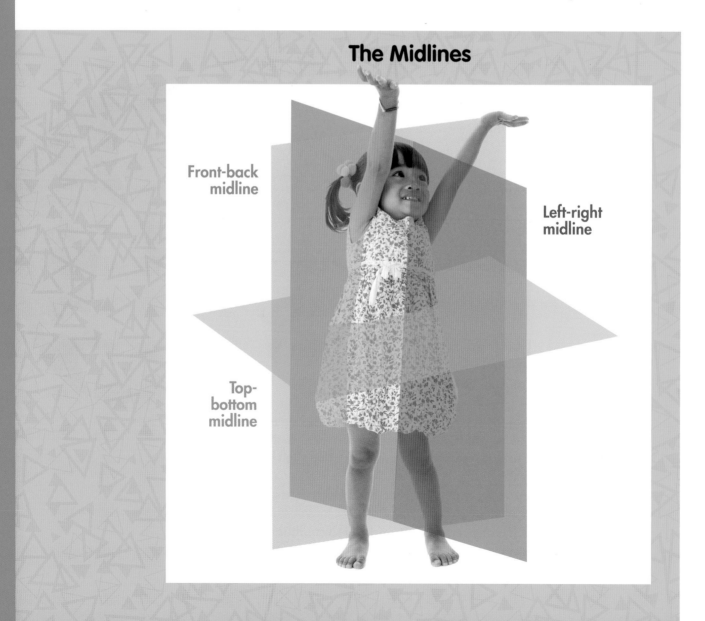

The Midlines

Front-back midline

Left-right midline

Top-bottom midline

from right. Another separates top from bottom. The third separates front from back. The midlines serve as the central pivot points for the body's sophisticated coordinated movement patterns.

Coordinated movements come in many forms:

- With mirrored or *bilateral* movement, both the left and right sides of the body move together in a similar way at the same time. For example, babies hold their bottles with both hands.

- One-sided or *homolateral* movement requires one half of the body to move while the other half stays still. Writing with one hand while the other hand remains still or scooting on a scooter are examples of homolaterality.

- Opposition or *lateral* movement occurs when one side of the body moves in the opposite manner of the other. Think walking—right foot front, left foot back.

- Crossover or *cross-lateral* movement is when one part of the body crosses over to the other side—as when you reach your left hand over your right shoulder to scratch your back.

Control

Self-control begins for children when they can master their own body and achieve the goals they set for themselves. This means highly refined control of muscle movement. And again, it doesn't matter whether the muscles are big or small. All muscles need the ability to adapt their speed, direction, and force, whether for running across a field or typing on a keyboard.

Language

Perhaps the most surprising element of the Kinetic Scale is the inclusion of language. Language in all its forms enriches the learning power of movement by providing the brain with the stimulation it needs to translate tangible experience into new concepts and, eventually, into abstract thinking. For instance, when a child lifts a heavy object, you might say, "The box is heavy. You are strong to lift that box." Three concepts come into play in that one scenario:

1. What does *heavy* feel like?
2. What does *strong* feel like?
3. The words *heavy* and *strong* relate to each other.

Later, the child may struggle to push open a door, and you might say, "That door is heavy. You need to be strong to open that door." Hearing *heavy* and *strong* in a different context gives him more physical evidence of the words' meanings. But more important, he begins to understand that those words can apply to more than one object or situation. And that is the very beginning of nuanced, conceptual thinking.

In short, continuous, in-the-moment exposure to rich and plentiful language optimizes and makes real a child's understanding of human communication. In other words, movement brings language to life. (Please see pages 36–38 for more information on how to supercharge learning with movement and language.)

Measuring Child Development: What Can the Child *Do*?

On its own, the Kinetic Scale provides broad guidance for planning the right balance of activities for young children. But of course, little ones are growing and changing all the time. And that means their movement needs are growing and changing, too. To provide for that, the Kinetic Scale is designed to "tilt" to meet those needs at each stage of development.

Now, the most common way to establish a child's stage of development is chronological age. But given all the "moving parts" of early childhood development, age may actually be one of the most misleading variables to consider in evaluating a child's movement needs. After all, some children walk at eight months, others at sixteen months. Some children can catch a ball when they're two years old, while some four-year-olds still can't. So instead of chronological age, the Kinetic Scale uses a criterion that is simple and easy to see: What can the child *do*?

The "Can-Dos" of Movement

As you know, there are many observable developmental changes in young children as they move through the early years, acquiring new levels of capabilities, or "can-dos," along the way. And while the exact progression of these can-dos may vary a little or a lot from child to child, nature's wisdom provides an orderly and cumulative sequence of events that occurs broadly across six stages of movement development:

Snugglers (birth to rolling over). The snugglers phase spans the time infants progress from nonmobile, full dependence on others to the first glimmers of **intentional, self-directed movement**—the very beginnings of self-discovery.

Squigglers (rocking, crawling, sitting up). Children discover **mobility independence** throughout this period, unlocking a wide range of early investigative explorations—the seeds of curiosity.

Scampers (pulling up to walking). The final evolutionary steps from horizontal to vertical occur in this period, bringing children to steady-on-their-feet upright— along with an explosive period of **new perspectives** and capabilities all now within reach.

Stompers (running and jumping). Full of experimental energy, children gain a larger sense of **confidence** as they test the limits of what their bodies can do. Speed, strength, and daring define this period, as stompers redefine what's possible and quite literally learn to defy gravity.

Scooters (hopping and climbing). Ever more complex and sophisticated whole-body **coordination** is emerging, sparking huge advancements in physical, cognitive, social, emotional, and communicative capabilities.

Skedaddlers (skipping, leaping, cooperative games, and dance). As the body and brain become one, **self-control** comes easier now. And with that control comes the freedom to achieve even more.

> Age may actually be one of the most misleading variables to consider in evaluating a child's movement needs.

The diagram on pages 12–13 vividly illustrates the journey of capabilities children follow as they progress from primitive reflexes to automated coordinated movement.

Tilting the Scale

With a baseline understanding of how children's can-dos unfold, we're ready to explore how the Kinetic Scale enables this progression. Note how the Kinetic Scale rebalances the physicalities as children move through each step. Broadly, a very young child's needs tilt toward the sensory tools—the senses, balance, and intuition. Over time and as she grows, the Kinetic Scale tilts toward the motor tools—power, coordination, and control.

But, the operative word here is *tilt*. This is *not* an on-off switch.

Nor is the Kinetic Scale a checklist. At every stage of development, reflexes, physicalities, and language are continuously interwoven, helping the child develop holistically as nature intended. The proportions change over time, but all of the ingredients are active parts of a daily, well-balanced physical diet throughout the early years.

Now, as we've said, the Kinetic Scale is guided by what the child can do, not by her age. But for clarity, in the diagram on pages 14–15 we have indicated approximate ages when these stages generally occur. For instance, we've identified the squiggler stage at approximately six to fourteen months. But please also note, the squigglers stage actually overlaps with the scampers stage at nine to twenty-four months. These overlaps are designed to account for the wide variation in children's individual developmental timetables.

And please remember, this or any other evaluation tool is just a guide. It's more important to be guided by the child. What a child does with her body tells you what her brain is trying to figure out. That is nature's course, and working "with the grain" of nature is the best course you can take.

The Journey of Can-Do

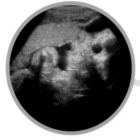

Prenatal primitive reflexes: involuntary movement

 Snugglers

Primitive reflexes in place at birth

Head control: first attempts

Awakening of senses with touch, massage, and skin-to-skin contact

Hand and foot recognition

Pincer grip

Crawling

Changing hands

Releasing grasp voluntarily

Sitting independently

 Scampers

Navigating small spaces

Pulling up to stand

Cruising

Hopping

Marching

Balancing on one foot

Handedness: early signs

 Scooters

Temporal awareness

Climbing in opposition

Galloping

Midlines developing

Hand and foot dominance developing

Skedaddlers

Hip tips: attempting to roll over

Sensory discoveries: especially mouth

Rolling over onto tummy

Pushing up from tummy

Squigglers

Postural reflexes emerging

Rocking

Up on all fours

Commando crawling

Mouthing things

Grasping

Studying facial expressions

Bobbing up and down, aided

Standing, unaided

Climbing up furniture or stairs

Eye-hand coordination: self-feeding

Walking unaided

Stompers

Manipulative skills emerging

Jumping forward on two feet

Upper body strength developing

Jumping on two feet

Bobbing up and down, unaided

Running

Leaping from standing

Crossing the midline

Leaping from running

Skipping

Automated coordinated movement

The Kinetic Scale Stage by Stage

Snugglers
Birth to rolling over
Approximate age: 0–6 months

Infants learn about the world largely through sensory information. Balance development is also essential right from the start to serve as the foundation for current and future whole-body movement.

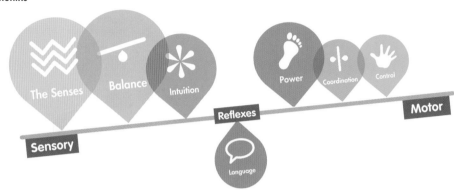

Squigglers
Rocking, crawling, and sitting
Approximate age: 6–14 months

Squigglers continue to understand their world principally through their senses. Balance and intuition development accelerates as rolling, sitting independently, and crawling emerge.

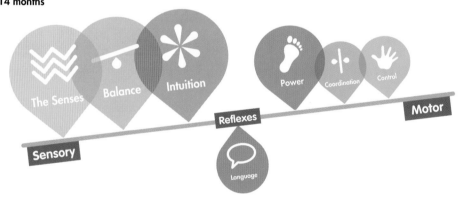

Scampers
Pulling up to walking
Approximate age: 9–24 months

The senses now act even more as the fuel for movement, and movement as the fuel for the senses. Balance, intuition, and power are in full gear as baby works toward vertical—standing and walking.

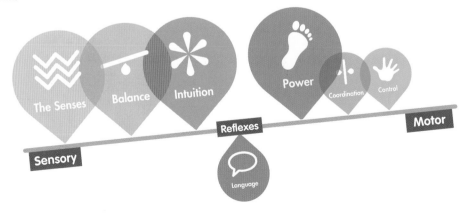

Stompers

Running and jumping
Approximate age: 20 months–3½ years

Stompers are picking up speed and endurance as they do more and more things on their own. Note how the scale now tilts to the motor side where whole-body coordination is emerging.

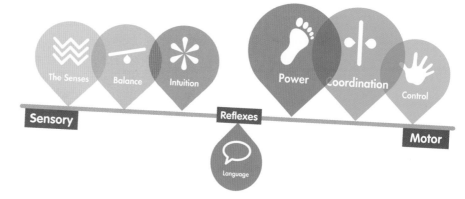

Scooters

Hopping and climbing
Approximate age: 3–4 years

Big, whole-body movements are the jet fuel for this stage, building power in the muscles to climb ever-more-challenging movement mountains. And of course, with power comes the important need for more and more control.

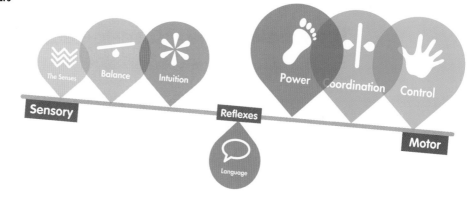

Skedaddlers

Skipping, leaping, cooperative games, and dance
Approximate age: 4 years and older

The three motor physicalities are in full focus for skedaddlers, who are nearing the finish line of foundational movement development and achieving full automaticity.

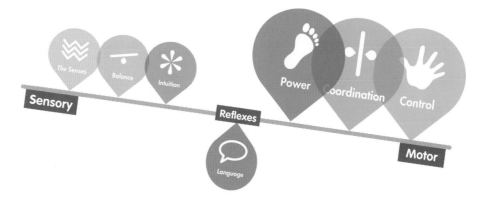

Move-to-Learn Activities Guide

The Move-to-Learn Activities Guide gives you a broad understanding and overview of how the Kinetic Scale translates into real-life play.

Note how these classic play patterns all have a role in developing the full range of physicalities. Of course, many of these play activities serve multiple developmental purposes. A great example is movement and music, which serves to draw out all six physicalities.

When you're planning movement activities for young children, be sure to first understand and respect their current can-dos. Always start there. Then gently encourage them to take the next step. In other words, approach movement the way kids do, *one step at a time.* And remember, always follow the child's lead.

Reading the Moves

Children often use movement as their primary means of communicating with us, so learning to read the moves makes it easier to understand what a child is thinking and feeling. For instance, have you ever had any of these children in your classroom (or living under your own roof)?

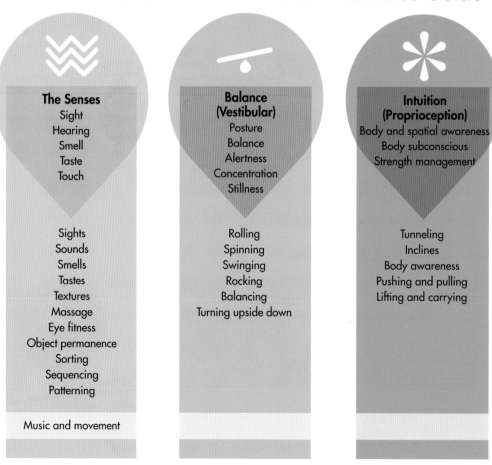

The Kinetic Scale: Move-to-Learn Activities Guide

The Senses
Sight
Hearing
Smell
Taste
Touch

Sights
Sounds
Smells
Tastes
Textures
Massage
Eye fitness
Object permanence
Sorting
Sequencing
Patterning

Music and movement

Balance (Vestibular)
Posture
Balance
Alertness
Concentration
Stillness

Rolling
Spinning
Swinging
Rocking
Balancing
Turning upside down

Intuition (Proprioception)
Body and spatial awareness
Body subconscious
Strength management

Tunneling
Inclines
Body awareness
Pushing and pulling
Lifting and carrying

The Eye Rubber might not be ready to read on his own. A child who rubs his eyes, blinks a lot, looks away from the page, or avoids reading altogether may need more time to develop his eye fitness before tackling the highly refined movements independent reading requires. To support this child, look for activities with lots of eye tracking to help build up his eye stamina.

The Ear Muffer covers his ears when the room is noisy. He may be struggling to make sense of the sounds, and when he can't, he tries to block them all out. He may need more quiet space in order to concentrate for now, as well as lots of musical experiences and games that focus on sound discrimination.

The Clean Freak avoids messy play. You can see "Yuck!" written all over his face. Patient, gentle exposure to a variety of tactile stimulation is in order. But always follow the child's lead.

The Fidgeter can't sit still. Fidgeting isn't necessarily a sign of disinterest. In fact, it may well be a sign that a child is trying to concentrate. (Or he might just need to go to the bathroom!) Balance activities are probably in order for him.

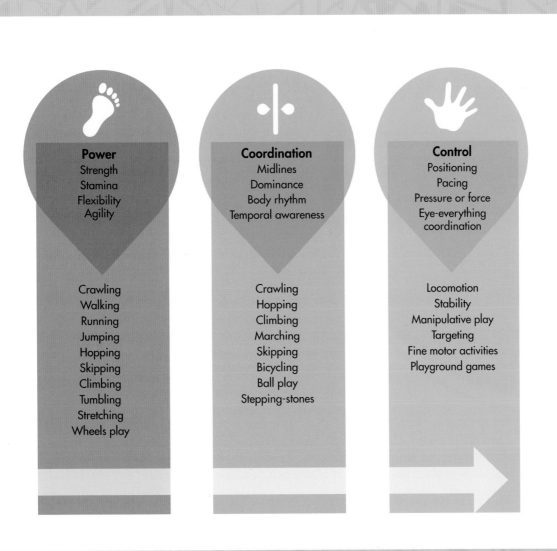

Power
Strength
Stamina
Flexibility
Agility

Crawling
Walking
Running
Jumping
Hopping
Skipping
Climbing
Tumbling
Stretching
Wheels play

Coordination
Midlines
Dominance
Body rhythm
Temporal awareness

Crawling
Hopping
Climbing
Marching
Skipping
Bicycling
Ball play
Stepping-stones

Control
Positioning
Pacing
Pressure or force
Eye-everything coordination

Locomotion
Stability
Manipulative play
Targeting
Fine motor activities
Playground games

The Spinner loves to make himself dizzy. This is not necessarily a sign of hyperactivity, but instead, an indication his brain craves vestibular (balance) stimulation. Slowing down the spinning will likely satisfy that craving.

The Chair Tipper, despite repeated reminders to be careful, may not be the daredevil he seems. Instead, he probably just needs the sensation of rocking. Try more balance activities with him.

The Kid Who Goes Bump into the furniture and into his friends isn't necessarily clumsy or unobservant. He just may not understand where his body begins and ends. Body awareness activities are probably a good idea, especially those that allow him to fit his body through, between, and under things such as tunnels and tables.

The Toucher touches everything. He's up close and leaning right into you. But that doesn't necessarily mean he's grabby or needy. More likely, he feels adrift without grounding himself through physical contact. He probably needs to develop more spatial awareness through fitting into things in his environment.

The Pencil Breaker breaks the lead in his pencil all the time. He may also be the kid who pushes or pulls too hard on the playground. This child seems aggressive, but he simply may not know his own strength. He might need experience with delicate tasks that require adapting and controlling his muscles, such as pouring water without spilling it.

The Clumper runs all his words and letters together when he's first learning to write. This is partly due to inexperience, of course, but it's also a sign that he needs more physical experiences moving his body in, out, over, under, through, and around different kinds of space.

The Slumper struggles to sit up straight for long periods of time. He looks bored, but he may just be tired. Good posture depends on core muscle strength. More whole-body movement—especially games and activities that challenge the core muscles—is probably a good idea.

The Jumper flits from activity to activity. It might look like he can't focus or lacks determination. But in early childhood, it's more likely that he switches gears a lot because his muscles lack stamina. Timed games may be in order here, to challenge him to use his muscles for longer and longer periods of time (such as jumping up and down for 15 seconds, then 30 seconds, then 45 seconds).

The Quitter asks if it's time to go home at 10:00 a.m. When this happens regularly, there's probably a physical reason for it. Chances are he's tired—not necessarily from lack of sleep but from lack of physical readiness for hours of activity in the classroom.

The Hand Swapper changes hands when he's drawing or writing across a page. This is a classic signal his midlines still need work, which means his hand dominance isn't fully in place yet. Spending some time doing cross-patterning activities will do him good.

The Letter Reverser writes his letters backward sometimes. This common mistake is probably not a matter of misunderstanding the letterforms. It may simply be a matter of immature midlines, which can result in misinterpreting the direction and order of things. Both lateral and cross-lateral movement patterns may be helpful.

When you're planning movement activities for young children, be sure to first understand and respect their current can-dos. Always follow the child's lead.

The Pretzel contorts his body to do simple tasks like writing his name. When children strike unnatural positions, they're likely working around or avoiding the midlines. Homolateral and cross-lateral activities may help. (For instance, have the child pretend his left hand is glued to his side and his feet are glued to the floor. Now tell him to try to use just his right hand to catch feathers before they fall to the floor. Be sure to repeat with the left hand.)

The Fist struggles with proper pencil grip. Chances are, he needs more time playing on the monkey bars and doing other activities that build strength in the upper body, hands, and fingers.

The Speed Demon does everything fast. When you ask him to slow down, he can't. Chances are, he's struggling with controlling his muscles. Challenge the speed demon to do things slowly. Try staging an entire "slow day" and see how long everyone lasts!

The Last Kid Picked for the Team is usually the one his peers see as the worst player in the group. Most team sports (soccer, T-ball, basketball, and so on) require manipulative skills. If a child struggles in this area, use bubbles, feathers, and other objects that move slowly so his eyes, hands, and feet have more time to work together.

CHAPTER 2

The Smart Steps Approach

There's more to active play than just running around and kicking a ball. In the early years, it's critical to provide children with a varied and well-balanced diet of physical experiences to build the foundations they need for physical, cognitive, emotional, and social development.

Smart Steps is about those foundations. And while general fitness and skill building are welcome by-products, the chief aim of Smart Steps is *automaticity*—helping young boys and girls make movement something they *don't* have to think about.

As we discussed on page 1, when a child automates control of her physical self, her brain can then turn to other matters—such as thinking and reasoning, creativity and invention, and strategies and tactics she will use in the classroom, on the playing field, or in any other endeavor she chooses to pursue. In other words, developing a smart relationship between the body and the brain makes everything else possible. And that happens step by step.

With automaticity as your goal, how do you know if a child has fully automated specific movements? The good news is: that's pretty easy to spot.

When a movement is fully automated, the child can both move and do a thinking task at the same time. For instance, she can walk on a balance beam and tell you what she had for breakfast. She can jump in place and count her jumps while she's doing it. She can dance and sing lyrics she's familiar with at the same time.

When a child hasn't yet automated a movement, she'll be fully engrossed and concentrating on that movement. She'll be quiet. She'll seem lost in thought. Her tongue might be sticking out. She won't make eye contact. In fact, she likely won't respond to you or to any other nonphysical

20

stimulation until she's completed the move. When a child is in the moment like this, adults often think she's not listening, when in fact she's listening intently to her body and brain, which are figuring out how to work together.

Here's a quick way to gauge automaticity. While a child is doing a movement, ask her to answer an easy question unrelated to what she's doing. For instance: "I can't remember. How old are you?" If the child can move and answer at the same time, it's a good sign she has automated that movement. Try to engage her in a little dialogue to see if she can still keep moving and talking. If she can't think of the answer, doesn't answer at all, or stops moving to answer your question, that's a sign that her brain is still prioritizing the movement over thinking, and she needs more time with that movement.

> When a movement is fully automated, the child can both move and do a thinking task at the same time.

As a teacher, caregiver, or parent, you know that guiding children toward new knowledge requires more listening than talking, more observation than demonstration, more exploration than instruction. So let's take a few moments to talk about how to approach the Smart Steps activities.

There are three major areas of consideration:

- creating a kinetic, "move-to-learn" environment
- managing safety
- activating the relationship between movement, language, and formal learning

Let's take a look at these one at a time.

Creating a Kinetic Environment

Perhaps more than any other area of early learning, physical development requires as much individualized attention as possible.

Respecting Individuality

In the early years, the brain makes movement one of its most important priorities. As a result, the child's idea of *self* is inextricably linked to his physical abilities, limitations, and aspirations. Think of it. When he can climb the monkey bars like the other kids, it's proof positive he's a big kid, too.

One-Size-Fits-All Fits No Child at All

With that in mind, the first rule of thumb for Smart Steps is this: a one-size-fits-all approach never fits any child perfectly. No two children are alike. Each child develops at his own pace, with waves of developmental ebb and flow throughout the early years. Put that together with the Herculean task of automating every single movement his body is capable of doing, and it's clear that no one-size-fits-all approach will be able to fit each child's unique needs. Furthermore, kids are growing and changing all the time, and so their needs are, too.

Ready When You Are

Automaticity takes time, repetition, and many varied contexts in order to fully master. And there's no one pattern to the way it unfolds for each child. One child may do something over and over for a long time. One may be quick to adopt crawling, but not walking. Another may skip crawling altogether.

The Smart Steps activity series has been designed to take that wide variance into account. The program begins where the child *is*, not where anyone thinks he's *supposed* to be, nor where any other child in the group happens to be. In that way, Smart Steps makes the activity fit the child, not the other way around. Aligning to the child's capabilities makes it easy to identify his immediate, near-term, and long-term movement needs. This ready-when-you-are approach naturally builds self-confidence. It puts new challenges and accomplishments within stretchable reach of his current capabilities while continuing to provide the time he needs for automaticity to occur.

Goldilocks Gauge

Frustration
(Too hard. I quit.)

Try, try again!
(I can do this if I just keep trying!)

Just right! Challenging and engaging
(Look what I can do!)

Experiment
(What else can I do?)

Boredom
(Too easy. I quit.)

The Goldilocks Gauge

An important part of keeping Smart Steps within a child's reach is to capture and keep his interest. Children check out when an activity is too difficult or too easy for them. The trick is to use the "Goldilocks Gauge" to find that just-right spot in which they are physically challenged, emotionally engaged, and intellectually stimulated. In other words, that place kids call fun.

Small Steps Are Big Steps

All effort—in any form, on any front—contributes to a child's developmental journey. Some children reach their goal on the first try, some on the third, some on the thirty-third. And just because a child "gets it" on the first try doesn't mean he can do it again and again with ease or automaticity. So, just like in any other area of learning, the key to Smart Steps is repetition. Build in lots of time for the try-try-again factor. After all, the brain learns as much (and sometimes more) from a perceived failure as from a recognized success.

Allowing time for effort is a great first step, but guiding and encouraging the process is equally important. Be sure to affirm a child's effort to advance his ability. Focus on the positive aspects of the child's actions and avoid calling out what you don't want to see. Be specific with purposeful encouragement rather than empty praise. "Well done" doesn't tell him what to do the next time.

Group Dynamics

As much as possible, manage the activities toward individual advances, not class-wide goals. Of course, that's easier said than done, especially when any group of young children is bound to include a wide range of differing abilities, from "speedsters" to "stragglers." Hurrying a child through an activity so that he can keep up with his peers not only shortchanges that child, it may impact the entire group dynamic. It serves no one well if some feel inadequate to the task while others are feeling held back.

Managing Children on the Move

Bearing in mind our goal of individual advancement, here are a few strategies for managing on-the-move group dynamics.

Leverage learning modalities. Be sure you're teaching to all learning styles—visual, auditory, and kinesthetic. Often it's most effective when you demonstrate and (when practically possible) participate in the activities yourself, so that children learn by:

- seeing what the movement looks like
- hearing the words and ideas associated with the movement
- doing the movement themselves (with you and on their own)

Be observant. It's natural for your eye to follow the children who are engaged and succeeding in an activity. But children who are struggling or afraid tend to avoid a task or do something they feel confident about instead. Pay special attention to the child who holds back, chooses the end of the line, or simply wanders off to do something else. Offer that child a special invitation to the activity. Reframe it in a playful way, such as relating it to something he enjoys. For instance, "I wonder how a baseball player would make it through that tunnel?" If the child continues to hesitate, find out what he'd like to try and follow his lead for now.

Warm up. It's always a good idea to refresh children on the skills they've been building, so when you feel it's necessary, do a warm-up by replaying the previous step in the activity sequence. (You'll see this is directly called for in some specific places, but of course, use this technique any time you feel you need it.)

Break it down. If a child continues to struggle with a movement or an activity, break it down and take it step by step. "Lift your right arm. Now lift your left arm." If equipment is involved, that may be adding to the struggle. Remove the equipment and practice just the movements.

Choose different leaders. For paired or group activities, be sure everyone gets equal turns in the leadership role.

Kids as crew. Involve all the children (especially the ones who tend to hold back) in the setup and cleanup of activities. The experience of working as a team, touching the equipment, and deciding how to set it up is an invitation to their curiosity.

Respect privacy. If a child is struggling or showing signs of getting upset, stop. Frustration yields aversion. And, of course, don't draw attention to it. Simply give the child a different activity to focus on and find time later to work with him individually.

Individualizers: The Six Ds

While Smart Steps provides a sequence of 18 progressions for each main activity, it would be hubris to suggest that those activities alone could fully account for each child's unique needs. Here is a handy list of ways to make just about any activity a little bit easier or a little bit more challenging. We call these individualizers.

Note: Take special safety precautions when using individualizers for activities in which the child is elevated off the ground, is inexperienced with the movement patterns, or is unfamiliar with the equipment in use. Prioritize safety at all times.

To change up an activity to suit a child's individual needs, we've created six rules of thumb we call the Six Ds: dynamics, distance, direction, duality, duration, and difficulty.

To increase the level of challenge, start by adding one D to the basic activity. For example, push the goal out farther. As the child masters each new level of challenge, change or add another D. For instance, have the child try reaching the goal using the other hand.

Similarly, if a child struggles with an activity, tamp down the level of challenge using the same Six Ds. For instance, move the goal closer, or have the child use both hands.

Here's a quick review of the Six Ds.

Dynamics. Young children tend to do things fast for the simple reason that *fast* is usually easier. The slower you go, the more balance and control are required. So, to increase challenge, encourage children to slow down. Ask, "How slow can you go?" To make an activity easier, encourage them to speed up. In addition, to challenge

Stragglers and Speedsters: How to Handle a Group with Varying Levels of Ability

For Stragglers

Explore progress. Keep track and show the child how much progress he's made since he started.

Explore options. Discuss alternative ways to achieve the same aim. "I wonder how else you might do it." "Can you show me what feels right (natural) to you?"

Explore alternatives. Distract the child away from the challenge. "Show me what else you can do."

For Speedsters

Authorship. Have the child show the others how he does it.

Leadership. Invite the child to mentor the others.

Partnership. Create paired or group activities to encourage children at different levels of ability to support one another.

And for all, consider ways to modify the activity to fit their at-the-moment needs by using individualizers (the six Ds).

children's control, at any point in the activity call out, "Freeze." The ability to stop and hold a pose supports and challenges listening skills, physical abilities, and emotional self-control.

Distance. The same activity can be easy or challenging depending on how far away the goal is. Move the goalposts, targets, and finish lines closer or farther away to make any game easier or more challenging.

Direction. Forward movement is the most natural movement, of course. When a child needs extra challenge, have him try the same movement using his body in different ways. For instance, when walking on a rope, he can try walking sideways or backward. Instead of a straight racecourse, add zigzags or patterns to encourage moving in different directions.

Duality. In the early years, using both the right and left sides of the body is important to balanced development. No matter the age of the child or whether hand or foot dominance has emerged, encourage him to try activities using both sides of his body together and separately. To start, watch to see which hand or foot he uses naturally. Then encourage him to switch to the other side. Then (when appropriate to the activity) have him use both hands or feet together.

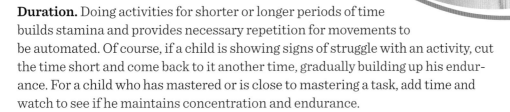

Duration. Doing activities for shorter or longer periods of time builds stamina and provides necessary repetition for movements to be automated. Of course, if a child is showing signs of struggle with an activity, cut the time short and come back to it another time, gradually building up his endurance. For a child who has mastered or is close to mastering a task, add time and watch to see if he maintains concentration and endurance.

Difficulty. To add challenge to an activity, change up the terrain or gradient. For example, if the child is running on a smooth, level surface, challenge him to run up a hill. Adding obstacles to navigate is another fast and easy way to add challenge. And when a child has mastered an activity, give him something else to consider. You might, for instance, have him hold an object or balance something on his head while doing the activity. Naturally, to make an activity easier, simplify the environment and remove obstacles and objects that get in the way of the basic movement pattern.

More Individualizers

In addition to the Six Ds, there are several other ways to change up activities and add challenge when a child is ready for this.

Make It Silly: Pretending. Kids love being silly, especially when they can put their whole body into it. To keep things fresh and add challenge, have them do activities pretending to be other things. For instance, they can walk like a duck, jump like a bunny rabbit, and dance like a robot.

Make It Silly: Minus One Sense. Some activities lend themselves to exploring the senses by actually depriving one of the senses. For instance, have the children close their eyes to play a game of pass the beanbag. This requires the other senses to do more of the work. In order to pass the beanbag, they have to listen carefully and feel for their partner's hands.

Make It Silly: Minus One Body Part. Some activities are great for exploring the body by holding one part of the body still or out of play. For instance, standing on one foot or passing the beanbag using only the right arm. This challenges the body and brain to find new ways to move and to discover new capabilities.

Make It Social. A great way to encourage teamwork and friendship is to have children work together, of course. But when it comes to movement, working in teams can actually make tasks more challenging, because children have to navigate their own bodies and space while being mindful of their partners'.

Make It Smart. Adding elements of formal learning into movement activities and games is fine, as long as you remember that the focus of the activity is movement and not the ABCs or 123s. Remember, like all of us, children can only do one thinking task at a time—and their minds will be on the movement.

Once a child demonstrates automaticity with an activity, adding a cognitive task is a great way to test that. For instance, have him count out loud as he's jumping. Or cue him with a memory task, such as: "Show me how you can jump from the red spot to the blue to the green." And add music to create a natural beat and rhythm for the movement while setting a soundtrack for children's language development.

Set the Tone: Be Kid-Logical

As you know, fun is the ultimate kid magnet, so when you introduce any Smart Steps activity, be sure to set a playful tone.

Be a movement role model. As we've said, demonstrate the activities yourself. Whenever it's practically possible, get in on the fun with them. Kids will follow your lead, so if you're active, they'll jump up and join in.

Change settings. When you're transitioning into Smart Steps activities, move to a new corner of the room or take children outside to rev up the energy. Sing a song or dance a silly dance. Just changing tempo will signal something exciting is about to happen.

Enchant and entice. Fantasy and storytelling motivate active role play, often turning children's *can'ts* into *cans*. Engage their imaginations with the story prompts provided. And of course, use the children's favorite stories and characters to add to the fun.

Guide, don't instruct. When presenting new activities, keep the ideas short, simple, and kid-logical. Take it one step at a time without overloading children with too much information. Show them how it's done, then step back and assist as needed. And remember, this isn't training camp. Precision drills are for older kids. Right now, inspiring effort and building muscle memory is plenty to be concerned with.

Wonder, don't instruct. Once children are actively engaged, they may need prompting from time to time. Avoid giving overt instructions (unless, of course, safety is an issue). Instead, work with the child by offering open-ended questions for them to try to solve on their own. (See page 33 for more ideas.)

Support as needed. Knowing the children in your care as you do, always be mindful of their emotional state as they try new things. Provide as much physical and emotional support as they need to build up their courage and confidence. It's okay if they need to rely on you at first.

Stay open to possibilities. When little ones are learning something new, sometimes they discover ways of doing things we weren't expecting. As long as safety isn't an issue, follow their lead.

Get silly. Kids love it when adults embrace their silly side. Talk in funny voices, dance in wacky ways, sing silly songs, and don't forget the sound effects (*quack, zoom, pffft*)!

Cue the Moves

When little ones are up and moving, all of their senses are engaged. To optimize these dynamics, make the directions as active and fun-filled as the kids! Whenever you can, use a combination of visual, auditory, and kinesthetic prompts to cue the moves.

A big rule of thumb when giving directions to little ones is this: keep it short and simple. Don't clutter their minds with information they don't need. Set up the premise of the activity (get over Sneaky Cheeky Creek) and the objective (we've got to cross the plank).

Once you've laid out the game play, encourage children to repeat it back to you so they have both your voice and their own in their short-term memory. And avoid interrupting them. This is their process for remembering, so it's important they find their own words for it.

Adults sometimes forget that children have limits to their ability to remember. They are growing the capacity to store more information and are still working out how to use it. A good rule of thumb to follow in giving directions is "age minus two": take the age of the child (say, three years) and subtract two to determine how many cues the child should be able to remember at one time. For instance, a three-year-old should be able to remember one cue, a four-year-old two cues, and a five-year-old three cues.

Here's a quick list of ideas for how you can cue the moves and get on with the fun!

Auditory Cues

Use verbal cues—your voice—to describe the movement. Substitute spoken cues with fun sounds like whistles, bells, or animal noises. Not only does this add to the atmosphere of fun and excitement, it makes the activity more challenging because kids have to remember what the sound means.

Visual Cues

Use colors, shapes, animals, letters, numbers, or any other set of visual aids to cue the moves. Combine these with auditory cues so the children can associate the visual cue and the sound to help them remember what to do.

Kinesthetic Cues

Teach children one or more specific poses or positions. For instance, "stand like a double-handled teapot" means to stand still with both hands on the hips. When you call out "double teapot," it's their cue to stop, put their hands on their hips, and listen. Again, add familiar visual and auditory cues to enhance the impact; for instance, whistle like a teapot, too!

Activity Set-Ups

Use cues to show children sequential patterns. For instance, when setting up a motory (obstacle course), put a picture of a tiger, lion, and bear on the different stations. Then explain to the children how to follow the route—tiger, lion, bear!

Start and End Points

Use a rope or a spot on the floor as a consistent place to start and end activities. For even more fun, put a bell or whistle near the start and end spots to ring when it's time for the fun to begin or end.

Grouping Children

Use different cues for grouping that challenge kids to observe and think. For instance, have the children wearing something red be in one group, and those wearing blue in another. Now the children have to stop and think about what they're wearing, while finding children who match them.

Using a Timer

Egg timers are essential for starting and ending game play, but more importantly, they teach time concepts in a tangible, physical way little ones will understand.

Personal Best (PB) Charts

Use PB charts to motivate children to try to better their own score. This gives little ones the chance to see their progress over time and the incentive to strive for even more growth. At the same time, it's essential in early childhood to *avoid* competition among kids. In the early years, a child's relationship to his body is central to his understanding of himself. So be sure the PB chart is just that: personal.

Set the Stage: Creating a Can-Do Environment

Little ones need room to move, so take a moment to get down on the floor and examine your space the way they see it. At kid-level, ask yourself:

- How much play space do I have? What obstacles are in my path?

- Can I run here? Tumble? Jump? Dance? Wiggle?

- Do I feel safe here? Do I feel happy? Am I excited? Enchanted? Intrigued? Can I be myself here? Can I be active the way I want to be?

Certainly, the four walls of your space will dictate what can be done to open up the environment for active movement and learning. Still, pretty much any space can be adapted for the Smart Steps activities. Consider the following:

Open up the floor space. A child's natural learning environment is the floor for two simple reasons: It's easy to get to, and you can't fall off.

Clear off as much floor space as you can (this includes getting rid of things like desks and chairs if need be). Indoor spaces should be as inviting to active learning as possible, and that means lots of elbow room for lots of elbows.

Don't just clear the space for Smart Steps. The floor is a great place for all kinds of movement and learning. It offers a child physical choices that make the learning feel right to his body. He can sit cross-legged, lie on his belly, crouch, stand, roll around, or do whatever suits him. Without physical obstacles in his way, he can simply drop to the floor and dig right into the learning.

Keep play at your fingertips. Make active play available to the children all day. In much the same way you stock your bookcase with books, have balls, beanbags, hoops, ropes, and the like visible and available all day long.

And use the equipment in unexpected ways. For instance, have the children sit on red rubber balls at storytime. This challenges them to focus on the story while maintaining their balance. Or, rather than count at the table, have them stand up and toss beanbags while they count. Put lines of different-colored masking tape down on the floor. This will come in handy for Smart Steps activities, of course, and also throughout the day when, for example, you can have the children walk along the red line to reinforce the color red. In other words, employ the high-energy principles and simple equipment of Smart Steps throughout your entire learning day.

And one more thing: be sure to also plan days where there's no equipment involved at all. For instance, create "Elbow Day." Instead of raising their hands, have children raise their elbows. Instead of walking across the room, have them use their elbows to scoot across. Line up elbow to elbow. Use all elbows all day long!

Be active indoors and out. Smart Steps activities are designed for any environment, indoors or out, for the simple reason that movement is a child's preferred means of learning. Take Smart Steps with you wherever you go. As much as you can, create a seamless indoor-outdoor transition to ensure the largest possible learning environment. The more room there is to move indoors or out, the more learning intensifies as children challenge their bodies in new and different ways.

Motorvators: A "Movement Snack" for Anytime

When you're little, the need to move doesn't wait until recess. And the need isn't shy about showing itself. Wiggling, fidgeting, slumping, hanging on classmates, hanging on you—all of these are signs that a child's brain is craving the kind of stimulation only movement can provide. And when that happens, why wait?

> The more room there is to move indoors or out, the more learning intensifies as children challenge their bodies in new and different ways.

When you're seeing those telltale signs that kids need to move *now*, it's time to pause and take a mini movement break. We call these breaks Motorvators—quick, easy, anytime, anywhere ideas for adding high-energy, purposeful activities to your day. Stop what you're doing and switch gears for one to two minutes by having the children sing a silly song, march or jump in place, stand on one foot, drop and roll, or do whatever your space allows. Spin like a top or look between your knees to see the world upside down. Like a rocket, squat down slowly to a countdown: five, four, three, two, one, blastoff! And, of course, put on some music and rock out for a few minutes!

Managing Safety

A child on the move is constantly pushing her physical boundaries—and undoubtedly that's going to cause a few tumbles along the way. Let's discuss the important matters of physical safety in guiding a moving child in these early years.

If you are a parent, you know your child better than anyone else. As an educator or childcare provider, you are trained to understand children's abilities and anticipate their needs. And you are responsible for their safety. So let's be clear: in matters of safety, the final call is always yours—child by child, day by day, situation by situation.

Managing Uncertainty

Most adults see risk on a straight-line continuum that looks something like this:

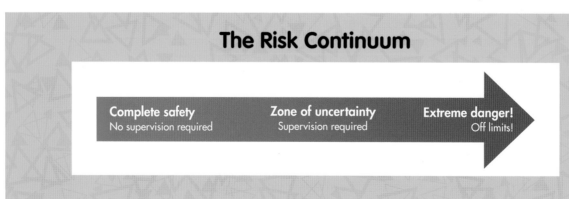

The Risk Continuum

Complete safety
No supervision required

Zone of uncertainty
Supervision required

Extreme danger!
Off limits!

Chances are, if you're in charge of active little ones, you spend at least part of your day in the zone of uncertainty—that place where there might be an issue with safety. And while physical safety is your first, most important job as a child's guardian, it's not your only job.

How you handle situations in that gray area between obviously safe and obviously dangerous—the zone of uncertainty—is critical not only for the child's physical safety, but for her intellectual and emotional growth. All learning takes some measure of risk, and all risk results in some measure of learning. Helping a child balance both rests with you as a teacher, caregiver, or parent.

Managing Risk: Pause, Prompt, and Praise

Children learn best by doing—by immersing themselves in whatever interests them, with their whole brain and body. There's just one problem. Young children don't have much experience, which means they have little sense of what is and isn't risky. Which brings us to the age-old, inevitable dilemma: How do I let a child try new things that may be risky while keeping her safe from harm?

You know the children in your care best, and hazard assessment is your call. If you decide to let a child try something risky, take a deep breath, drum up your courage and common sense, and consider this classroom mantra: *pause, prompt, and praise.*

1. **Pause.** Knowing the child as you do, when you see a potential problem that is *not immediately hazardous,* pause for a moment before reacting. For instance, a child may get stuck on a piece of playground equipment. If there's no obvious, immediate danger, give her time to work through the problem herself.

2. **Prompt.** Then, if you feel the need to step in, do so. Try not to do everything for the child. Instead, gently prompt her with ways to solve the situation. Be the helper, not the leader. For instance, you might say, "I wonder how we can help you get unstuck. What if I hold your arms while you lift your leg?"

3. **Praise.** As the situation resolves, affirm the actions the child took to solve her own problem. Be specific. As we've said, "Good job!" doesn't tell her what to do next time. Review the situation verbally so she knows what she did well. For example: "I love the way you lifted your knee up to get unstuck." Chances are, the next time she gets stuck, she'll remember to lift her knee.

The Balance of Play

Identifying the risk of play without valuing its rewards is like tying one hand behind a moving child's back. Instead, let's look at the whole picture. The Balance of Play diagram on page 32 illustrates what happens when we evaluate both the physical risk (the zone of uncertainty) *and* the learning rewards (the Goldilocks gauge) of movement.

The Balance of Play (with the Goldilocks Gauge)

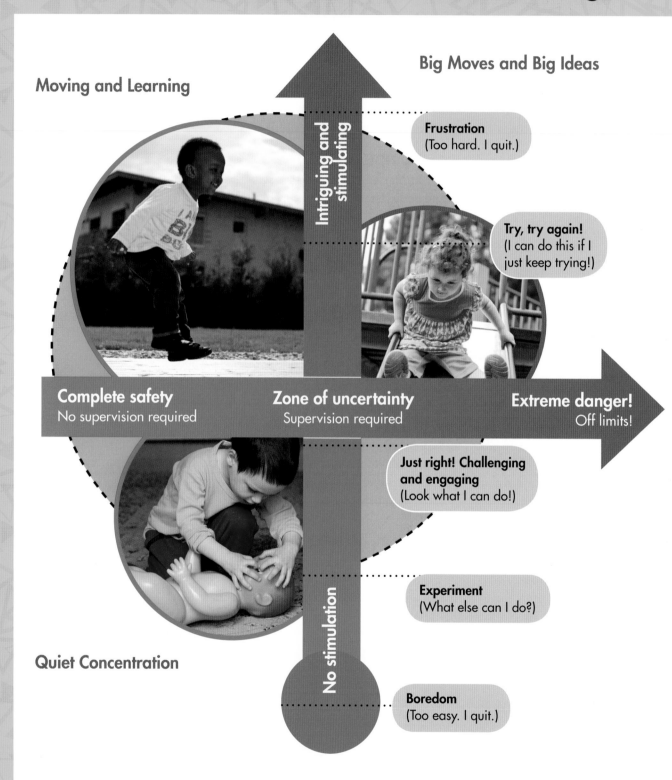

Note how the diagram reveals three essential types of play: moving and learning, big moves and big ideas, and quiet concentration. The Smart Steps activities present a balanced menu of all three styles of play for you to choose from.

Teaching Children About Safety: Take a Safety Safari

With active learning, safety should always be your guiding principle. And of course, explaining why some things are off-limits is a great way to help children understand why they can't always do what the big kids do.

But what about the times when you aren't there to provide guidance? To manage these situations, help them learn to think through the safety assessment process—the idea of consequences. And that begins with the simple question "What would happen if . . . ?"

Take the children on a safety safari. Tour your environment together and ask what they think is safe and unsafe to do in different areas. Gently prompt if necessary, and praise the children when they correctly identify an area for play that is safe or unsafe.

Offer open-ended questions that help them imagine consequences. For example:

- "I wonder if chasing games would be a good idea in the play kitchen? What do you think would happen if the floor was wet and you ran on it? I wonder where would be a better place to play chasing games?"

- "Remember the time I dropped the cup and it broke into lots of sharp pieces? The cup was made of glass. What else is made of glass? What would happen if someone bumped into something made of glass, like the window?"

- "You're really good at doing somersaults. I wonder if this would be a good place to somersault? Why wouldn't this be a good place? I wonder where would be a better place?"

Getting children to think about safety in this way will not only help them understand what to look out for, but might also lead them to think safety is *their* idea. And when it's their idea, it's bound to be a good one!

Next, let's talk about the physical support children need as they develop new capabilities and conquer new skills.

Safety Holds: Supporting a Moving Child

Children learning new movement skills need lots of encouragement, of course, and often need our physical support to build up their abilities and confidence. How much support a child needs depends on her stage of development and prior experience.

Following are ways in which you can support and hold young children as they are making their way through the learn-to-move years, from infancy all the way through the preschool and early primary years.

Note: Of course, as a teacher or childcare provider, you need to know and adhere to the safety licensing regulations of your state, province, region, or country. In your day-to-day work with children, you must individualize safety protocols to each child's capabilities and comfort level. Whenever you're unsure, begin with the highest level of support and gauge from there. And remember, the final call on safety is always yours. If you're uncertain of the child's ability, support as you see fit, even if the child feels she's ready to go solo.

Support for Snugglers, Squigglers, and Scampers

Head and neck support. At all times, support the child's head and neck when lifting and holding her.

Rock-a-bye hold. Sitting or standing, lay baby on her back, cradling her with both of your arms so that you are face to face.

Snuggle hold. Sitting or standing, hold baby to your chest in a vertical position, facing you. Support baby under the arms and bottom, with your hand on the back of her head for support.

Kangaroo hold. Sitting or standing, hold baby to your chest in a vertical position, facing away from you. Support baby around her chest and under her bottom. Lean baby's head against your chest for support, supporting her head with one hand as needed.

Baby airplane. Hold baby in your arms on her tummy, looking toward the floor. Support her under the chest and thighs. Ensure there is no bow in her back. Hold her close to your body at first, then very slowly move her a few inches away from your chest so that she is supported only by your arms.

Baby glider. Hold baby in your arms on her back, looking toward you. Support her under her shoulders and legs. Hold her close to your body at first, then very slowly move her a few inches away from your chest so that she is supported only by your arms.

Burp hold. Sitting or standing, hold baby to your shoulder in a vertical position. She should be high enough up to peek over your shoulder, her face looking down at the floor. *Note:* Baby should *not* be upside down in this position. Support baby around her chest and legs.

Baby pull-up. For an older baby who has demonstrated muscle control of her head and neck, when assisting and supporting her to pull herself up into a sitting position, be sure her elbows are locked, her arms are straight, and her head is not dropping forward, backward, or to the side.

No propping! *Never* put a young child in a position she cannot get herself into or out of. For instance, do not use pillows to prop baby into a sitting position.

Support for Stompers, Scooters, and Skedaddlers

As children become independently mobile, they continue to need our support, especially when they're trying new things for the first time. Your support gives them the added strength and steadiness they need to find their way toward doing these new things on their own. And of course, your encouragement gives them the confidence they need to try.

Most children need more support at first and less as time passes. Here's a step-by-step approach to help you help them on their journey toward independence.

Balanced support. If a child needs your help, support her on both sides of her body. Supporting a child on one side, such as holding one hand, gives the child's brain an unbalanced message. It may skew how the child moves.

I won't let you fall. Often children need support when they're nervous or uncertain. Stand in front of the child so she can see you at all times. Make eye contact and talk supportively about her efforts. Fold your arms in front of you, bend down, and offer them to the child as a handrail. Keep your arms steady and walk backward in pace with her forward movement. This provides physical support and a connection between you in an important emotional moment.

Helping hands. As the child's confidence grows, try the activity holding *both* her hands. Stay in front of her so she can see you're her partner in the process. But now, she is doing more of the work.

Don't worry, I've got you. Once the child is confident in her abilities, it's important she take the lead. Move to her back and support her with your hands on either side of her waist.

I'm here just in case. As the child progresses, she'll need less and less support from you but will likely still need reassurance. Now gently hold onto the back of her shirt at the middle of her back on the midline. This gives her freedom to move without help but lets her know you're there. It's also a great way to help her slow down a bit without interrupting her movement.

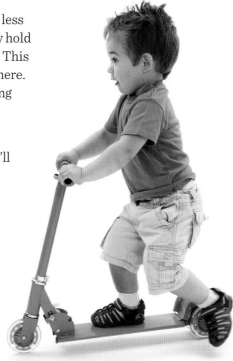

Soloing. When the child feels confident enough to go solo, stand behind her with your hands near her waist—but not touching. She'll sense that you're there while proving to herself that she can do it!

A Note About Landings

When children begin to defy gravity (jumping, hopping, climbing), landing becomes an important tool in their movement toolbox. Here's how to teach the motorbike landing technique.

Feel the position first. Start by having the child stand straight with her feet shoulder-width apart. Have her bend her knees slightly (as if on a motorbike) and hold her hands out in front (as if she were holding the handlebars). Have her bob up and down to get a feel for the position.

Pretend motorbike. Next, the child pretends she's mounting a motorbike. She lifts one leg up, stretches it over the pretend bike, and puts her foot back down so that her legs are shoulder-width apart. She then grabs the handlebars with both hands straight out in front. Then she takes a seat on the motorbike, bending her knees slightly and bobbing up and down.

Jump and motorbike land. Now it's time to put that into action. Have the child jump up in the air and land in the motorbike position! (Kids love to make *vroom vroom* sounds when they land their motorbikes.)

Each time you work with activities or equipment that require landing, practice motorbike landing before you tackle the activity as a physical reminder of the position.

Language: The Link to Formal Learning

It will come as no surprise that language is pivotal to learning. But when put in context with physical, tangible experiences, language in all its forms—verbal, nonverbal, musical, and symbolic—has the power to transform what children do into what children think.

That's why language is quite literally the pivot point of the Kinetic Scale. Of course, the words you use become the tools the child needs to express himself and understand others. When you provide the language and the child provides the action, together you are forming a deep bedrock for his understanding of himself and his world. And the result is a simple, dynamic, and endlessly repeatable formula:

Experience + Language = Understanding

The Smart Steps activities give you an ideal opportunity to put words and physical experiences together.

The Kinetic Scale

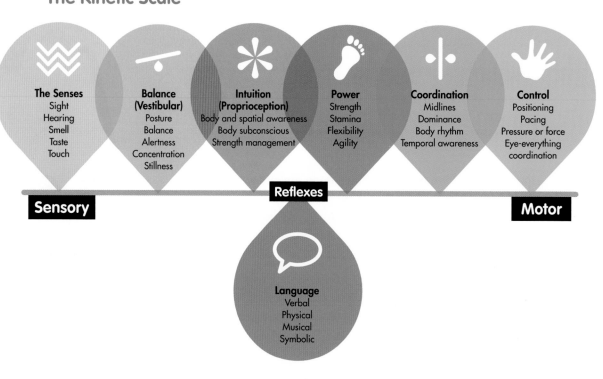

The Senses
Sight
Hearing
Smell
Taste
Touch

Balance (Vestibular)
Posture
Balance
Alertness
Concentration
Stillness

Intuition (Proprioception)
Body and spatial awareness
Body subconscious
Strength management

Power
Strength
Stamina
Flexibility
Agility

Coordination
Midlines
Dominance
Body rhythm
Temporal awareness

Control
Positioning
Pacing
Pressure or force
Eye-everything coordination

Reflexes

Sensory

Motor

Language
Verbal
Physical
Musical
Symbolic

Some Rules of Thumb

Consider these rules of thumb as you put the activities into action:

Words! Words! And more words! Narrate everything. "I like the way you lift your knee to climb up the ladder." "I see you jumping up and down." "When you look up, can you touch the branch?" All of those words are sinking in, whether the child is preverbal or verbal. Just keep talking.

Directionality. Notice in the preceding paragraph that the word *up* appears three times in three different contexts. *Up* can be a word about climbing. *Up* can be a word about jumping. And *up* can be a place you look and reach to. So where is *up?* As you can imagine, for young children, language can be very confusing. Children need to hear words over and over in lots of different contexts to understand the nuances of language.

As you review the Smart Steps activities, note the Language Focus section. As you take children through the *activity sequence*, use these key words repeatedly throughout the play to help little listeners hear, feel, and experience directional concepts in context. And consider ways to reinforce the Language Focus words after playtime, too.

You will notice that many of the words are repeated in different activities. This is so children can experience the same words in many different contexts. When this happens, they learn that one word can mean many different things, depending on how it is applied.

Knowledge of context is also necessary as children learn to apply this language in their early writing experiences. Having experienced words in the real world, they can more easily transfer that learning into the written world. And of course, in different contexts, words mean different things, so in *Move, Play, and Learn with Smart Steps* we aim to provide children with a plethora of experiences.

Use nutritious language. Use a wide variety of words within the child's reach, and be descriptive in how you paint verbal pictures. Of course, use proper grammar and pronunciation. And, whenever you can, show him how much fun words are. Invite discussion. Encourage him to tell you where he is during the play (or immediately after the play). When he says, "I'm walking on the rope," he's reinforcing his own learning.

Stay open to his questions. And whenever you can, let the child teach you. After all, nothing's more empowering than a listener interested in what you have to say.

Nursery rhymes. The rhyming and the timing of spoken rhymes or poems makes language playful to the ear. The short-form, repetitive nature of rhymes gives children lots of practice with a few words, while building up auditory discrimination and association for increasing vocabulary (for example: *rhyme, time, slime,* and so forth).

> Language in all its forms—verbal, nonverbal, musical, and symbolic—has the power to transform what children do into what children think.

Music and movement. You'll see that the Smart Steps activities provide many opportunities for music and movement. The beat, rhythm, tempo, melody, and harmony of music, when combined with movement, double the brain's potential to understand the complexities of sound. Add lyrics, and language comes to life and embeds deeply into children's memory for later recall (sometimes for a lifetime . . . *e-i-e-i-o*).

Teaching Left and Right

Teachers often ask for ideas on teaching the concepts of left and right. Left and right are tricky bits of business for young children, actually requiring advanced directional reasoning to master. That's probably why it takes a long time (or a lifetime) to master.

As an early childhood teacher, author Gill Connell took a perpetual-focus, consistent-learning approach. For the first 10 weeks of kindergarten, Gill would focus on the concept of left. When a child earned a sticker, she put it on his left hand and foot. When children wanted to participate or ask a question, she had them raise their left hand. She had them write their names on the left side of their paper, stand to the left of her, jump to the left, and shake hands with their left hand. Left. Left. Left. She'd tell parents to keep "left" at home, too.

Gill employed the concept in everything she did throughout each day before, during, after, and between units. And while she recommends this for classroom use, she also recommends it for home use even with younger children.

For instance, when dressing, put the left sock on first and reinforce it by saying, "Let's put your sock on your left foot." Put a bracelet on the child's left arm and say,

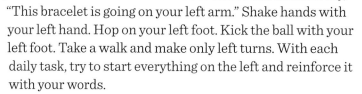

"This bracelet is going on your left arm." Shake hands with your left hand. Hop on your left foot. Kick the ball with your left foot. Take a walk and make only left turns. With each daily task, try to start everything on the left and reinforce it with your words.

Through consistent, daily repetition, a physical connection will begin to form between the left side of the child's body, the word *left,* and eventually, the concept of left. After

a while, switch to the right. The important thing here is prolonged consistency for both left and right.

The principle is simple. Use every sensory, motor, visual, and auditory cue to constantly reinforce the association between the body and the concept of left. For instance, "I'm putting this sticker on your *left* hand." "You did a good job of writing your name on the *left* side of your paper." "Can you show me how you jump on your *left* foot?" In other words, employ this principle:

Experience + Language = Understanding

Over time, and with lots of practice, left will become a firm, fixed concept. And with the foundations you provide, children will then be ready to apply the idea of left to other things, such as putting their left shoe on their left foot.

And over the next 10 weeks, of course, the focus is on the concept of right. Right. Right. Right.

CHAPTER 3

Implementing Smart Steps

//

Smart Steps are developmentally appropriate, step-by-step activities designed to leverage young children's natural need to move in preparing the body and brain for early learning and school readiness—while instilling the confidence children need to tackle challenges head on.

The activities are designed for use with children one on one or in groups, in preschool, childcare, or home settings.

Three key elements make up the Smart Steps activities:

- the Movement Can-Do Guide, an observational evaluation tool
- a series of 50 Smart Steps activity sequences, each offering 18 sequential steps of incremental challenge
- Teaching GEMs (Get 'Em Moving!), teaching tips and techniques for ensuring positive movement experiences that advance and automate children's foundational physical capabilities

And there are three key steps to implementing the activities:

- observational evaluation
- get moving—select and play the activities
- review

Before we get into the details of implementing Smart Steps, let's take a look at a sample activity to give you a sense of how the program lays out.

Step 1: Observational Evaluation

Sequential teaching takes the learner step-by-step from the known to the new. It's widely used in academics, but less so for children's physical development. So to begin implementing Smart Steps, the first step is to identify where to start the child within the activity sequence.

For this step, we've taken the can-dos of movement discussed in Chapter 1 and broken them down even further into what we call the Movement Can-Do Guide (pages 44–45). Note how this guide builds a continuum of progress—On the Move, Watch Me Grow, and In the Know—with three progressions per developmental stage from snugglers to skedaddlers—resulting in 18 progressions of children's movement development. Correspondingly, each of the 50 Smart Steps activity sets follows the same progressive track, with 18 steps from the snugglers through the skedaddlers stages.

Activity Number
For easy reference

Kinetic Scale Category
Indicates main learning outcome

On the Move
Introduces key movements and movement patterns

In the Know
Challenges key movements toward automaticity

Story Suggestion
Inspires the imagination to motivate movement

Activity Name
Ties together the sequence of 18 activities

Teaching GEMs
Suggestions for best teaching practices

Watch Me Grow
Reinforces key movements and advances skills

Equipment
Materials needed for entire activity set

Key Benefits
Indicates the learning outcomes derived across the activities

Language Focus
Directional and relational concepts reinforced through the activities

Critical Safeguards
Safety considerations for implementing activities

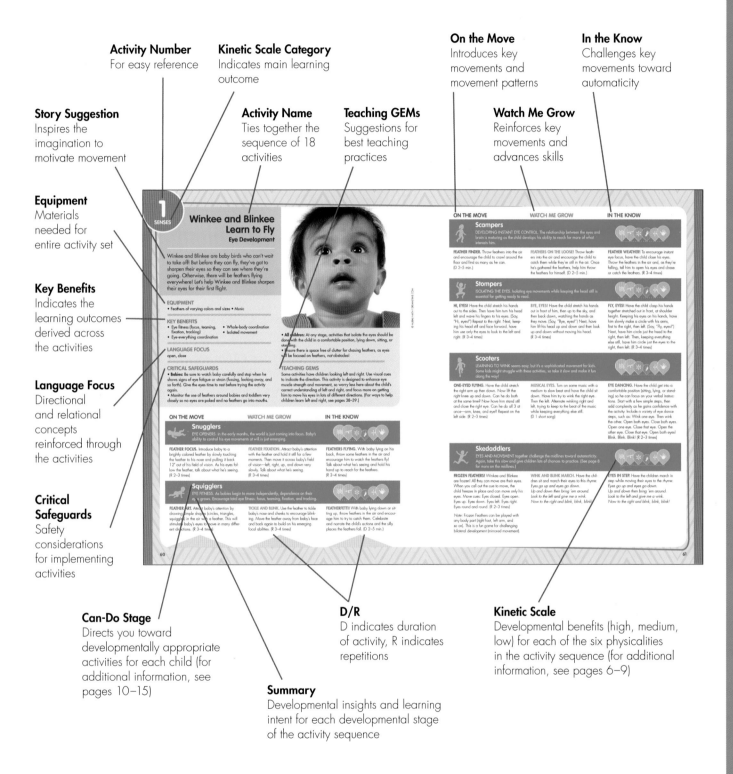

Can-Do Stage
Directs you toward developmentally appropriate activities for each child (for additional information, see pages 10–15)

Summary
Developmental insights and learning intent for each developmental stage of the activity sequence

D/R
D indicates duration of activity, R indicates repetitions

Kinetic Scale
Developmental benefits (high, medium, low) for each of the six physicalities in the activity sequence (for additional information, see pages 6–9)

Note: In even-numbered activities, children are referred to as female; in odd-numbered activities, children are referred to as male. All activities are appropriate for boys and girls alike.

Defining a Daily Balanced Diet

- Before you begin, simply observe what the child *can do* at this moment and identify where she belongs on the guide. For instance, if a child is sitting up by herself but hasn't yet started crawling, she would be at the midpoint (Watch Me Grow) of the squigglers stage.

- Next, identify the tilt of the Kinetic Scale that is most optimal to the child's stage of development. Note the proportions of each of the physicalities she needs for her well-balanced movement diet. For example, our squiggler would benefit most from activities with high values of Senses, Balance, and Intuition.

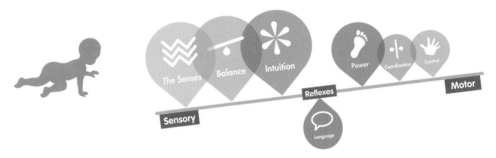

With that information in hand, you're ready to select your activities. As you do, let the Movement Can-Do Guide on pages 44–45 help in your selection. Please note that the guide is *not* meant for comparing children of the same age, nor is it meant to be used as a gauge for where a child *should* be in her development. She is where she is. Start from there.

Selecting a Daily Balanced Diet

Ideally, children should be up and active as much as possible throughout the day so they get a wide variety of physical experiences. But even with lots of free-play time, they may not get the full balance and variety of activity their bodies and brains need. The Smart Steps activities are designed to help you ensure that children get the right mix of physicalities daily, weekly, monthly, and across an entire year.

> The Movement Can-Do Guide is *not* meant for comparing children of the same age, nor is it meant to be used as a gauge for where a child *should* be in her development. She is where she is. Start from there.

Once you've identified the daily balanced diet of physicalities a child needs, look for activities rich in those physicalities for her to play and enjoy. As you select activities, your first criterion should be variety. For instance, in week one you might look for activities that emphasize the senses, balance, and intuition. However, the Kinetic Scale allows you to be more precise in your planning.

Kinetic Groupings

As you thumb through the activities, you'll notice they are grouped according to the six physicalities of the Kinetic Scale. This should make your planning easier. But notice that a single activity may have multiple development benefits. For that reason, we've coded each activity with an at-a-glance visual guide to all of the kinetic benefits at each stage.

The kinetic code is based on a simple three-point scale—high, medium, and low—which you'll see depicted visually through three different-sized icons.

Consider the whole value of an activity in your planning. Every activity has many bonus benefits beyond supporting those most-emphasized physicalities.

low   medium   high

Step 2: Get Moving

Now comes the fun. Start by selecting an activity that closely matches the developmental needs of the stage of the child. For instance, squigglers need lots of sensory, balance, and intuition activities, so you will want to choose one of these to begin with.

Next, identify the child's can-do level within the activity. In the example we've been following, our squiggler is in the Watch Me Grow stage. Now, go play!

If the activity appears too difficult at first, back up a step or two until the activity is within a comfortable stretch of the child's abilities. Never stay with an activity that frustrates a child for too long. Take a step back (for example, from Watch Me Grow to On the Move) or switch activities and come back another time. Confidence is the fuel for Smart Steps, so try not to dent it.

Likewise, if a child breezes through the activity many times with little effort, individualize the activity with increased challenge or advance him forward to the next step. Boredom defeats motivation just as much as frustration does.

Step 3: Review

As we've noted, Smart Steps isn't training camp. Instead, the activity sequence is designed so children can follow nature's plan, advancing along their own course and at their own pace. So, how do you know when a child is ready to advance to the next step?

When a child is becoming confident and capable with an activity, you'll notice one or more of these things:

- She'll do the activity without asking for help.
- She'll do it faster.
- She'll do it with less concentration (automatically).
- She'll want to show you what she can do.
- She'll go back to that same activity repeatedly.
- She'll seek out, investigate, and invent new ways to do it on her own.

When you see these signs, it may be time to bump up the challenge one step. In other words, advance her when she's developmentally ready.

The Movement Can-Do Guide

On the Move

Play by Play		Moving into new skills and abilities
Snugglers Birth to rolling over Approximate age: 0–6 months		Primitive reflexes in place Head control (first attempts) Enjoys touch, massage, and skin-to-skin care
Squigglers Rocking, crawling, and sitting Approximate age: 6–14 months		Grasping Mouthing (mimicking mouth movements) Commando crawling (beginning to explore the floor)
Scampers Pulling up to walking Approximate age: 9–24 months		Learning navigation (small spaces) Pulling up to standing (aided) Cruising Bobbing up and down (aided)
Stompers Running and jumping Approximate age: 20 months–3½ years		Running Bobbing up and down (independently)
Scooters Hopping and climbing Approximate age: 3–4 years		Early signs of handedness Balancing on one foot (dominant hand and foot awakening)
Skedaddlers Skipping, leaping, cooperative games, and dance Approximate age: 4 years and older		Leaping (from standing) Cross-walking (crossing one foot over the other)

Watch Me Grow	In the Know
Growing through practice by playing, exploring, and experimenting	**Automating skills while building confidence to try more**
Hand and foot recognition starts Hip tips (attempting to roll) Discovery through senses emerging (especially mouth)	Fascinated by faces (studies facial expressions) Rolling independently Pushing up (from tummy) Postural reflexes emerging (primitive reflexes abating)
Up on all fours Rocking Releasing grasp (voluntarily) Changing hands	Crawling Pincer grip Pushing into sitting position
Standing independently Climbing on furniture or stairs	Eye-hand coordination emerging (self-feeding) Toddling and walking
Jumping (on two feet) Upper body strength (beginning to hold own weight)	Jumping (forward or backward) Manipulative skills (using objects to affect other things) Temporal awareness emerging (attempts to catch, bat, or kick moving ball)
Marching Hopping on one foot Coordinated climbing	Galloping Midlines sharpening Dominant hand and foot developing
Leaping (from running) Skipping (no rope)	Automated, coordinated movement such as dance, skipping rope, and playground games

Implementation Strategies

Smart Steps has been designed to integrate with and add value to your policy and curriculum goals. Here are recommended guidelines for implementing the activities along with a list of suitable alternatives to adapt to your unique learning environment.

Recommended Implementation: Snugglers and Squigglers

- **What: small bites.** Use Smart Steps several times a day for 10 minutes at a time (depending on the child). Repeat the same activity multiple times for baby's benefit, responding to the child's reactions as you play.

- **When: tone and time of day.** Identify high-energy, fun games for times when babies are awake and active. Select quiet-time activities before naptime.

- **Where: outdoors and indoors.** Whenever possible, bring Smart Steps outside. By the same token, don't limit activities just to outdoors. Active learning can happen in any environment.

- **How: daily balanced diet.** Select activities that create a balanced diet of movement by choosing those with high values of Kinetic Scale physicalities that meet each child's current needs.

Recommended Implementation: Scampers, Stompers, Scooters, and Skedaddlers

- **What and when: multiple small sessions.** Use Smart Steps several times a day for 15 to 30 minutes at a time. These sessions may be part of your scheduled mat time or any other time of the day you choose when the energy level is high, or when you want to lift energy levels.

- **Where: outdoors and indoors.** Whenever possible, bring Smart Steps outside. By the same token, don't limit activities to just outdoors. Active learning can happen in any environment.

- **How: daily balanced diet.** Select activities that create a balanced diet of movement by choosing activities with high values of Kinetic Scale physicalities that meet each child's current needs.

- **How: variety.** Choose two or three activities to focus on each day and repeat them several times throughout the day. Beyond that, repeat activities multiple times, modifying to each child's responses and emerging competencies as you play.

Other Considerations

- **One-on-one time.** Take time to work individually with children who are struggling with an activity. Your time and attention will bolster their confidence.

- **Perpetual Smart Steps.** Make activities available for the children to return to throughout the day.

- **Motorvators.** Use any single Smart Steps activity as a movement snack throughout the day. See page 30 for more on Motorvators.

- **Create a circuit of activities.** Reinforce the learning by mixing and matching activities you've been learning over the course of a few days or weeks to create a circuit challenge.
- **Smart Steps at home.** Encourage families to play Smart Steps at home with their children. Repetition is key to helping children automate movement, so continuing the play at home continues the learning, too.

Learning Stories to Share with Families

The Smart Steps activities present detailed, progression-by-progression insights into the developmental value of each activity. These highlight the links between play and movement and learning. Make it a point to share these insights with families through daily or weekly learning stories. Not only will this help parents see the value of movement in their child's development, it also gives you a place to celebrate children's achievements.

Keep your learning stories simple. Focus on one outcome at a time. Relate one success at a time. And encourage families to play the Smart Steps activities at home as much as possible (see page viii for information on downloading and printing the activities).

Photograph the child in action and build a photographic review of his progress over time. It will be fun for him to go back and see his own progress.

Here's an example of a Smart Steps learning story, written from the child's point of view:

Today I was having a great time sliding down the slide headfirst and landing on the safety mat. Doing activities with my head lower than the rest of my body helps me learn to control my body better. It also helps my balance, and it might even help me concentrate for longer periods of time. At home it would be great if I could do things with my head lower than the rest of my body. For example, I could bend over and look at you from between my legs. If we're watching TV, I could watch upside down.

Equipment List

Smart Steps activities are designed to be used with readily available equipment. Following is a list of many of the items you will want to have on hand. The equipment lists included with the activities cite additional materials you will need. Before you begin, use this handy checklist to be sure you have everything you need.

- Animal cards
- Apples (varying colors and sizes)
- Art materials for decorating boxes
- Balance beam
- Balloons and balloon bags*
- Balls (all types, sizes, and textures)
- Bar from which a child can hang
- Baskets
- Bath sponge
- Bathtub
- Bats (plastic or cardboard tube)
- Beads
- Beanbags
- Bell
- Bench
- Bike tires (small and large)
- Blankets
- Blindfolds
- Blocks
- Books or other reading material
- Broom handle
- Brush
- Bubble gun or machine
- Bubble solution
- Bubble wand
- Bubble wrap
- Bucket stilts
- Buckets
- Buzzer
- Camera
- Car tire
- Cardboard boxes
- Cardboard tubes
- Cardstock
- Carriage or stroller
- Cellophane
- Chair (office spinning chair and table chairs)
- Child-safe shiny objects

- Children's family photos
- Climbing equipment
- Clothespins
- Coins
- Cones
- Directional arrows (cut from cardboard with a picture of a hand or a foot on each)
- Dowels
- Drawing implements
- Drums (toy drums, plastic or tin containers, or whatever you have on hand)
- Drumsticks (toy drumsticks or other readily available implement such as wooden or plastic utensils)
- Fabric (various kinds)
- Fan
- Feathers of varying colors and sizes
- Finger cymbals
- Finger paints
- Fitness ball or other large ball, such as Moonhopper
- Flashlight
- Flyswatters
- Foam roller
- Food coloring
- Frisbee
- Glitter
- Gloop (see recipe on page 198)
- Glue
- Gymnastic wedge
- Hairdryer
- Hat
- Hoops
- Ice-cream sticks
- Index cards
- Jumping sacks (pillowcases)
- Large cardboard cylinder
- Laundry basket
- Log
- Mats (varying sizes)

---

*Safety regulations may prohibit or limit the use of balloons with young children. Check your local standards for guidance. As an alternative, balloon covers or bags could be used to cover the balloon and still achieve the slow, floating bounce of a balloon. Do not use balloons with children who have a latex allergy. A beach ball is another alternative.

- Metal objects (such as spoons or coins)
- Milk bottle
- Mirror
- Mud
- Natural objects such as stones, pebbles, pinecones, leaves, and sticks
- Net
- Nimble sticks (1-inch or ¾-inch diameter solid wood dowels, cut to 8½-inch length, sanded and shellacked for smoothness)
- Paddle (tennis or Ping Pong type)
- Paint
- Paper (tissue, newsprint, letter-sized, drawing-sized, notebook, and so on)
- Paper plates
- Parachute
- Pictures cut from magazines or on picture cards
- Pillowcases
- Pillows
- Pipe cleaners
- Planks
- Plank saddles
- Plastic balls
- Plastic bat (wide, lightweight)
- Plastic bottles with secure lids
- Plastic containers of varying sizes
- Plastic cups
- Plastic sheet
- Plastic spoons
- Plastic tub
- Play dough
- Play foam
- Pool noodles
- Pots and lids
- Printer
- Rattles
- Recorded music
- Ribbons
- Rice
- Rope
- Rug
- Sand
- Sandbox
- Scarves
- Scissors
- Scoop

- Sheets
- Shoeboxes or other containers for children to store objects they've collected for exploration
- Shoes
- Slide
- Slime
- Socks (varying colors and sizes) and other clothing
- Stickers (arrows, adhesive dots)
- Stilts
- Straight wooden ladder (6 feet to 8 feet long)
- Straws
- Streamers
- String
- Stroller
- Suitcases
- Swing
- Tape
- Ticking clock
- Timer
- Torch
- Towels
- Toys (various kinds)
- Traffic-light cards
- Tunnel
- Vinyl or paper circles
- Washcloths
- Water
- Whistle
- Wooden spoon
- Wrist or ankle bells

The Smart Steps Activities

At-a-Glance Guide to Smart Steps

Part 2 consists of a series of 50 Smart Steps activity sequences, grouped according to the Kinetic Scale. Each sequence presents a continuum of 18 activities tailored to use with snugglers, squigglers, scampers, stompers, scooters, and skedaddlers. (See the Activity Preview on page 41.)

	Activity	Topic	Language Focus
The Senses	1. Winkee and Blinkee Learn to Fly	Eye development	open, close
	2. Listening Mice	Ear development	toward
	3. Different Drummers	Auditory learning concepts	same, different
	4. The Out-of-Order Border	Visual learning concepts	same, different, before, after
	5. The Great Crinkle Cleanup	Developing the sense of touch	up, in, on
	6. The Sensory Garden	Multisensory processing	wide, narrow, top
	7. Let's Have a Color Party	Perpetual-focus learning; color recognition	same, different, names of colors
	8. Cardboardia	Asensory play: leaving room for imagination	inside, outside, through
Balance	9. Happy Hatchling	Dynamic equilibrium: balance in motion	on

Summary	Kinetic Scale Emphases*	Page
A comprehensive approach to eye fitness: focus, fixation, teaming, and tracking		60
Good listening skills begin with the process of hearing: exploring auditory development and sound filtering		62
Learning through the senses: auditory discrimination as a tool for developing critical reasoning and problem-solving skills		64
Learning through the senses: abstract concepts become real through sensory-rich physical experiences		66
Experiencing touch as a powerful learning tool		68
Learning through the senses: putting multisensory experiences to work in developing classroom readiness		70
Immersion works: how to use and infuse the classroom with perpetual learning		72
Less-is-more learning: fostering self-guided learning through imagination and free play		74
Steadiness: challenging children's balance in active situations helps steady them physically, cognitively, and emotionally		76

* In this At-a-Glance Guide, the sensory and motor physicalities depicted on the Kinetic Scale reflect the overall balance of the 18 activities within the sequence. Each of the 18 individual activities includes a Kinetic Scale graphic illustrating the sensory and motor physicalities in more nuanced ways, based on the capabilities and needs of children at the particular stage and phase addressed in that activity.

	Activity	Topic	Language Focus	
Balance	10. Roll-Over Rover	Rolling over: horizontal orientation	over	
	11. The Spinnagans	Spinning: challenging orientation	around, front and back, side to side	
	12. Do the Elvis	Spinning: vertical orientation	around, left, right	
	13. The Go-Over Game	Balance beam: building concentration	over, along, across	
	14. Hello, Octopo	Balance and positioning: meeting gravity in new ways	stop, go, around	
	15. Tortoise and Hare: After the Race	Dynamic equilibrium: going fast, going slow, and stopping	fast, slow, stop	
	16. Tortoise and Hare: On the Road Again	Dynamic equilibrium: managing terrain	up, down, on, across, over, under	
Intuition	17. Wiggle Where?	Body awareness: body design	inside, outside, match	
	18. Getting to Know Me	Body awareness: body mapping	around, through, over, under	
	19. Tunnel Trek	Spatial awareness: tunneling	through, in, out	
	20. Sardines in a Can	Understanding size and volume	small, medium, large, long, tall, wide, too little, too much, just right	
	21. Two Worms on a Plank	Strength management: pushing and pulling	across, along, up	
	22. Jack and Jill	Strength management: understanding varying weights	push, pull, light, heavy	
	23. Game Day	Understanding boundaries	around, inside, outside	

Summary	Kinetic Scale Emphases	Page
Leveraging balance development for optimal learning		78
Natural movement patterns: leveraging children's natural inclination to spin to help them stay grounded and engaged		80
Incorporating dance: exploring the learning benefits of dance beyond the dance floor		82
Be careful where you step: active, deliberate play builds focus and concentration for the classroom		84
Developing self-control: challenging balance and orientation		87
Speed impacts control: developing the ability to maintain balance at any speed		90
Developing the ability to maintain balance while navigating different environments and terrains		93
My body as a tool: developing an automatic sense of all the parts of the body and how they work together		96
Self-awareness: developing a deep, intuitive sense of one's own body and its internal GPS system		98
Understanding space: physical experiences with space lay the foundations for conceptual learning later on		100
Pre-math skills: physical, whole-body experiences with the abstract concepts of size and volume		103
Developing the body's intuitive sense for fine-tuning and adjusting movement leads to a sense of incrementalism		106
Tangible, physical experiences with weight to explore the concepts of similarities and differences		109
Exploring game play: essential life lessons in understanding boundaries, limits, and fair play		112

	Activity	Topic	Language Focus
Intuition	24. Steposaur Steps	Directionality	in, out, front, behind, between, through, under, over, around
Power	25. Ultimate Tug-of-War	Upper-body strength	up, over
	26. On the Road to Cartwheeling	Developing core strength	side to side, upside down, over, right, left
	27. Grabbypillar	Hand strength	up, down
	28. Don't Drop Fidgety Fox	Knowing your own strength	under, between, around
	29. Escape from the Zoo	Building stamina	up, down, in
	30. Let's Go to Hopscotch Camp	Whole-body development: jumping and hopping	in, out, around, on
	31. Mixed-Up Motories	Whole-body coordination: overcoming obstacles	high, low, over, under, through
	32. Pop Go the Bubbles	Flexibility and agility	through, into, off
Coordination	33. Crawlimals	Coordinated movement: crawling for all ages	all directional language
	34. The 3-Legged Triple-Toed Triopsicle!	Midline development: homo-laterality (moving a single body part)	left, right, top, bottom, front, back
	35. Crocodile Flop	Midline development: laterality (opposite movements)	left, right
	36. The Beanbaggles Brigade	Midline development: cross-laterality (crossing arms or legs over midlines)	over, across, behind
	37. Farmer Gates	Complex coordinated movement	open, close, left, right

Summary	Kinetic Scale Emphases	Page
Where is "top"? Exploring and making sense of the many meanings of contextual language through physical context		115
Understanding my own strength: developing the physical strength and stamina needed for learning		118
Skill preparation: developing the underlying physical foundations necessary for more advanced skills such as cartwheeling		121
Fine muscle control: building the strength and stamina needed to control hands and fingers		124
Self-awareness: understanding one's own strength		127
Stick-to-it-ive-ness: developing the physical strength and emotional mindset necessary for perseverance		130
Expanding capabilities through new movement patterns (hopping on one foot)		132
Whole-body coordination: mixed movement patterns (obstacle courses) to develop confidence with complexity		134
Maneuverability: learning to move the body with precision and at will with ease and speed		137
Crawling: a power tool for physical and cognitive development		139
Developing the ability to control, isolate, and move each part of the body independently from the rest of the body		142
Opposing sides: developing opposition movement patterns (such as left-right, left-right) supercharges brain development		144
Getting ready for thinking: cross-lateral movement patterns prepare the body and brain to manage complexity both physically and cognitively		147
Patterned movement requires "instant messaging" between the body and brain for on-demand control of all the body's moving parts		150

	Activity	Topic	Language Focus
Coordination	38. Put Your Tap Shoes On	Body rhythm	along, light, soft
	39. Food Fight	Judging external distance and timing	stop, go, now
	40. The Beanbaggles Juggle	Sequential movement	side, front, back
	41. Hopper Frog	Complex coordinated movement: learning to skip	forward, backward, on
Control	42. My First Volleyball	Eye-everything coordination and control	over, up, on
	43. Finger Fun	Manipulative play	up, in, on
	44. My First Rodeo	Learning to change direction	left, right, forward, back
	45. Traffic Jam	Pacing: changing speed and stopping	stop, go, wait
	46. Squish!	Understanding pressure and force	pull, push, roll
	47. Trusty Yellow Rope	Dynamic equilibrium: stability in motion	wide, narrow, on, over
	48. Incredible Shrinking Target	Incrementalism: adjusting movement by degrees	center, middle, between, forward, back, left, right
	49. Chicken Switch	Physical problem solving	through, inside, between
	50. Mission: Possible	Synchronization (putting all the moves together)	under, over, through

Summary	Kinetic Scale Emphases	Page
Getting in sync: developing an internal sense of timing fosters coordination, collaboration, and cooperation		153
Dynamic judgment: gauging speed and distance in static and dynamic situations		156
Physicalizing learning concepts: laying the groundwork for critical reasoning and thinking skills through physical experiences with patterns and sequences		159
Body and brain as one: preparing for high-level reasoning and creativity through whole-body movement and whole-brain engagement		162
Seeing and doing: synergizing the brain, eyes, hands, feet, and body for precision and accuracy		164
Finger dexterity: developing the hands and fingers (and feet and toes) as tools for learning		166
Decision making: learning to think on one's feet		169
Learning how to manage speed and negotiate the speed of others		172
Understanding impact through the use of manipulative materials		175
Maintaining control: understanding how to manage changing situations		178
Mastering control by degrees		181
Fast thinking, reasoning, and adapting in dynamic situations		184
Getting the job done: working in sync with one's environment and in collaboration with others		187

1
SENSES

Winkee and Blinkee Learn to Fly
Eye Development

Winkee and Blinkee are baby birds who can't wait to take off! But before they can fly, they've got to sharpen their eyes so they can see where they're going. Otherwise, there will be feathers flying everywhere! Let's help Winkee and Blinkee sharpen their eyes for their first flight.

EQUIPMENT
• Feathers of varying colors and sizes • Music

KEY BENEFITS
• Eye fitness (focus, teaming, fixation, tracking)
• Eye-everything coordination
• Whole-body coordination
• Isolated movement

LANGUAGE FOCUS
open, close

CRITICAL SAFEGUARDS
• **Babies:** Be sure to watch baby carefully and stop when he shows signs of eye fatigue or strain (fussing, looking away, and so forth). Give the eyes time to rest before trying the activity again.
• Monitor the use of feathers around babies and toddlers very closely so no eyes are poked and no feathers go into mouths.

• **All children:** At any stage, activities that isolate the eyes should be done with the child in a comfortable position, lying down, sitting, or standing.
• Ensure there is space free of clutter for chasing feathers, as eyes will be focused on feathers, *not* obstacles!

TEACHING GEMS
Some activities have children looking left and right. Use visual cues to indicate the direction. This activity is designed to enhance eye muscle strength and movement, so worry less here about the child's correct understanding of left and right, and focus more on getting him to move his eyes in lots of different directions. (For ways to help children learn left and right, see pages 38–39.)

ON THE MOVE   **WATCH ME GROW**   **IN THE KNOW**

 ### Snugglers
EYE OPENERS. In the early months, the world is just coming into focus. Baby's ability to control his eye movements at will is just emerging.

FEATHER FOCUS. Introduce baby to a brightly colored feather by slowly touching the feather to his nose and pulling it back 12" out of his field of vision. As his eyes follow the feather, talk about what he's seeing. (R 2–3 times)

FEATHER FIXATION. Attract baby's attention with the feather and hold it still for a few moments. Then move it across baby's field of vision—left, right, up, and down very slowly. Talk about what he's seeing. (R 3–4 times)

FEATHERS FLYING. With baby lying on his back, throw some feathers in the air and encourage him to watch the feathers fly! Talk about what he's seeing and hold his hand up to reach for the feathers. (R 3–4 times)

 ### Squigglers
EYE FITNESS. As babies begin to move independently, dependence on their eyes grows. Encourage total eye fitness: focus, teaming, fixation, and tracking.

FEATHER ART. Attract baby's attention by drawing simple shapes (circles, triangles, squiggles) in the air with a feather. This will stimulate baby's eyes to move in many different directions. (R 3–4 times)

TICKLE AND BLINK. Use the feather to tickle baby's nose and cheeks to encourage blinking. Move the feather away from baby's face and back again to build on his emerging focal abilities. (R 3–4 times)

FEATHERFETTI! With baby lying down or sitting up, throw feathers in the air and encourage him to try to catch them. Celebrate and narrate the child's actions and the silly places the feathers fall. (D 2–5 min.)

Scampers

DEVELOPING INSTANT EYE CONTROL. The relationship between the eyes and brain is maturing as the child develops his ability to reach for more of what interests him.

FEATHER FINDER. Throw feathers into the air and encourage the child to crawl around the floor and find as many as he can. (D 2–5 min.)

FEATHERS ON THE LOOSE! Throw feathers into the air and encourage the child to catch them while they're still in the air. Once he's gathered the feathers, help him throw the feathers for himself. (D 2–5 min.)

FEATHER WEATHER! To encourage instant eye focus, have the child close his eyes. Throw the feathers in the air and, as they're falling, tell him to open his eyes and chase or catch the feathers. (R 3–4 times)

Stompers

ISOLATING THE EYES. Isolating eye movements while keeping the head still is essential for getting ready to read.

HI, EYES! Have the child stretch his hands out to the sides. Then have him turn his head left and wave his fingers to his eyes. (Say, "Hi, eyes!") Repeat to the right. Next, keeping his head still and face forward, have him use only the eyes to look to the left and right. (R 3–4 times)

BYE, EYES! Have the child stretch his hands out in front of him, then up to the sky, and then back down, watching the hands as they move. (Say, "Bye, eyes!") Next, have him lift his head up and down and then look up and down without moving his head. (R 3–4 times)

FLY, EYES! Have the child clasp his hands together stretched out in front, at shoulder height. Keeping his eyes on his hands, have him slowly make a circle with his arms, first to the right, then left. (Say, "Fly, eyes!") Next, have him circle just the head to the right, then left. Then, keeping everything else still, have him circle just the eyes to the right, then left. (R 3–4 times)

Scooters

LEARNING TO WINK seems easy, but it's a sophisticated movement for kids. Some kids might struggle with these activities, so take it slow and make it fun along the way!

ONE-EYED FLYING. Have the child stretch the right arm up then down. Now lift the right knee up and down. Can he do both at the same time? Now have him stand still and close the right eye. Can he do all 3 at once—arm, knee, and eye? Repeat on the left side. (R 2–3 times)

MUSICAL EYES. Turn on some music with a medium to slow beat and have the child sit down. Have him try to wink the right eye. Then the left. Alternate winking right and left, trying to keep to the beat of the music while keeping everything else still. (D 1 short song)

EYE DANCING. Have the child get into a comfortable position (sitting, lying, or standing) so he can focus on your verbal instructions. Start with a few simple steps, then add complexity as he gains confidence with the activity. Include a variety of eye dance steps, such as: Wink one eye. Then wink the other. Open both eyes. Close both eyes. Open one eye. Close that eye. Open the other eye. Close that eye. Open both eyes! Blink. Blink. Blink! (R 2–3 times)

Skedaddlers

EYES AND MOVEMENT together challenge the midlines toward automaticity. Again, take this slow and give children lots of chances to practice. (See page 8 for more on the midlines.)

FROZEN FEATHERS! Winkee and Blinkee are frozen! All they can move are their eyes. When you call out the cue to move, the child freezes in place and can move only his eyes. Move cues: Eyes closed. Eyes open. Eyes up. Eyes down. Eyes left. Eyes right. Eyes round and round. (R 2–3 times)

Note: Frozen Feathers can be played with any body part (right foot, left arm, and so on). This is a fun game for challenging bilateral development (mirrored movement).

WINK AND BLINK MARCH. Have the children sit and march their eyes to this rhyme:
Eyes go up and eyes go down.
Up and down then bring 'em around.
Look to the left and give me a wink.
Now to the right and blink, blink, blink!

EYES IN STEP. Have the children march in step while moving their eyes to the rhyme:
Eyes go up and eyes go down.
Up and down then bring 'em around.
Look to the left and give me a wink.
Now to the right and blink, blink, blink!

Listening Mice
Ear Development

Whenever you want children to listen closely, sing the "Listening Mice" song (page 190).

EQUIPMENT

- Blanket
- Rattle toys
- Music
- Quest Chests (see page 190)
- Sticks, leaves, pinecones, and other natural materials

- *Optional:* Various items for sound cues (bell, whistle, buzzer)
- Metal objects (such as spoons or coins)
- Blindfold

KEY BENEFITS

- Sound identification and discrimination
- Auditory figure ground (ability to tune in and tune out sounds)

- Ear tracking
- Auditory sequencing
- Cooperation

LANGUAGE FOCUS

toward

CRITICAL SAFEGUARDS

- **Babies:** Do not let babies or toddlers handle small objects such as stones, sticks, coins, or other objects that may be easily put into their mouths or swallowed. Supervise closely whenever small objects are used.

- **Older children:** Ensure natural materials (sticks, pinecones, and so forth) are well rounded and not too sharp.
- **All children:** Do not blindfold children or cover their eyes if they are not comfortable with this. Supervise and support activities when children close their eyes or are blindfolded. Be sure the room is clear of obstacles when children are blindfolded.

TEACHING GEMS

Unlike visual stimulation, we don't always think about our auditory landscape as a learning experience. Even incidental exposure to sound helps develop auditory processing skills, which will one day play a major role in children's verbal and written skills. Create a sound-rich environment. Talk a lot. Narrate everything. And don't forget to sing, too!

ON THE MOVE   **WATCH ME GROW**   **IN THE KNOW**

 ## Snugglers
SOUND AWARENESS. Giving baby different experiences with the sound of your voice starts to build her understanding of sound differentiation.

THESE ARE YOUR EARS. Softly touch the contours of baby's ears while talking and singing. Watch for baby's reaction. Gently blow on her ears. Encourage her to touch her ears and yours. Talk about what you hear. (D 5 min.)

SOUND GOES UP AND DOWN. Lay baby on her back and gently massage her from top to toe. As you move down baby's body, lower the pitch of your voice. Next, massage up her body, raising the pitch of your voice as you go. Repeat with baby lying on her tummy. (D 2–3 min.)

FOLLOW THAT SOUND! Lay baby down on a blanket on the floor. Talk, sing, or make a sound as you move around the room, encouraging her to look toward the sound. Be sure to let her find you and see the sound coming from you. (D 2–3 min.)

 ## Squigglers
SOUND AND MOVEMENT. Exploring sounds by using the body stimulates multiple senses while building sound discrimination and listening skills.

EAR-A-BOO. Sing a song to the child. At different intervals, gently cover the child's ears to muffle what she hears. This will give her the sense that sound continues even when she can't hear it clearly. Repeat several times so she hears the difference in volume throughout the song. (D 1–2 min.)

SHAKE! SHAKE! SHAKE! Give the child 1 or 2 rattle toys and assist her to shake them in different ways: high, low, to the front, out to the side, and so forth. Turn on music and shake to the beat! (D 2–5 min.)

SOUND AND SEEK. Once baby is up and crawling around, duck out of sight and call to her to encourage her to head toward the sound of your voice. If baby is having difficulty locating your voice, reveal yourself several times until she grasps the game. Repeat by hiding in a new spot for baby to find you. (D 2–5 min.)

Scampers

SOUND DYNAMICS. Understanding that sound varies in volume and intensity is the beginning of a child's understanding of how to modulate her own sound-making efforts.

QUEST CHEST: SOUNDS. Fill your Quest Chest with things that make sounds. Encourage the child to listen to the sounds, identifying the qualities of the sounds for her. For instance, "That sound is loud" or "That sound is high." Once she's explored each sound individually, assist her to create several sounds at once. (D 2–5 min.)

WHAT DOES A STICK SOUND LIKE? Take a walk outdoors and find a stick. Explore all the sounds the stick can make on the ground, on tree bark, and so on. Repeat with different objects, such as leaves or pinecones, listening closely for the differences. (D 5–10 min.)

QUIET AND LOUD. Ask the child to show you what a quiet mouse does. Talk in whispers. Tiptoe. Be very, very quiet. Then ask what a noisy cat does when it comes toward you. Shout loud. Stomp your feet! *Meow! Meow!* Be very, very loud! (D 2–5 min.)

Stompers

LISTENING MEANS HEARING. As children develop mastery over their soundscape, learning to focus on specific sounds (known as auditory figure ground) is the next step.

SOUND SAFARI. Take a sound safari outdoors, listening for different natural and human-made sounds. "Can you hear the sparrow? Can you sound like a sparrow? Where is the sparrow? Let's walk toward it. Listen. It's getting louder!" (D 10–15 min.)

SOUND REBOUND. Present the child with a sound (such as a bell ring or whistle). Each time she hears that sound, have her make a sound back by moving (for example, by clapping or stomping). Once she gets the idea, introduce a second "sound rebound." (D 2–3 min.)

LISTENING MICE. Give the child 1 or 2 sounds to make by moving (such as clapping or stomping). Then sing the "Listening Mice" song, making the sounds throughout the song. ("Listening mice." Stomp. "Listening mice." Clap. "Turn on your ears." Stomp.) With a group, give different children different movement sounds to create a party-sized sound game! (R 2–3 times)

Scooters

UNDERSTANDING COMPLEXITIES IN SOUND underpins important classroom and life skills such as recognizing the inflections in speech that aid in understanding other people's meaning.

PINDROPS. Listening mice are so quiet they can hear a pin drop! Have the child close her eyes. Drop a spoon on the floor at different spots around the room. Have the child point toward the sound. Repeat at different distances and with different objects, making softer and softer sounds, until the child can hear a pin drop! (R 2–3 times)

WHO'S GOT THE CHEESE? Form a circle and assign each child a sound to make. Ask for 3 volunteers to wear blindfolds and play the mice in the middle. Give 1 child in the circle a beanbag to represent the cheese. The child holding the cheese makes a funny noise of her choice while the mice in the middle listen for the sound and point to it. Pass the cheese to another child in the circle and continue the play. (D 3–5 min.)

HIDE AND HEAR. Present a silly sound (such as quacking like a duck) and have all the children repeat it. Select 3 children to play the noisy mice. Have the mice hide while the others shut their eyes. Then the others go and find the noisy mice by moving toward the sounds they hear. For added challenge, repeat the game with different sounds for each of the mice, and have children find the sounds in sequence. (R 3–5 times)

Skedaddlers

SOUND IN CONTEXT is the way we hear everything, so encouraging children's hearing skills in a noisy environment is real-life practice for building good listeners.

NOISY BARNYARD. Assign animal sounds to children, making sure 2 or more children each have the same sound. Have them make their sounds while moving around the room looking for their matching sounds. Have them try moving like the animal, too! (D 2+ min.)

SOUND CIRCLES. Select 3 children to be mice; assign each of the other children a barnyard sound. Barnyard animals stand in a circle; the mice stand in the center with their eyes covered (or blindfolded). The barnyard animals make their sounds all at the same time. Call out different sounds for the mice to point to. "Where's the rooster?" "Can you find the cow?" (D 3–5 min.)

SOUNDS-GO-ROUND. Repeat "Sound Circles," only this time the barnyard is moving, circling left then right. Call out different sounds for the mice to find. Next, have the barnyard children move like their animal while making the sound. Change the pace from slow to fast. Change the volume from loud to quiet. (D 5–7 min.)

Different Drummers
Auditory Learning Concepts

Rum-a-tum-tum! Rat-a-tat-tat! Nothing's more exciting than waiting for a parade to begin! Can you hear it coming?

EQUIPMENT
- Music (of different genres)
- Wrist or ankle bells or finger cymbals
- Feathers
- Bath sponge
- Drum
- Drumsticks
- Plastic spoon
- Brush

KEY BENEFITS
- Temporal awareness
- Auditory discrimination
- Auditory memory
- Music: feeling the beat
- Language or musical dynamics: fast, soft, slow, etc.

LANGUAGE FOCUS
same, different

CRITICAL SAFEGUARDS
- Monitor the use of feathers around babies and toddlers very closely so no eyes are poked and no feathers go into mouths.

- Ensure drumsticks are kept away from eyes and mouths.
- Ensure there is enough room for children to play their drums without banging into others.

TEACHING GEMS
- Keep cans, pots, pans, wooden spoons, brushes, and other similar items on hand for these activities and for any time you want to strike up the band!
- Use plastic containers with removable lids to make drums.
- Encourage children to make and decorate their own drums.

SARAH ALICE LEE

ON THE MOVE | **WATCH ME GROW** | **IN THE KNOW**

Snugglers
SOUND EXPOSURE. Because the ears are always on, build children's auditory library by devoting a few minutes each day to the playful exploration of sound.

ONE EAR AT A TIME. Gently prop baby up on his side to partially muffle 1 ear. Be sure to keep 1 hand on baby at all times to avoid rolling. Play music, sing, and talk. Repeat on his other side. (D 2–5 min.)

DANCE, BABY, DANCE. Hold baby in various positions (upright, lying down, on his tummy), always supporting his whole body, especially the head. Move your body and his to the dynamics of the music—fast and slow, high and low, and so forth. (D 2–5 min.)

FOOT CYMBALS. Attach ankle bells or finger cymbals to baby's legs. Encourage baby to kick. Hold his feet up and gently jingle them to show him where the sound is coming from—his feet! (D 2–5 min.)

Squigglers
UNDERSTANDING BEAT, RHYTHM, AND TEMPO creates the early beginnings of many sophisticated reasoning skills such as sorting, patterning, and sequencing.

TUMMY DRUM. Turn on some music and gently tap out the beat on the child's tummy with something soft like a feather. Repeat with different textures such as a sponge at bath time, or just your fingertips. Repeat on baby's back during tummy time. (D 2–3 min.)

MY FIRST DRUM. Sit with baby between your legs and introduce a drum. Assist baby to tap the drum with his fingers. Drum fast. Drum slow. Then put on some music and tap the drum to the beat. (D 2–5 min.)

MY FIRST DRUM SET! Introduce a variety of drums (pots or pans, a plastic homemade drum, and so on) to create different sounds. Explore the different sounds each drum makes with your hands. Put on some music and assist him to tap out the beat. When baby's ready, introduce drumsticks (real drumsticks, wooden spoons, plastic utensils). (D 2–5 min.)

ON THE MOVE	WATCH ME GROW	IN THE KNOW

Scampers

BODY SOUNDS. Making sounds and music with the body combines physical and sensory experiences—which gives little ones a deeper understanding of both experiences.

I HEAR DRUMMERS. With the child sitting or lying down, sing and tap out the "I Hear Drummers" song (page 190) on his back, tummy, or any other part of his body. Use the palm of your hand for the *rum-a-tums* and your fingertips for the *rat-a-tats*. (R 2–3 times at different tempos)

CLAP! CLAP! Sing "I Hear Drummers" for the child while encouraging him to clap to the beat. Start by clapping hands, then try clapping with your feet, elbows, knees, and so forth. Clap your hands on your knees. Clap your hands on your tummy. Clap any which way you can think of! And when you're done, give yourselves a big round of applause! (D 2–3 min.)

ECHO! ECHO! Make silly sounds (clapping, animal sounds, raspberries, a great big smooch) and encourage the child to mimic you. Follow his lead, too, repeating sounds he makes so he understands communication is a 2-way street. (D 2–3 min.)

Stompers

CLASSIFYING SOUND. We often think of sorting and classifying as a visual activity, but comparing sounds offers children a unique way to explore the concept of comparisons.

SOUND AROUND. Place different sound-making objects around the room. Talk about what each sounds like: How are they the same? How are they different? Encourage the child to make up his own "song" by running from sound to sound. (D 5–10 min.)

SOUND-ALIKES. Gather objects that make a variety of sounds. Explore the sounds individually; then assist the child to find objects that sound alike. Which ones are loud? Quiet? Which sound high? Low? Then sort the objects for their differences. (D 5–10 min.)

DIFFERENT DRUMMERS. Have children explore the different sounds they can make on a single drum. Have them tap it with their fingers, elbow, foot, and so forth. Experiment with a wooden drumstick, plastic spoon, brush, or feather. How many ways can they make the drum sound? (D 5–10 min.)

Scooters

SOUND VARIATION. Manipulating words and sounds challenges sound discrimination while giving kids ways to experiment with all the ways they can express themselves.

SILLY SPEAK. Make up a silly word or sentence and experiment with it in lots of ways. Talk very slowly. Or superfast! Talk high. Talk low. How would a parrot say it? How would Mommy say it? (D 2–3 min.)

MOODITUDES. Using the silly word or sentence from "Silly Speak," explore ways to express it in different moods, such as happy, sad, excited, silly, angry, and worried. Use broad verbal and body cues so that children clearly see the distinctions among emotions. (D 2–3 min.)

FILL IN THE _____. Pick a familiar song and have the child sing it with you. Sing the song again, randomly "forgetting" 1 of the words. Ask him to fill in the blank for you. This challenges auditory memory skills, while empowering the child to show you what he knows. (R 3–4 times)

Skedaddlers

PATTERNS AND SEQUENCES with sound support children's innate understanding of the rhythms of life, while underpinning emerging verbal and written communication skills.

DRUMSTICKS. Sing a song and have the child clap to the beat. Sing it again and use drumsticks to tap out the beat on the floor. Then, tap out familiar phrases such as a child's name or a favorite rhyme. What else has the same beat? (D 2–5 min.)

WORD FOR WORD. Sit in a circle with children and sing a favorite song together. Next, have the children take turns singing 1 word of the song: Child 1 sings "three," Child 2 sings "blind," and Child 3 sings "mice." (If working with a single child, alternate the words back and forth between you.) This builds listening, memory, sequencing, and patterning skills. (D 3–5 min.)

DRUM CORPS! Have the children sit in a circle, each with his own drum. Have 1 child tap out a beat; then all the other children repeat the same beat. Give everyone a turn setting the beat. After that, it's time to jam! (D 3–5 min.)

The Out-of-Order Border
Visual Learning Concepts

SARAH WHITING

When things are out of order, we need a sorter. Are you up for the job?

EQUIPMENT

- Tape and string
- Children's family photos
- Plastic cup
- Water
- Straw
- Large plastic bowl and pebbles
- Rainbow streamers (to make your own, cut 12"–18" strips of different-colored cellophane or sheer fabric and attach them to a stick to create a streamer)
- Chair or box
- Flashlight
- Music
- Stones of different sizes and weights
- Buckets
- Red and green apples
- Socks and clothing
- Paper and drawing implements
- Pictures cut from magazines or on picture cards

KEY BENEFITS

- Sequencing
- Locomotion
- Eye fitness
- Object permanence

LANGUAGE FOCUS

same, different, before, after

CRITICAL SAFEGUARDS

- Keep small objects out of the reach of young children.

- Watch for children putting things in their mouth. In the case of the "Taste Test" game, be sure to check for food allergies first.
- When children are moving quickly, ensure there is enough room for them not to collide.

TEACHING GEMS

- Life repeats itself. Some may call this routine. However, for a child, discovering repetition, pattern, and order in the things around her is a puzzle to be solved—a fascinating task that yields important life-management skills.
- Explore patterns with children as a way to explore the concept of order. Assist them to make discoveries and create new order for themselves.

ON THE MOVE	WATCH ME GROW	IN THE KNOW

Snugglers

VISUAL DEVELOPMENT. Baby's sensory understanding of the world is enhanced through simple, up-close stimulation and interactions with parents and caregivers.

PHOTO MOBILE. Tape string to the back of several of baby's family photos and dangle each photo for baby to see (approx. 8"–12" away). Talk about her family and tell her how she fits in: "This is your brother Marco." (D 2–3 min.)

MEET THE BUBBLES. Hold baby on your lap and show her how to make bubbles! Fill a plastic cup with water and use a straw to blow bubbles. Make big and small bubbles, go slow and fast, and so forth. (D 2–3 min.)

MAKE A SPLASH! Sit on the floor with baby between your legs. Place a wide plastic bowl filled with water in front of you. Assist baby to throw small objects in the bowl to make a splash. Cheer when you both get splashed! (D 3–5 min.)

Squigglers

FILTERS. Sensory development is like a series of filters that change the child's interpretation and understanding of things.

RAINBOW STREAMER. With baby on her back, dangle a rainbow streamer for her to see and explore. With baby on her tummy, dance your rainbow streamer in front of her to encourage her to reach and crawl. (D 3–5 min.)

RAINBOW PEEKABOO. Tickle baby with a rainbow streamer, encouraging her to see the world through the different colors. Get eye-to-eye close and play peekaboo with the ribbons. (D 3–5 min.)

RAINBOW TUNNEL. Drape the rainbow streamer over a chair or an open box to encourage baby to crawl to and through the streamers and into the tunnel. (D 3–5 min.)

ON THE MOVE	WATCH ME GROW	IN THE KNOW

Scampers

CHANGING ENVIRONMENTS. Simple changes to the environment, like changing the light, challenge the senses to tune in and sense things differently.

LET THERE BE LIGHT. Dim the lights a bit and use a flashlight to make shapes and patterns on the floor. Encourage the child to crawl and catch the light. (D 3–5 min.)

RAINBOW DISCO. Turn on the music, dim the lights, and shine a light through your rainbow streamer onto the wall. Dance the light and encourage children to sit or stand and catch the colors as they dance. (D 3–5 min.)

SHADOW HUNT. On a sunny day, go outside to find your shadows. Have children see if they can stand on their shadow. Can they stand on another person's shadow? What happens when children stand in the shade? Now go back into the sunshine on a shadow hunt to find your missing shadow! (D 5–10 min.)

Stompers

CONSTANCY is the study of categories—that 2 things can be different but still be part of a group. (For example, apples and oranges are both fruit.)

SAME BUT DIFFERENT. Collect stones in 3 buckets (flat stones, round small stones, heavy stones, and so on). Then make a stone pile using the qualities of the sorted stones for different purposes. For instance, what happens when you put the round stones on the bottom? What happens when you put the heavy stones on top? What's the best way to make the tallest pile? (D 10–15 min.)

STOP AND SMELL THE GARDEN. Go into a garden to smell the flowers. (Be careful to tiptoe so you don't wake up the weeds!) Identify children's favorite flowers. Talk about how each favorite flower smells, looks, feels. Then make up a dance to discover how the flower dances! (Indoors, try this with fruit.) (D 10–15 min.)

TASTE TEST. Start by tasting a red apple, then a green apple. Be sure the skin is on so children can see the difference. Talk about how the apples differ in taste, texture, and color. Next, offer 2 more pieces, this time without the skin. Encourage children to tell the difference and identify which is red and which is green. (D 3–5 min.)

Scooters

VISUALIZATION is based on prior knowledge. Being able to see what's "right" or "wrong" with something is great practice for memory and reasoning skills.

DIZZY DRESS-UP. Gather pieces of clothing and have 1 child put the clothes on in the wrong order (sock on her head, pants on her arms, and so forth). The sillier the better! Have the other children help re-dress her in the right order. (D 5–10 min.)

VANISHING ACT. Place 5 items on a table. Talk about them with the child, but don't touch them. Have the child close her eyes. Remove 1 item. When she opens her eyes, ask her which item is missing. Add a sixth item and play again. Each time you play, add another item to the table or remove more than 1 item to challenge the child's memory skills. (R 2–3 times)

SOCK SPIN. Call out a color and piece of clothing (for example, "white socks"). Have every child wearing white socks do a movement ("white socks spin!"). Call out another combination ("red shirts jump!"). Once everyone's engaged, repeat the call-outs using just the clothing to see what they remember about the moves. This is a great transition activity. (D 5–10 min.)

Skedaddlers

PATTERNING AND SEQUENCING. Developing an understanding of patterns and sequences builds memory capabilities and critical reasoning skills.

PATTERN PATH. Have the child draw shapes on separate pieces of paper, then create a repeat pattern with those shapes on the floor (such as circle, square, triangle, circle, square, triangle). Next, have the child step on the shapes, calling out the shapes as she goes. Try color patterns, too. (D 3–5 min.)

BEFORE AND AFTER. After an event, have the child draw pictures of what happened. Lay the pictures on the floor and have her put the pictures in the order in which they occurred. Talk about what happened using the words *before* and *after*. For example: "You and Gina played at the sand table. What did you do before that? What happened after that?" (D 5–10 min.)

PHOTO MATCH. Gather 12 pictures and place them on the floor in a grid. Name 3 pictures. Have the child step on the pictures in the same order you called them out. Next, try a new sequence of 4 pictures, then 5, and so on. See how far she can go, changing the pictures and sequence each time. (R 2–3 times)

The Great Crinkle Cleanup
Developing the Sense of Touch

Crafty Mr. Gummer Upper is at it again, wrinkling up the works at the paper factory! Do you know what happens when paper gets wrinkled? It turns into crinkles! Now we've got crinkles all over the place! It's time to bring in the recycling truck and begin the Great Crinkle Cleanup! Can you help out?

SARAH WHITING

EQUIPMENT

- Tissue paper
- Newspaper or newsprint
- Hairdryer or fan
- Letter-sized paper or note-book paper
- Basket or bucket

KEY BENEFITS

- Touch and texture
- Pincer grip

LANGUAGE FOCUS

up, in, on

CRITICAL SAFEGUARDS

- For younger children, use soft paper textures such as tissue or newsprint. For older children, use letter-sized or notebook paper for more precise folding and ripping activities.
- Be sure there's unobstructed room on the floor for all floor activities.

TEACHING GEMS

Once the games are done, show the children how to upcycle the crinkles by using them to do an arts and crafts project such as papier-mâché.

| ON THE MOVE | WATCH ME GROW | IN THE KNOW |

Snugglers
INTRODUCING THE WORLD OF TOUCH. Gently stimulating baby's sense of touch awakens him to his own body and to the world around him.

TISSUE BALLS. Roll a soft tissue into a ball or tube. Open baby's hands and roll the tissue on and between his hands. Repeat with the feet, legs, arms, tummy, back, and so forth. (R 2–3 times)

TISSUE SPRINKLES. Take some tissues and sprinkle them on baby. Talk about where the tissues land: "Look, they landed on your hand (leg, feet)." (D 2–3 min.)

TISSUE TICKLES. Place a soft tissue on baby's arm or hand and roll it up into a long tube. Gently thread the tube between baby's fingers and pull it through for a 3-D sensory experience. Repeat with baby's toes. (R 2–3 times)

Squigglers

EXPLORING TEXTURE. Crinkled papers present multisensory (sight, sound, texture) experiences while giving the child a taste of effecting change for himself.

MY FIRST CRINKLE. Explore soft papers such as tissue or newspaper. Help the child crumple the paper into a ball to create a soft crinkle. Roll it over the child's body to explore the texture. (D 2–3 min.)

CRINKLE CRAWL. Help the child make some soft crinkles; use them to create a big pile in the center of the floor. Encourage him to crawl through the crinkles. Sprinkle them over the child for fun. (D 2–3 min.)

CRINKLE PIT. Help the child make some soft crinkles. Then help him drop them into a large box. When the box is full, encourage the child to crawl in and explore the crinkly sensations with his whole body. (D 3–5 min.)

Scampers

MOVEMENT AND TEXTURE. Combining whole-body movement with texture helps the brain develop motor and sensory processing simultaneously.

CRINKLE STOMP. Roll a soft crinkle over the child's bare feet. Next, encourage him to stand and step on the crinkle. Celebrate the textures and sounds crinkles make when you stomp on them! (D 3–5 min.)

FIND THE CRINKLES. Lay out soft crinkles in a path all over the room and guide the child to crawl or walk along the path. Encourage the child to step on each crinkle or scoop them up as he goes. (D 3–5 min.)

OH! IT'S WINDY! Put some soft crinkles in a pile in the middle of the floor. Using a hairdryer or fan, scatter the balls around the room and have the child scoop them up or stomp on them with his bare feet. (D 3–5 min.)

Stompers

WHOLE-BODY TEXTURE EXPLORATION. Textural play is often associated with the hands, but the whole body should be involved in the exploration of texture.

CRINKLE-MAKING. Have the child make soft crinkles with his hands. Then show him how to make crinkles with other parts of his body (wrists, elbows, feet). Help him make tiny crinkles with his fingertips. (D 3–5 min.)

DON'T DROP THE CRINKLE. Have the child pass a crinkle to you or another child without dropping it on the floor. Use different body parts to do the passing, such as hands, feet, head, or knees. (D 3–5 min.)

CRINKLE SQUASH. Create a big pile of crinkles on the floor and have the child pencil roll over them to flatten them. Encourage him to explore all the ways he can squash the crinkles! (D 3–5 min.)

Scooters

ROLE-PLAYING WITH TEXTURE. Present sensory experiences through storytelling and role-play activities to engage the imagination and ramp up the excitement.

FOLD AND RIP. Show the child how to fold letter-sized paper into quarters and tear it into 4 equal pieces. Have the child crinkle the small paper pieces with 1 hand until he can no longer see it in his hand. Repeat with the other hand. (D 5–10 min.)

THE RECYCLING TRUCK. Put a big pile of crinkles on the floor; place a basket a little ways away to serve as the recycling station. Have the child be the recycling truck, bringing 1 crinkle at a time to the station using different ways of moving, such as crawling, jumping, or crab-walking. (D 3–5 min.)

THE BIG SCOOP. Put a big pile of crinkles on the floor and place a bucket next to the child. Have the child sit and be a recycling truck, scooping up the crinkles with his bare feet then dropping them into the bucket. Vary the speed for extra challenge. (D 3–5 min.)

Skedaddlers

PRECISION ACTIVITIES. Paper balls are ideal for exploring the effects of texture and mass on performance.

CRINKLE TOES. Have the child fold and tear the paper, then use his toes to make crinkles! Encourage him to roll the paper between his feet, then try crinkling the paper with just his toes. (D 3–5 min.)

CRINKLE FLICK. Set up a goal a short distance away. Show the child how to flick crinkles with his thumb and middle finger (similar to shooting marbles). Explore what happens with crinkles that are tightly or loosely wadded, and have children adapt their finger movements accordingly. (D 3–5 min.)

CRINKLEBALL. Set out a basket on the floor and have the child shoot crinkles (like shooting baskets) with his hands. Next, have him place a crinkle on the top of his foot and flick it into a bucket. Then have him pick up a crinkle with just his toes and dunk it in the basket. (D 3–5 min.)

The Sensory Garden
Multisensory Processing

Outdoors or in, our senses teach us what we need to know about our world (and a whole lot about ourselves, too). So follow the butterflies through the gates of the Sensory Garden to discover a world of sights, sounds, smells, tastes, and textures.

EQUIPMENT

- Feathers
- Terrycloth washcloths
- Paper
- Finger paints
- Sponges
- Play foam
- Bathtub
- Sandbox
- Sand or mud
- Water
- Variety of sensory materials (see "Texture Prints" activity)

KEY BENEFITS

- Real-to-symbolic play
- Teamwork
- Sensory awareness
- Physical numeracy
- Physical literacy
- Imagination

LANGUAGE FOCUS

wide, narrow, top

CRITICAL SAFEGUARDS

- Monitor the use of feathers around babies and toddlers very closely so no eyes are poked and no feathers go into mouths.
- Make baby-safe foam by whipping baby shampoo.

- Adult supervision is required at all times to prevent children from putting paints or other art materials in their mouths. Always use nontoxic materials.

TEACHING GEMS

- RULES TO 1 POTATO, 2 POTATO. Have the children stand in a circle with both hands in fists (potatoes). Select a child to count the potatoes. Using his fist, he counts each potato by gently tapping the other fists with his: "1 potato, 2 potato, 3 potato, 4. 5 potato, 6 potato, 7 potato, more." On "more," that potato is withdrawn from the game, and the count begins again with the next potato. Continue to count until only 1 potato is left.
- For mud activities, choose a rainy day or add water to the sandbox.

ON THE MOVE   **WATCH ME GROW**   **IN THE KNOW**

 ## Snugglers

THE GRASPING REFLEX is nature's way of encouraging baby to build the muscles in her hands and fingers.

BUTTERFLY KISSES. Gently open baby's hands and "butterfly kiss" the palms with your eyelashes. Repeat with the feet. (D 1–2 min.)

FEATHER FINGERS. Slowly run a feather between baby's fingers. Tickle the palm with the feather to encourage grasping, then tug gently on the feather so the fingers feel the tension. Repeat with the other hand, then both hands. Repeat with the toes. (D 2–3 min.)

ROUGH PATCH. Dampen and freeze a small patch of terrycloth or other textured fabric. Explore the rough, cold texture with baby on her hands and feet. Play a gentle game of tug-of-war with each hand, then with both hands at once. Be sure to warm up baby's fingers and toes when play is done. (D 2–3 min.)

 ## Squigglers

IMPRINTING. Early explorations of messy-play materials provides important new sensory experiences while showing baby how to leave her mark on the world.

FOOTPRINTS. Sit baby on your lap in front of a blank sheet of paper. Dip her toes in finger paint and assist her to "walk" her feet on the paper. Tiptoe to create dots. "Dance" to create swirls. (D 3–5 min.)

SPONGE PRINTS. Assist baby to explore finger paints with her fingers. Next, introduce soft sponges to paint with. Explore dabbing, swirling, and stroking the paint in different colors and directions. (D 3–5 min.)

TEXTURE PRINTS. Lay out a large sheet to protect the space. Explore painting with textured materials such as knees, elbows, bubble wrap, crinkled papers, feathers, or streamers to create different effects on the page. (D 5–10 min.)

ON THE MOVE	WATCH ME GROW	IN THE KNOW

Scampers

SENSORY TRANSFORMATION. The senses give children tangible experiences with changing circumstances.

FOAM SQUEEZE. Put a dollop of play foam in the child's hand and encourage her to squeeze. Rub her hands together. Encourage her to rub the foam on her knees, feet . . . even on you! Paint with the foam on the wall or sides of a bathtub. (D 3–5 min.)

DRY TO WET. Sit the child in the sandbox. Encourage her to explore the sand with her hands and feet. Pour a little water on the sand and repeat the exploration. Continue to add water a little at a time to explore the changes in texture. (D 3–5 min.)

PAINT ON. PAINT OFF. Sit the child on your lap and do some finger painting together. Have a clear bowl of water nearby. Rinse her hands with the water. Show her how her hands change from messy to clean as the water changes from clean to messy. (D 3–5 min.)

Stompers

SENSORY IMMERSION. Exploring 1 sensation in multiple ways refines and sharpens a child's ability to detect nuances.

MUD PRINTS. Explore making footprints in the mud. Find different ways to make imprints—with tiptoes, stomping, zigzags, and so on. Point out the trails the child leaves behind so she can see where she's come from. (D 3–5 min.)

IMAGINE MUDDO. Encourage the child to imagine Muddo the Mud Monster. How big are Muddo's feet? What do Muddo's footprints look like? How many feet does Muddo have? How does Muddo move through the mud? Where is Muddo going today? (D 3–5 min.)

MEET MUDDO! Encourage the child to draw a picture of Muddo the Mud Monster in the mud. What does Muddo like to do in the mud? Can you show me? Does Muddo like to run in the mud? Stomp? Sit? Jump? Roll over? Just how muddy can Muddo get? (D 3–5 min.)

Scooters

SENSORY PHYSICS. Physical concepts are more easily understood when a child explores them with her senses.

WHAT'S WIDE OR NARROW? Explore the concepts of *wide* and *narrow* with children, using examples in your environment. Next, ask children to show you how narrow or wide they can be using their bodies. Demonstrate to give them the idea. Repeat with other size concepts such as *tall, short, big, small, high,* and *low.* (D 5–10 min.)

WHAT'S ON TOP? Put your hand out and have the child put her hand on top of yours. Put your other hand on hers, and have her top your hand. Continue the game to show him how *top* changes. Where else is *top*? Put your hand on top of your head, your foot, the table, and so forth. Repeat with other directional concepts such as *bottom, next to,* and *across from.* (D 2–3 min.)

SQUASH SANDWICH. Repeat the "What's on Top?" activity to start. Next, play the game with your feet. Then, with a group of children, have 1 child lie flat on the floor, layer another child across the first child, and add a third child to the top of the pile. Discuss who's on top, who's in the middle, and who's on the bottom. Repeat, switching the parts of the sandwich around. (D 3–5 min.)

Skedaddlers

SENSORY LEARNING. Children learn with their bodies first, so adding physical sensations to academic subject matter puts the learning in their language.

1 POTATO, 2 POTATO. This classic playground mediator is a great example of physicalizing numeracy. Encourage the children to count aloud as the potatoes are counted. Next, use feet (tomatoes) to play the game. (D 3–5 min.)

X MARKS THE SPOT. Have the child sit on the floor and cross 1 leg over the other. This is the X position. What other X's can they make with their bodies? Have them cross their arms, fingers, and toes, or cross their arms behind them. Next, have them try the game with a partner to see how many X's they can make together. Repeat with any other letter of the alphabet. (D 3–5 min.)

SENSORY GARDEN. Gather a wide range of sensory materials into a pile. Child 1 takes any material and does something with it (such as shake the maraca). Child 2 repeats what Child 1 did and then takes a different object and decides what to do with it (such as wave the streamer). Child 3 uses her memory to repeat the first 2 actions and adds her own sensory experience to your growing sensory garden. (D 5–10 min.)

Let's Have a Color Party
Perpetual-Focus Learning: Color Recognition

Learning colors is pretty tricky when there are colors all around us. So what would happen if we just paid attention to one color at a time? Let's have a color party and see what happens.

SARAH WHITING

EQUIPMENT
- Items of different colors: cellophane, papers, streamers, scarves, feathers, plastic balls, circles (vinyl or paper)
- Plastic tub
- Socks and other clothing articles
- Objects for sorting
- Quest Chest
- Paper plates of different colors
- String
- Beanbags
- Index cards
- Hat

KEY BENEFITS
- Visual discrimination
- Fine-motor development
- Locomotion

LANGUAGE FOCUS
same, different, names of colors

CRITICAL SAFEGUARDS
- Always be present when children are playing in and around water. Never leave the children unattended.
- Ensure small objects are kept away from baby's mouth.

TEACHING GEMS
- **Perpetual-focus learning:** "Let's Have a Color Party" is an example of what we call *perpetual-focus learning* (PFL). It's based on the idea that children can learn deeply when they have repeated and varied experiences with a concept over an extended period of time. For instance, here the topic is color. Notice that the core of each activity focuses on a single color rather than presenting the entire color spectrum all at once. As

you approach these activities, it's natural to want to explore all the colors one after another so that children are learning colors contextually. PFL is designed to augment that contextual learning through immersive focus. Begin with these activities, then let them spill out into your daily routine. For example, if your focus is the color red, hold up a red stop sign to get the children to stop and focus, have children gather on the red carpet or near the red teddy bear, ask children to clap whenever they see red on a page or hear the word *red* in the text, and so forth. As you integrate red throughout your day, verbalize *red* over and over. "I'm holding up the red stop sign. What does that mean?" "Can you stack the red blocks all together?"

Or consider staging a "Red Day" during which all the children wear red, eat red snacks, count with red numbers, play with red toys, write with a red pencil, and draw red pictures. Explore variations of the topic. For instance, is pink part of the red family? This immersive experience with the color red, without the distraction of the rest of the rainbow, is a great way to reinforce important concepts that translate to multiple learning and life situations. And once the children demonstrate mastery over the topic (for example, by being able to transfer their learning of *red* to new and unknown red objects), that's your cue to move on to another PFL topic.

Note: Perpetual-focus learning can be applied to any area of conceptual learning, such as numbers, letters, shapes, or left and right.
- **Talking to children about color:** Studies have shown that how we present and talk about color to children can make a big difference in their learning. Avoid always using color as an adjective before a noun, such as "the red ball." Children tend to confuse the adjective and the object when color is presented to them this way. To counter this, be more deliberate and specific as often as you can. "The ball is red."

ON THE MOVE
WATCH ME GROW
IN THE KNOW

Snugglers
COLOR EMERGING. The ability to see color fully emerges over the early months. Exploring color gives the eyes a clue to what will come into focus soon.

COLOR LENS. Each week, try covering the outside windows with different-colored cellophane. Take baby over to the window and look out at the world through a different lens. (D 2–3 min.)

INTRODUCING COLOR. Lay baby on his back and dangle different brightly colored objects within his line of sight. Choose 1 color a week to focus on. Talk to him about the objects and the colors. Encourage him to reach for them. (D 2–3 min.)

COLOR SAFARI. Carry baby around the room, home, playground, or garden and point out objects of the same color. For example: "This pillow is red." "This apple is red." "This flower is red." (D 3–5 min.)

Squigglers

EXPERIENCING COLOR. Color is one of the first ways baby begins to see differences and similarities between things.

COLOR PATH. Create a sensory path on the floor using papers, streamers, scarves, feathers, or other material, all of the same color. Talk about the color as baby explores with his eyes, hands, and body. (D 3–5 min.)

COLOR TUB. Fill a small tub with plastic balls or crinkled papers that are all the same color. Seat baby in the tub and talk about the color as he explores. (D 3–5 min.)

COLOR BOUNCE. Lay out different-colored spots on the floor. Hold baby under his arms and bounce him from spot to spot, calling out the color names. Next, bounce on only 1 color, skipping all the others. (D 3–5 min.)

Scampers

COLOR IDENTIFICATION. Talking about color, even at these early ages, plants seeds for color identification and recognition.

EARLY COLOR MATCHING. Put colored socks on the child. Take a color safari, touching his socks to other objects of the same color. (D 3–5 min.)

ALL DRESSED IN. Dress the child and yourself in the same color and wear it all day. Spend time in front of the mirror. Talk about his shirt, his pants, his socks, his hat. Talk about yours, too. "Your shirt is red. My shirt is red."

WASHING DAY. Use finger paints to mess up your socks. Wash your socks in bubbly water and watch the water turn red. Hang them on the line with red clothespins to dry.

Stompers

COLOR PATTERNING. Color is one of the first ways children begin to recognize patterns. Patterning is an early precursor to higher thinking and reasoning skills.

COLOR MAPPING. Create patterns on the floor using circles of 1 color. Create straight lines, circles, zigzags, and so on. Encourage children to follow the path. (D 3–5 min.)

COLOR STEPS. Choose 2 different-colored circles and create patterns on the floor. Encourage the child to follow the path, calling out the 2 colors as he steps. Next, encourage him to step on only 1 of the colors, skipping the other. (D 3–5 min.)

COLOR MOVES. Repeat the "Color Steps" game, but this time have the child do 2 different moves on the different colors (such as wiggle on the red circle, then jump to the yellow circle). Next, have him skip 1 color and do *both* moves on the other color. (D 3–5 min.)

Scooters

COLOR DISCRIMINATION AND SORTING. Sorting things by color is one of the earliest ways children learn about putting things in groups and sequences.

COLOR QUEST. Assemble various objects in the Quest Chest. Have the child pick out only the objects of 1 color. (D 5–10 min.)

COLOR REMOVAL. Assemble various objects of different colors in the Quest Chest. Have the child remove anything that isn't the specified color. (D 5–10 min.)

COLOR SEQUENCING. Collect a pile of objects all the same color. Discuss how all of the things are different, but they all share the same color. Sequence the items, such as from biggest to smallest or tallest to shortest. (D 5–10 min.)

Skedaddlers

PHYSICALIZING COLOR. Active games in which color is the target work to cement children's understanding of color while building important matching skills.

COLOR TARGETS. Tie same-colored paper plates along a string and hang the string at eye level for the child. Give the child matching colored beanbags. Take a few steps back and have the child throw the beanbags and try to hit a plate. Next, replace 1 plate with a plate of another color. Now try the game again, avoiding the odd-colored plate. Continue to add paper plates of other colors until there is only 1 target left. (D 5–10 min.)

COLOR CHARADES. Identify objects that are all the same color and have the children draw them on separate index cards. Put the cards in a hat and have each child draw 1 card. Have each child take turns acting out their card while the others guess what they are! (D 5–10 min.)

LET'S HAVE A COLOR PARTY! Create a Color Day. For instance, on Red Day, everyone wears all red (including face paints), eats red food, creates red art, makes red hats, builds red towers, tells red stories, and so forth. Make up a song about *red*. Create a red dance. Walk on red lines on the floor. Create a red code word. In short, make absolutely everything red all day!

Cardboardia
Asensory Play: Leaving Room for Imagination

Something's terribly wrong in Cardboardia! Mr. Gummer Upper has stolen all the imagination. And now the whole place is turning into cardboard—even the people! Quick, we've got to get some imagination to Cardboardia. Can you help?

EQUIPMENT
- Large cardboard boxes
- Blanket
- Music
- Art materials for decorating boxes

KEY BENEFITS
- Asensory play
- Spatial awareness
- Imagination

LANGUAGE FOCUS
inside, outside, through

CRITICAL SAFEGUARDS
- Ensure the play happens in a space where children have room to move.

MOVING SMART

- For "Mailbox Mania," make a simple mailbox by cutting slots and holes in a cardboard box. Children can decorate it if they wish.

TEACHING GEMS
- Use different sizes, shapes, colors, and textures of boxes to provide different experiences.
- Take time to decorate the boxes together, then use them for other activities to show children how 1 object can have many purposes.

ON THE MOVE	WATCH ME GROW	IN THE KNOW

 ## Snugglers
ASENSORY PLAY. Low-stimulation experiences give the senses a much-needed rest and provide an important contrast with our sensory-rich world.

ISOLATING THE SENSES. Sit still and silent with baby in your arms. Engage her eyes with your smile. Next, turn baby so she can't see you and sing a quiet song. Then, without visual or auditory stimulation, gently rock her. (D 5–10 min.)

THE SENSES IN SPACE. In a quiet room, lay baby on a blanket on the floor and step out of sight. Allow her time to explore the space with her eyes. Staying out of sight, sing a song. Then, rejoin baby on the floor. Quietly touch her from head to toe. (D 5–10 min.)

SENSES IN A BOX. Find a clean box and cut off the top. Place a blanket in the box and lay baby down inside. Step away to give her time in this space. Staying out of sight, sing to her. Then gently push the box forward and backward and from side to side. (D 5–10 min.)

 ## Squigglers
NESTING. Right from the start of life, children are soothed by a sense of being bundled up or embraced.

WHAT'S INSIDE? Scatter several boxes on their sides on the floor near baby. Place a toy inside each box and encourage baby to reach and crawl for the toy. Repeat, putting the toys further and further inside the boxes to encourage baby to crawl inside. (R 3–4 times)

BOX CARS. Sit the child in a cardboard box and slide the box around the room. Start slowly so she adjusts to the motion. Add fun sound effects, such as a car (*vroom!*), a train (*toot toot!*), or a dragon (*roar!*). (D 3–5 min.)

POP GOES THE WEASEL. Sit the child in a box in front of you. Sing "Pop Goes the Weasel." On the word *pop*, lift baby up and add a big "whee!" Repeat. Watch to see her anticipate the pop. (D 3–5 min.)

ON THE MOVE   WATCH ME GROW   IN THE KNOW

Scampers

EMPOWERMENT. Imagine what it's like to always be the smallest person in a room. Everything is sized for big people. In small spaces, kids feel big.

BOX TOWER. Demonstrate how to stack boxes and give the child time to experiment on her own. Build a tower and encourage her to knock it over. Cheer each time a tower goes up, and when it comes down! (D 5–10 min.)

BOX MAZE. Scatter boxes around the floor to create a maze around the room. Encourage the child to navigate the maze by crawling around, in, and through the boxes. Encourage her to use the boxes to stand up, too. (D 5–10 min.)

BOX TUNNEL. Open both ends of a cardboard box and entice the child to crawl through. Add another box to create a longer tunnel. Use different sizes to challenge her movements. (D 5–10 min.)

Stompers

ROLE PLAY. When children pretend, they challenge themselves to move in different ways, which gives them a deeper sense of what they can do with their own bodies.

MAILBOX MANIA. Have the child gather objects to post in the mailbox. Encourage her to post objects in different ways—with the right hand, left hand, feet, elbows, and even upside down from between her knees! Make a game out of delivering the objects (the "mail") back to where they came from. (D 5–10 min.)

ROBOT GREETINGS. Have the child put her arm through a small box (like a cereal box) and then try moving stiffly like a robot. Ask the child to shake hands and talk like a robot. Create your own robot secret greeting. Then try the other arm. (D 5–10 min.)

ROBOT STOMP! Encourage the child to cover her body with boxes on her arms, legs, torso, and head. Have her try walking and talking like a robot. Then introduce a few simple dance steps. Put on some music and do the Robot Stomp! (D 5–10 min.)

Scooters

HIDING GAMES. When children are tucked down out of sight, they have a powerful sense of being in control, because they know something you don't know!

STOP, TURTLE, STOP! Have the child get on her hands and knees; place a box over her back. As she crawls like a turtle, she'll need to move slowly so the box doesn't tip over. Then, when you give the cue to stop, have her duck down and hide inside her shell. (R 3–5 times)

TURTLE TEN! Scatter boxes upside down around the room. Have 1 child hide like a turtle while the others close their eyes and count to 10. Then, start the countdown to go find the turtle: 10, 9, 8. . . . The seeker who finds the turtle gets to hide next. (R 3–5 times)

MUSICAL BOXES. Take a selection of different-sized boxes and put them in a circle. When you start the music, have the children step in the boxes, moving from box to box. When the music stops, they all stop, duck down, and hide! (R 3–5 times)

Skedaddlers

IMAGINATION. Cardboard boxes are a perfect blank canvas for children's imaginations. Stand back and let imagination take the lead.

ON THE ROAD TO CARDBOARDIA. Cut off the top and bottom panels of boxes big enough for children to fit in. They can use art materials to decorate their boxes to be cars, trucks, or whatever they want to drive. Then decide the rules of your roadway—speed limits, stoplights, passing lanes—and take a trip to Cardboardia! (D 10–30 min.)

WELCOME TO CARDBOARDIA. Give each child a box and have children draw different buildings on each of the 4 sides. Assemble Cardboardia City by lining up the boxes, stacking them, creating roadways, and so forth. Encourage role playing and telling stories about what happens in Cardboardia. What do people do there? What jobs do they have? (D 10–30 min.)

MEET THE CARDBOARDIANS. Stack 3 boxes. On each box panel, have the children draw pictures of themselves, their family, animals, creatures, and so on. Have them draw heads on the top box, torsos on the middle box, and the legs and feet on the bottom box. Now pivot the boxes to mix and match the pictures and invite children to tell stories about the Cardboardians! (D 10–30 min.)

Happy Hatchling
Dynamic Equilibrium: Balance in Motion

Mama Cluck is hatching the biggest hatchling you've ever seen. She's been at it for months. She rocks her egg. She rolls her egg. She sits on her egg. She stands on her egg. She even bounces on her egg! Can you help Mama Cluck hatch her Happy Hatchling?

EQUIPMENT
- *Optional:* music
- Fitness ball or any other large ball such as a Moonbouncer
- Toy
- Beanbag or other toy that is easy to grasp

KEY BENEFITS
- Balance and orientation
- Body control

LANGUAGE FOCUS
on

CRITICAL SAFEGUARDS
• **At all times:** When working on any unsteady surface, use secure holds appropriate to children's sizes and capabilities. (See "Safety Holds," page 33). Never leave the child unattended.
• When introducing new positions (such as kneeling or squatting), start on the floor to give the child a sense of what it feels like on a steady surface. This instills physical confidence while giving the brain time to understand the sensations before moving to a dynamic experience.

TEACHING GEMS
• When tipping the child, move slowly so that he doesn't startle. Follow the child's lead and adjust play according to his comfort level.
• If a child shows resistance to any activity, stop and return to it another time.
• When introducing a new sensation, start with small movements and do the activity only once to avoid overstimulation. This is especially important with infants. Offer small, short experiences repeated several times throughout the day.

SARAH ALICE LEE

ON THE MOVE | WATCH ME GROW | IN THE KNOW

 Snugglers
INTRODUCTION TO BALANCE. Helping baby experience different sensations of movement primes his sense of balance for the day he'll confront gravity all by himself.

SWING AND SWAY. Lay baby in your arms facing you, supporting his head and neck at all times. Slowly and gently tilt baby upright so his head is above his feet; then tilt the other way, raising his feet above his head for a few moments. (D 1–2 min.)

TUMMY TIME SWING AND SWAY. Repeat the "Swing and Sway" activity, positioning baby on his tummy. Playing music or singing a song enhances the experience by providing a natural beat or rhythm to the movements he's feeling. (D 1–2 min.)

MY FIRST EGG RIDE. Lay baby on his tummy on top of a fitness ball, securely supporting him at all times. Very slowly and gently, rock baby side to side, backward and forward, and diagonally. Keep movements very small. (D 1–2 min.)

Squigglers

THE PUSH-AWAY REFLEX helps baby navigate the birth canal. After birth, this reflex gives the body and brain their first sensations of independent movement.

EGGSTRA! Repeat the "My First Egg Ride" activity, increasing the depth of the movements forward and backward for a bigger ride. Encourage baby to touch the floor with his hands and feet as you rock. (D 1–2 min.)

EGGSTRA! EGGSTRA! Repeat the "Eggstra!" activity, focusing this time on rocking the ball side to side, encouraging the child to touch and push away from the floor with his hands. This activity encourages the parachute reflex (see Glossary) to emerge as well. (D 1–2 min.)

3-2-1 EGG! Repeat "Eggstra! Eggstra!" while rocking baby down to a slightly crouched position (feet on floor, knees bent). Watch to see if he pushes away from the floor on his own, then give him a slow, gentle ride back up to the top of the ball. Whee! (D 1–2 min.)

Scampers

VERTICAL BALANCE. Experiences with vertical sensations will give children the tools and confidence they need for those precious first steps.

EGG-AROUND. Sit the child on the fitness ball and securely hold him under the arms facing you. Gently rock him forward and backward, side to side, then round and round. (D 1–2 min.)

EGG BOUNCE. To start, give the child an "Egg-Around" ride. Next, gently bounce him on his bottom a few times on the top of the ball. Repeat, having him face away from you. (D 1–2 min.)

GETTING MY WINGS. Hold the fitness ball still with your knees. Stand the child on the ball and hold him securely around the waist. Bob the child up and down, building up to a gentle bounce. (D 1–2 min.)

Stompers

DYNAMIC ORIENTATION. Experiencing different positions while in motion is great practice for the more complex, whole-body movements to come.

EGG STRETCH. Securely hold the child on his tummy on the fitness ball. Tilt the ball all the way forward, then back to the center. Place a toy in front of the ball. Tilt forward again, encouraging the child to try to reach the toy. (D 1–2 min.)

UPSIDE-DOWN EGG STRETCH. Repeat the "Egg Stretch" activity, with the child lying on his back. Try it with his feet, too. (D 1–2 min.)

EGG ROLL. Hold the ball still with your knees. Lay the child on his tummy on the ball. Assist the child to tilt or roll to the left and hold for a few seconds. Roll back to the center and now roll to the right. (R 2–3 times)

Scooters

DYNAMIC EQUILIBRIUM is the ability to maintain balance while moving, no matter whether you're right side up, upside down, or somewhere in between.

TUCK AND CLUCK. Sit the child on the fitness ball and have him crouch in a full tuck position. Hold the child securely by the waist and have him close his eyes. Go for an "Egg-Around." Next, have him open his eyes and tuck his hands under his arms like chicken wings. (Don't forget to cluck!) (D 2–3 min.)

GETTING READY TO HATCH. Kneel the child on the ball, and have him sit on his heels. Hold him securely and go for an "Egg-Around." Next, have him tuck his arms up like chicken wings and take another ride. (D 1–2 min.)

CRACKING THE SHELL. Put the child on the ball in the upright kneeling position. Hold him securely and go for an "Egg-Around." Next, have him tuck his arms up like chicken wings. Finally, have him put his arms in the air ("Blast off!") and go for another ride. (D 2–3 min.)

Skedaddlers

CONTROL AND CONFIDENCE. Creating opportunities for children to practice control on an uneven or moving surface doubles the effect of the practice!

CHICKEN STEPS. Starting on the floor, have the child squat, tuck his arms into the chicken-wings position, and waddle like a chick. Once he has the feel for chicken steps, put him on the ball in the same squat position. Support him under his chicken wings and go for an "Egg-Around." (D 3–5 min.)

HATCHING DAY. Start on the floor again, this time standing with feet apart and arms in the chicken-wings position. Have the child rock from side to side, then all around. Next, stand the child on the ball, holding him by the waist. Gently go for an "Egg-Around" while he flaps his wings. (D 2–3 min.)

HAPPY HATCHLING. Repeat "Hatching Day." Next, keeping the ball still with your knees and feet, securely hold the child by the waist and let him bounce on the ball, building up to a full jump. That's how the chickens hatch! (R 2–3 times)

Roll-Over Rover
Rolling Over: Horizontal Orientation

Roll-Over Rover is a doggie who loves to roll. When he walks, he rolls. When he fetches, he rolls. When he sits up, he rolls. When he sleeps, he rolls. He even rolls when he's reading! And of course, his favorite song is "Roll Over" (page 190).

EQUIPMENT
- Blanket
- Soft toy
- Ball
- Rope
- Standard-sized parachute
- Book or other reading material
- Scarves

KEY BENEFITS
- Balance
- Core strength
- Body awareness
- Visual development
- Body control

LANGUAGE FOCUS
over

CRITICAL SAFEGUARDS
- Ensure there is ample space for children to roll around and that the floor surface is appropriate and free of obstructions.
- Be on hand when children are standing and turning in case they get dizzy.
- *Never* do rolling activities on an elevated surface such as a bed.

TEACHING GEMS
- Take time each day, every day, and multiple times a day to stimulate the vestibular system.
- To ensure well-balanced development, be sure each rolling activity is done in both directions (rolling right and left).
- To ensure 2 or more children roll in the same direction, use a sticker on the left or right hand or foot to allow children to check their direction. For older children, verbally reinforce *left* and *right*.

SARAH ALICE LEE

ON THE MOVE	WATCH ME GROW	IN THE KNOW

Snugglers
RELEASING REFLEXES. In the early months, nature is working to use and release primitive reflexes in order to make way for the postural reflexes that allow upright posture and independent mobility to emerge.

SPINETINGLER. Slowly run 2 fingers down the right side of baby's spine, then the left side, beginning at her shoulder and all the way down to her toes. Apply enough pressure to avoid tickling. *Note:* You will likely see baby squirm a bit—a sign her primitive reflexes are still active. (R 1 time)

HIP TIPS. Place baby on her back and gently lift her right leg over her left, tilting her body up on her side. Repeat on the other side. When baby is fully comfortable with these movements, assist her to roll all the way over onto her tummy. (R 2–3 times)

JELLYROLLS. Lay a blanket on the floor and lay baby on one end. Ever so gently, encourage and assist baby to roll over onto her tummy. As she does, wrap the blanket around her back. Next, gently continue to roll baby in the same direction and wrap the blanket around her, creating a swaddle. *Note:* Never leave baby unattended when she is swaddled. Next time, roll in the opposite direction. (R 1 time)

Squigglers
ROLLOVERS. To get little ones ready for the sensations of rolling all on their own, they need to be better acquainted with both the front and back of themselves.

YOU-AND-ME FLIP. Lay baby on the floor and prop yourself up on your elbows over her. Gather her under your arms and slowly flip over on your back so that now she's on top of you, tummy to tummy. Be sure to roll in both directions. (R 2–3 times)

ROLL-OVER ROVER. Lay baby on her back on the floor and put a favorite toy just out of reach. Encourage her to roll over to reach the toy—from tummy to back and back to tummy. (R 2–3 times)

ROVER'S ROLL AND SEEK. Lay baby on her back on the floor. Duck out of sight and call to her, encouraging her to roll over and crawl toward your voice. From your hiding place, roll a ball to entice her to chase after it. Now the choice is hers. Does she come and find you or chase after the ball? (D 3–5 min.)

Scampers

INDEPENDENT ROLLING. Controlling the roll all by oneself is empowering and a signal that the child's vestibular system is beginning to mature.

PUPPIES IN THE BED. Lay the child on the floor (*not* on a bed). Sing the "Roll Over" song twice, first having the child roll only to the right, then only to the left. (D 3–5 min.)

DO THE ROVER ROCK! Have the child lie on her back on the floor and assist her to rock her body side to side. Repeat on her tummy. Next, have her rock side to side and assist the child to roll up on her side and hold for few moments. (D 2–3 min.)

ROVER IN THE MIRROR. Sit in front of the child and encourage her to mimic your Roll-Over Rover moves. For example, crawl on all fours, sit up and beg, scratch behind your ear, and of course, roll over. Don't forget to woof! (D 3–5 min.)

Stompers

CONTROLLED ROLLING enhances a child's overall sense of body control by strengthening the core muscles and providing new vestibular (balance) stimulation.

SHARPEN YOUR PENCIL. Have children stand and hold their hands together above their heads like a pencil point. Then have them look right and turn around slowly. (R 2–3 times right and 2–3 time left) Next, have children look up at their hands as they spin around, then down at their toes. (R 2–3 times)

LOOK, MOM, NO PAWS! Have children lie on the floor with their hands at their sides, legs straight, and ankles together. Using the shoulders and hips for momentum, have them roll in one direction, trying to keep their bodies straight. Reverse direction. Next, have children concentrate on keeping their legs straight and ankles together as they roll. (R 5 times in both directions)

PENCIL ROLLING. Lay a long rope down on the floor. Have children lie down perpendicular to the rope, reaching over their heads to touch the rope with both hands. Then have them roll first to the right, then left, keeping their fingertips on the rope. As they roll, ask them to concentrate on keeping their body straight. Then ask them to focus on keeping their knees straight and ankles together. Now try it without the rope to see if they can roll straight like pencils. (R 5 times)

Scooters

DEVELOPING CONCENTRATION. Vestibular (balance) development underpins a child's ability to focus and concentrate on cognitive tasks.

ONE PIG IN A BLANKET. For each child, lay out a large blanket or parachute on the floor. Have the child lie at one end, with her shoulders on the fabric and her head on the floor. Have her hold the edge of the fabric and roll herself all the way up, then all the way back. (R 2–3 times)

TWO PIGS IN A BLANKET. Repeat "One Pig in a Blanket," only this time, have 2 children on either end roll toward the middle. When they meet up, have them roll back. Encourage the children to try rolling fast. Then try it rolling very, very slowly. (R 2–3 times)

ROLL-OVER READING. At storytime, have children lie on the floor on their backs. They'll need to listen very carefully, because each time they hear you turn the page, they need to roll over (from back to tummy or tummy to back). At the end of the story, have children roll as far as they can roll. (D 5+ min.)

Skedaddlers

TEAMWORK. When children work together, they're beginning to understand how to include others in their thinking and their actions. And it tends to slow them down, which means more deliberate and measured movements.

ROVER, ROVER, ROLL ON OVER. Have 2 children lie on the floor with the tops of their heads facing each other. Have each hold one end of a scarf with both hands so they are tethered together. Stand a few feet away and encourage them to roll toward you *together*. Once they can roll in unison using the scarf, have them hold hands to roll. (R 3 times in both directions)

TEAM ROLLING. Have children lie down on the floor shoulder to shoulder. Be sure there's no space between them. When you clap, have them all roll in the same direction at once. When you clap again, they stop. Repeat in the other direction. (R 3 times in both directions)

CONVEYOR BELT ROLLING. Repeat "Team Rolling" to warm up, then introduce the idea of a conveyor belt: "All *together*, we have to get Rover from one end of the room to the other." Place a soft toy (to represent Rover) on the first child's tummy. Have the children roll and watch as Rover makes his way down the conveyor belt. (R 3 in both directions)

The Spinnagans
Spinning: Challenging Orientation

SARAH WHITING

Meet the Spinnagans—they spin everywhere they go! And you can hear them coming from a mile away because when they spin, they sing their favorite song, "Spinnagans Go Round and Round" (page 190).

EQUIPMENT
- Spinning chair, such as an office chair
- Hoop
- Adhesive spot sticker

KEY BENEFITS
- Core strength development
- Balance
- Body control
- Stamina

LANGUAGE FOCUS
around, front and back, side to side

CRITICAL SAFEGUARDS
- Always be guided by the child. If it appears the child isn't enjoying the activity, stop and try again later. Do not overspin.
- Ensure spinning is done slowly to prevent the child from becoming dizzy and losing control. The recommended pace is 1 complete revolution per 8 seconds. If a child becomes dizzy, stop and let him regain his bearings before trying again.
- Support the child when he's spinning on things like an office chair.

TEACHING GEMS
The most advanced form of balance is the ability to be still. That's why it's hard for young children to stay still for very long. Spinning slowly enhances the vestibular (balance) system, which is one of the main reasons little ones like the sensation of spinning. So if you want a child to sit still, let him spin when he feels like it!

ON THE MOVE | **WATCH ME GROW** | **IN THE KNOW**

Snugglers

EARLY BALANCE. The sense of balance is developed through movement, which actually begins through the natural process of carrying baby in your arms.

EARLY TURNS. Hold baby close against your body and turn very slowly (1 revolution per 8 seconds). Turn in both directions. Next, hold baby away from your body and turn in both directions. (D 1–2 min.)

EARLY TWIRLS. Sit on the floor with baby enclosed in your lap. Support baby's head and neck as you gently rock your body backward and forward, then from side to side. (D 1–2 min.)

EARLY BOUNCES. Sit baby on your knee facing you. Support him under his arms and bounce him up and down. Sway your knee side to side. Turn baby away from you and repeat the ride. (D 1–2 min.)

Squigglers

SPINNING. Spinning—especially slow spinning—helps the brain understand the dynamics of motion and balance.

MY FIRST OFFICE CHAIR. Sit on a spinning chair and sit baby up in your lap facing you. Spin very slowly (1 revolution per 8 seconds) in both directions. Turn baby away from you and repeat. Repeat again with baby lying on his back and then on his tummy. (D 1–2 min.)

UPSIDE-DOWN ROUND AND ROUND. Sit on a spinning chair and lay baby on his back with his feet up against your chest. Support his head and neck as you spin very slowly in both directions. Repeat with baby's head tilted back over your knees to give the sensation of spinning upside down. (D 1–2 min.)

AIRPLANE RIDE. Hold baby away from your body supported under his chest and hips. As you spin slowly, change his orientation—head down for landing and head up for takeoff. *Zoom, zoom!* (D 1–2 min.)

| ON THE MOVE | WATCH ME GROW | IN THE KNOW |

 ## Scampers

ORIENTATION. A finely tuned sense of balance means understanding the sensations of movement in any position and at any angle.

UPRIGHT SPINS. Hold the child under his arms and slowly spin around in both directions. Next, have the child bend his elbows. Pick him up by the elbows and slowly spin him in both directions. (R 2–3 times)

HORIZONTAL SPINS. Hold the child in your arms facing upward, supporting him under his back and knees, and spin slowly. Then hold him facing downward, supporting him under his chest and thighs, and spin slowly some more. Next, hold him lying horizontally (your tummies touching) and give him a slow spin. Finally, hold him facing out (his back to your tummy) and spin again. Be sure to spin in both directions slowly in each position. (R 2–3 times)

UPSIDE-DOWN SPINS. Hold the child by his hips upside down and slowly spin in both directions. If this position isn't comfortable for him, try holding the child over your shoulder to go for a spin. (R 2–3 times)

 ## Stompers

DYNAMIC BODY CONTROL. As children begin to spin themselves around, the brain is absorbing important new information about orientation, equilibrium, and self-control.

WHERE'S MY TAIL? Pretend to pin a tail on the child. Have the child kneel inside a hoop on the floor. Have the child stay inside the hoop and crawl in circles to the left and right, trying to find his tail. (D 2–3 min.)

NOSE SPINS. Put an adhesive spot sticker in the center of a hoop on the floor. Have the child kneel inside the hoop and put both hands on the dot. Staying inside the hoop, have him crawl around the dot. Next, have him put his nose on the dot and repeat the game. (D 2–3 min.)

MY FIRST SPINNAGAN! Have the child lie on his back and tuck his arms under his legs. Gently spin him around by his feet, first to the left then to the right. Start slowly, changing up the speed as you go. Sing "Spinnagans Go Round and Round" as he spins. (D 2–3 min.)

 ## Scooters

RHYTHM, TIMING, AND BALANCE. Full-body coordination requires a complex set of skills and abilities to come together, all while in motion.

HIGH-FLYING FIVE. Sit the child on a spinning chair and slowly spin the chair to the right. Sing "Spinnagans Go Round and Round" to match the pace of his spin. On each rotation, have the child high-five you as he passes. Repeat, spinning to the left. (D 2 min. in each direction)

LOW-FLYING FIVE! Repeat "High-Flying Five" with the child lying on his tummy on the chair so his head is below his feet, slowly spinning to the right. Sing "Spinnagans Go Round and Round" to match the pace of his spin. On each rotation, have him "low-five" you as he passes. Repeat, spinning to the left. (D 2 min. in each direction)

THE SPINNAGANS SPIN. Sing "Spinnagans Go Round and Round." On each lyric, have children spin first to their left then to the right. On "Let's get dizzy!" fall to the ground with a great big giggle. Next, have the children make up their own choreography to the song. Invite them to pair up to spin around, too. (D 3–5 min.)

 ## Skedaddlers

CORE MUSCLE MOMENTUM. Strong core muscles work in conjunction with the rest of the body and the brain to create dynamic equilibrium.

SPINNAGANS GO FRONT AND BACK. Have children sit on the floor and lock their hands under their bent knees. Have them rock forward and backward, using their feet to propel the movement. Next, have them try it without touching their feet to the floor. Then have them extend their legs straight out and try it again. (D 2–3 min.)

SPINNAGANS GO SIDE TO SIDE. Have children sit on the floor and lock their hands under their bent knees. Have them rock side to side while keeping their feet off the floor. Next, have them extend their legs out straight and try it again. (D 2–3 min.)

SPINNAGANS GO ROUND. Sitting on the floor with their hands locked under their bent knees, have children roll forward, then to the side, then backward, then to the other side, and then return to center without touching their feet to the floor. Create a full 360-degree rotation. Next, encourage them to try to go from one side of the room to the other like Spinnagans! (D 3–5 min.)

Do the Elvis
Spinning: Vertical Orientation

SARAH WHITING

Music is a natural movement motivator, especially when you learn to move like Elvis. Come on, let's dance!

EQUIPMENT
- Blanket
- Carriage or stroller
- Swing
- Music

KEY BENEFITS
- Balance
- Body rhythm
- Body control

LANGUAGE FOCUS
around, left, right

CRITICAL SAFEGUARDS
- When children are spinning, there is always a chance they might fall. Be sure there is plenty of room. Stand by for support. Ensure there is something soft for them to land on.
- Children differ when it comes to knowing when they have had enough. Be guided by the child and do not overstimulate or push for more rotation than she wants to do.

TEACHING GEMS
- Spinning slowly offers optimal developmental benefit. Slowly is defined as 1 revolution per 8 seconds.
- Take several spins in one direction, then reverse direction.
- Children have different spin tolerances. Be aware that some children will enjoy spinning activities while others may shy away or even refuse. If spinning is uncomfortable for a child, stop the activity for now. Next time, try an earlier progression at a very slow pace, always being mindful of the child's comfort level.

ON THE MOVE	WATCH ME GROW	IN THE KNOW

Snugglers
SIMULATING THE WOMB. Young infants are comforted by slow, gentle movements similar to those they became accustomed to in the womb.

STEP AND TURN. Hold baby in your arms and rock back and forth from foot to foot. As you rock, slowly turn in circles, several times in one direction, then the other. (D 1–2 min.)

SHOULDER SPIN. Hold baby over your shoulder so that she's still upright but she's looking down toward the floor. Repeat "Step and Turn." Be sure to talk and sing to baby reassuringly. (D 1–2 min.)

TILT SPIN. With baby on her back in your arms, very slowly tilt her so that her feet are above her head for a few moments as you repeat "Step and Turn." Alternate between upright and tilted positions as you turn. Repeat with baby lying on her tummy. (D 1–2 min.)

Squigglers
SOOTHING MOVEMENTS. Slow spinning provides a calming effect while stimulating the vestibular (balance) system.

BLANKET SPINS. Lay baby on a blanket on a smooth, hard floor. Gently and slowly spin the blanket around so baby gets a new sensation of mobility without being held. Repeat with baby lying on her tummy. (R 2 times in each direction)

STROLLER SPINS. When you take baby for a walk in her stroller, occasionally spin the stroller slowly 1 full rotation. Be sure to tell baby what you're going to do beforehand, and reassure her with your voice as you turn her around. Whee! (R 1–2 times per walk)

SIDE SPINS. Stand holding baby facing you. Tilt her sideways so that her right ear is parallel to the floor. Slowly spin around several times in each direction. Reverse position (left ear toward the floor). (D 2–3 min.)

Scampers

VERTICAL SPINNING. As the child is beginning to find her feet, she needs practice in turning herself to help ready her balance for those big first steps.

SWING STAR. While at the playground, seat the child in a baby swing and give her a gentle swing ride. From time to time, twist the swing 180 degrees then slowly twist it back to center. *Never let go of the swing.* (R 1–2 times)

DANCE STAR. Support the child to stand on your feet facing out. Hold her against your body and slowly "Step and Turn" as she rides on your feet. (R 1–2 times in each direction)

SKATE STAR. Hold the child in your arms, wrapping her feet around you. Spin slowly in both directions. Invite her to lie back so that her head is parallel to the ground. Over time, encourage her to hang upside down as you spin very slowly. (Stop if either of you is getting dizzy.) (R 1–2 times)

Stompers

INDEPENDENT SPINNING begins with strong core muscles, which align the body to help maintain balance.

SWIVEL ARMS. To build momentum, show children how to swivel their arms to the right and left in front and back of them as if they're dancing the Twist. Put on some music and twist away! (D 2–5 min.)

TORSO TWIST. Assist children to plant their feet and twist only the torso in both directions. Next, add "Swivel Arms," keeping feet still with just the opposite heel coming off the floor. (D 1–2 min.)

DO THE TWIST! Repeat "Torso Twist," only this time allow the feet to swivel left and right as children twist. (Think Elvis or Chubby Checker!) Next, as they continue to twist, have them bend their knees to a full squat position and come back up. Turn on some music and do the Twist! (D 3–5 min.)

Scooters

TANDEM MOVEMENTS. Doing activities with a partner creates important verbal and nonverbal social dynamics for young children.

MAKING CIRCLES. Have 2 children hold hands and sidestep around in circles. Next, still holding hands, have them jump together in a circle. Then have them stand back to back, hold hands, and sidestep in circles. (D 2–3 min.)

SPIN ME! Have 2 children hold hands. As 1 child sidesteps in circles, the other stands on her heels and spins around. Reverse roles. Have them also try spinning on their toes or with 1 foot on top of the other. (D 2–3 min.)

CROSS AND TURN. Show the child how to cross her right foot over her left. When the child can maintain her balance in this position, demonstrate how to pivot by standing up on her toes and turning her body so that she's facing the opposite direction. Stand by for support. Repeat in the other direction. (D 2–3 min.)

Skedaddlers

CONTROLLED SPINNING is an advanced form of balance and signals that the child is in command of her body.

SPINNING TOPS. Demonstrate how to 1-foot spin: Twist your arms and torso to the right with the right foot behind the left. Push off with the right and swing the arms to the left to spin on one foot. Encourage children to spin as far around as they can. Repeat in the other direction. (D 3–5 min.)

LEARNING TO "SPOT." Pick a spot on the wall and have children focus their eyes on that spot. Tell them you'll be asking them to move, and encourage them to keep spotting—not to take their eyes off the spot—as they move. Call out instructions, such as *step forward, step to the side, crouch, crawl, stand and bend to the side.* (D 2–3 min.)

SPIN AND SPOT. Pick a spot on the wall. Encourage children to turn around, keeping their eyes on the spot for as long as they can. As they come back around, show them how to find the spot again by using the head and neck to lead the body through the turn. Repeat while doing "Cross and Turn." Then repeat while doing "Spinning Tops." Take it slow and repeat the activity over many sessions. (D 2–3 min. each session)

The Go-Over Game
Balance Beam:
Building Concentration

Do you know about the stream called Sneaky Cheeky Creek? Unlike other streams, the Sneaky can change course any time it wants. And when it does, there's only one way past: the "Go-Over Game"! You need to walk across a plank—and each time you do, Sneaky Cheeky Creek throws a new challenge your way.

SARAH ALICE LEE

EQUIPMENT

- Music
- Fitness ball
- Plank (approximately 8" wide)
- Toys
- *Optional:* chalk
- Beanbags
- Balance beam (approximately 4" wide)
- Blindfold
- Buckets

KEY BENEFITS

- Balance
- Spatial awareness
- Body control

LANGUAGE FOCUS

over, along, across

CRITICAL SAFEGUARDS

- Be sure to support the child at all times, particularly when moving along a raised surface.
- Support both sides of the body evenly. For instance, hold the child at the waist on both sides, or hold both hands simultaneously (rather than hold just 1 hand).
- For activities using a plank or beam, have 1 child on the equipment at a time. *Note:* We usually recommend using a wide plank beginning at the scampers stages (when a child is able to crawl and is getting ready to walk). Supervision is required at *all* times whenever a child is on equipment that takes him off the ground.
- Do not blindfold children or cover their eyes if they are not comfortable with this. If using a blindfold or if both eyes are shut, allow children to do this *only* while you are using a safety hold (pages 33–35).

TEACHING GEMS

- Do all activities in bare feet.
- When presenting inclines to children, begin with a slight angle and increase the incline as the child demonstrates proficiency.
- Always support and guide the child on raised surfaces and inclines.
- Some children need to move along the plank quickly. Moving quickly requires less balance. Encourage the child to go slowly to give his body and brain more balance practice.

Snugglers

FOOT AWARENESS. An important precursor to 2-footed balance is a strong, sensory understanding of the feet.

HELLO, TOES. Gently introduce baby to his toes, wiggling each toe individually as you talk or sing. For instance, play the classic "This Little Piggy" game, first on his right foot, then his left, then with both feet simultaneously. (D 1–2 min.)

FOOT TAPS. Lay baby on his back. Remove his socks. Gently tap baby's toes together in a rhythmic pattern *(tap tap tap)* as you sing to him. Tap his heels together *(tap tap tap)*. Then alternate heel-toe, heel-toe, heel-toe. Put his socks on your fingers for a different sensory experience. (D 1–2 min.)

HEEL, MEET TOES. Lay baby on his back. Remove his socks. Bring his right foot in front of his left, tapping his right heel to his left toes rhythmically *(tap tap tap)*. Reverse with left foot in front and right foot in back *(tap tap tap)*. Then alternate left-right, left-right. (D 1–2 min.)

Squigglers

BODY ALIGNMENT. Balance for crawling and walking requires controlled head movement aligned upright over the shoulders and torso.

BABY STRETCH. Lay baby on his back. Slowly and gently raise his arms above his head and give him a little stretch. Return to his natural position. Next, hold his ankles and give him a gentle stretch. Repeat on tummy. (D 1–2 min.)

BABY ROCK. When babies are getting ready to crawl, they work their way into the crawling position (on all fours). You may see babies rock on all fours without actually crawling at first. This helps create independent movement of the head. Turn on some music, put baby on all fours, get down on the floor with him, and have fun rocking to the beat together. (D 2–3 min.)

BABY BUNT. Place a large ball (fitness ball) in front of baby. Encourage him to push the ball with his head as he moves forward. (D 2–3 min.)

Scampers

DIMENSIONALIZED EXPERIENCES. Moving along a raised surface helps children learn their world is not flat and introduces them to depth and height perception.

CRAWL THE PLANK. Place a wide plank on the floor and entice the child to crawl across. Support him so he doesn't slip. When he's ready, elevate the plank a few inches off the ground and support him at the waist as he crawls across. (R 2–3 times)

CLIMB THE PLANK. Raise the plank to the child's waist height. Place several toys along the plank. Encourage him to cruise alongside the plank, knocking off the toys as he goes. His instinct may be to climb on it. Support him as he climbs, helping him turn his body around so that he can climb down the other side feet first. (R 2–3 times)

WALK THE PLANK. Place a wide plank on the floor. Stand in front of the child and hold both of his arms for support. Encourage him to walk across the plank. When he's ready, elevate the plank a few inches off the ground and repeat, continually supporting him at all times. When he gets the idea, help him take a few steps backward, too! (R 2–3 times)

Stompers

FOOTFALLS. Paying specific attention to where you place your feet challenges the body and brain to maintain balance.

STEP ON THE CRACK. Draw a chalk line on the pavement or floor (or find a crack to follow). One at a time, encourage children to walk along the line, keeping 1 foot on the line at all times. (D 2–3 min.)

SIDESTEPPING. Draw a line on the pavement or floor (or find a crack to follow). Encourage children to step sideways by stepping the right foot out to the right and then bringing the left foot together with the right. Challenge children to try to stay on the line. Repeat in both directions. (D 2–3 min.)

PASSING TRAFFIC. Draw a line on the pavement or floor (or find a crack to follow). Have 2 children start at either end, walking on the line toward each other. When they meet, encourage and assist them to work out how they will pass each other while still keeping 1 foot on the line at all times. (D 2–3 min.)

Scooters

CHANGING PERSPECTIVE. Something as simple as changing the terrain challenges the child to think differently about how he's moving.

HEEL-TO-TOE WALKING. Draw a line on the pavement or floor (or find a crack to follow). Demonstrate how to walk heel-to-toe, being sure to always touch your heel to your toes as you go along, staying on the line at all times. One at a time, have children walk heel-to-toe along the line. Have their arms in airplane position to start, then challenge them to lower their arms as they progress. (D 2–3 min.)

TIGHTROPE WALKING. Place a wide plank several inches off the ground and, one at a time, encourage each child to walk heel-to-toe across. Use the safety holds on page 34. As each child gains proficiency, switch to a narrower plank, again, supporting him to be sure he's comfortable and gaining confidence with each try. (D 2–3 min.)

RAMP WALKING. Create a 45-degree incline using a wide plank. Using the appropriate safety holds for the child's ability (see page 34), encourage the child to walk up, turn around, and walk back down the plank. Repeat the activity, this time using heel-to-toe walking, always supporting the child. (D 2–3 min.)

Skedaddlers

BALANCE PLUS. As basic balance abilities are put in place, new and bigger challenges continue the process of fine-tuning and automating the brain's ability to maintain balance.

STEP-OVERS. Place beanbags at even intervals along a narrow balance beam. Encourage the child to walk across the beam, stepping over the beanbags as he goes. Use the appropriate safety hold (see page 34). Next, have him do heel-to-toe walking, again stepping over the obstacles in his path. (D 2–3 min.)

FLAMINGO WALK. On a narrow beam, have the child walk heel-to-toe to the center and stop. Next, encourage him to stand still, lift 1 knee, and hold that position. Repeat with the other knee. Next time, have him strike the flamingo pose (1 foot pressed against the side of the knee). (D 2–3 min.)

THE GO-OVER GAME. Create a mix of challenges on the beam, adding 1 new challenge each time the child goes across. (D 2–3 min. each) Some ideas:
- Sweeps—kick beanbags off the beam.
- Beanbag Balance—balance a beanbag on your head as you cross.
- One Eye Shut—cross with 1 hand over 1 eye; repeat with the other eye.
- Both Eyes Shut—walk the plank blindfolded or with both eyes closed; do not allow children to do this without your support.
- Off Balance—carry a small weighted bucket in 1 hand to add weight to 1 side; repeat with the bucket in the other hand.
- Sidestep—sidestep to the left; repeat to the right.
- Backward—repeat any activity backward, supporting the child at all times.

SARAH ALICE LEE

Hello, Octopo
Balance and Positioning:
Meeting Gravity in New Ways

Say hello to Octopo,
A friend of smiles and charm.
When Octopo calls out, "Hello,"
He waves with all eight arms!

With all those arms and legs going every which way, it's no wonder Octopo is a little bit clumsy. Let's see if we can help Octopo keep his balance.

EQUIPMENT
- Laundry basket
- Blanket
- Spinning chair, such as an office chair
- Small toys
- Bucket
- Scoop
- Basket
- Pillows
- Drawing implements
- Cardstock
- Towel or sheet

KEY BENEFITS
- Teamwork
- Strong posture
- Alertness and concentration

LANGUAGE FOCUS
stop, go, around

CRITICAL SAFEGUARDS
- Ensure that an adult is lifting the child only slightly off the ground. Slow spinning should be carried out at 1 revolution per 8 seconds.
- Whenever a child is upside down, maintain personal supervision at all times.

TEACHING GEMS
- Orientation matters, so throughout the day give children opportunities to do routine activities from different perspectives. For instance, they can draw pictures while lying on their backs or listen to a story while lying upside down.
- Balance and orientation are inseparable forces that underpin virtually everything we do. Key off of these and other balance activities in this section to provide small bites of balance activity throughout the day.
- When pairing up children for Smart Steps active movement activities, keep in mind their physical size and build and current level of capabilities, so that they are evenly matched.

SARAH WHITING

ON THE MOVE | WATCH ME GROW | IN THE KNOW

 ### Snugglers

ORIENTATION. From the very start, moving in our 3-dimensional world gives the brain many different orientations to better develop a well-rounded sense of balance.

GENTLE WAVES. Line a laundry basket with a soft snuggly blanket. Place baby in the basket on his back. Very gently tip the basket from side to side. Make sure you keep eye contact at all times. (D 1–2 min.)

OCTOSPIN. Sit on an office chair and hold baby vertically, close to your chest. Gently stretch her arms and legs out, like in the spread-eagle position. Support her head and back. Slowly spin to the right, then to the left. (R 2–3 times) Repeat with baby facing away from you.

OCTOCLAP. Lay baby on her back. Gently stretch her arms out to her sides, then bring them back to center. *Clap!* Next, gently bring both arms to the right. *Clap!* And then to the left. *Clap!* Repeat with the feet. When the game is done, support or assist baby to roll over on her tummy. (D 2–3 min.)

Squigglers

VERTICAL BALANCE. As baby works toward independent, vertical orientation, she's developing balance that will keep her upright.

UP AND AT 'EM, OCTOPO! Lay baby on her back. Fully support her under her back and neck and lift her parallel to the floor. In a very slow and gentle swinging motion, glide her up to a vertical position, hold for a few seconds, then bring her back down between your legs. Return baby to the floor. Rest and repeat, this time starting her on her tummy so she's looking away from you during the ride. (R 2–3 times)

OCTO-CLOCK: Sit down and hold baby facing you. Very slowly, rotate her 360 degrees like the hands of a clock from 12:00 to 3:00, 6:00, 9:00, and back to 12:00. Repeat very slowly, going the other way. (R 1–2 times).

FLYING OCTOPO. Hold the child in the flying position and slowly lower her down toward some toys scattered on the floor. Encourage her to reach for any toy. When she grabs hold of one, lift her back and admire her prize! Repeat in an upside-down flying position. *Note:* As the child learns how the game is played, encourage her to drop the toy back on the floor or into a basket. (D 1–2 min.)

Scampers

ROLLING. SPINNING. UPSIDE-DOWNING. These 3 movements pay big dividends to children's balance at any stage of development.

SPINNING OCTOPO. Hold the child under the arms securely facing you. Lift her up and spin her slowly around once. Stop and repeat, going the other way. As she gains confidence, spin a little longer in each direction. To end the game, spin the child around one more time fast. Whee! (D 1–2 min.)

OCTOROLL. Lay the child on her back. Place a favorite toy to her right just out of reach. At the same time, tilt her legs and hips to the left to encourage her to look in 1 direction while moving her body in the other. Encourage or assist the child to roll left, then go find her toy. Repeat in the other direction. (D 2–3 min.)

SCOOP IT UP! Give the child a bucket or scoop and hold her in the flying position. Slowly lower her down toward some small toys scattered on the floor. Encourage her to scoop up as many toys as she can. Lift her back and admire her prize! Repeat in an upside-down flying position. *Note:* As the child gains confidence, encourage her to drop the toys into a basket or back down on the floor. (D 1–2 min.)

Stompers

OFF BALANCE. Learning balance means conquering off-balance moments.

HELLO, OCTOPO. Get down on the floor with the child. Have her get on all fours. Tap 1 hand and have her wave while balancing on her other hand and knees. Return to all fours. Now tap the other hand. Return to all fours. Continue the game, lifting 1 arm or 1 leg off the ground at a time. (D 2–3 min.)

DOUBLE OCTOPO. Repeat the "Hello, Octopo" game. Next, tap 2 limbs at once and have the child lift them both, balancing on the other 2. For instance, tap the right hand and left foot. Then tap the left hand and left foot. Tap both hands or both feet. (D 3–5 min.) For added challenge, tap both hands and 1 foot (for a 1-legged kneel).

UPSIDE-DOWN OCTOPO. Have the child stand, bend over to put her hands on the floor, and look between her legs. Now play "Hello, Octopo" and "Double Octopo" again, only this time upside down. (D 2–3 min.)

Scooters

POSTURE CONTROL. Being able to adopt and hold unusual positions demonstrates good balance, body control, and a high level of concentration.

GONE FISHIN', OCTOPO. Scatter toys on the floor. Have the child lie down and explain you're going to go fishing upside down. Lift her around or above the thighs. Support her with your body. Have her pick up the toys and put them in a bucket. Then have her form her fingers into hooks to try to hook the toys. (D 2–3 min.)

SURFING OCTOPO. Have children lie on their tummies and lift their arms and legs in the air (parachute position). Have them wave their arms and legs like Octopo. When you call out, "Swim," have them roll in one direction until you call out, "Stop." When they stop, have them return to the parachute position and wave some more. For added challenge, place pillows on the floor for children to roll over. (D 3–5 min.)

MEMORY OCTOPO. Have or help the children draw pictures on cardstock of hands and feet creating 4 cards total—2 hands and 2 feet. Now play a game of "Hello, Octopo," only this time using the cards and calling out, "Hand," or "Foot." Next, create a short sequence to follow, such as: "Wave your hand." "Now wave your hand and wave your foot." "Wave your hand, your foot, and your other foot." (D 3–5 min.)

Skedaddlers

COMPLEX COORDINATED MOVEMENTS challenge the brain to maintain its sense of balance no matter which end is up!

WAVE AROUND, OCTOPO. Have 2 children stand back to back and lock arms. Now have them turn round in a circle, waving their arms like Octopo. Be sure to have them turn in both directions. (D 1–2 min.)

THE TANGLED TANGO. Repeat "Wave Around, Octopo." Then, while still with their arms locked, have the children lean back on each other and slide to a sitting position on the floor. Once seated, have them turn themselves in a circle, waving all 8 arms and legs at once! Be sure to turn in both directions. When done, have them lean back on each other and return to a standing position. (D 2–3 min.)

HANGING OUT WITH OCTOPO. With 8 arms at the ready, Octopo loves to hang out! Assist and support the child to hook her arms and legs over a straight bar and hang for 10 seconds. (R 2–3 times)

SARAH ALICE LEE

Tortoise and Hare: After the Race
Dynamic Equilibrium: Going Fast, Going Slow, and Stopping

Do you know the story of the race between the tortoise and the hare? After their race, Tortoise and Hare sat down under a tree for a well-deserved rest. They got to talking about where they'd like to go and what they'd like to see if they ever had a chance to go on an adventure. And then the idea struck them: they could go on an adventure *together!*

See page 190 for the lyrics to "Tortoise and Hare," the song for this activity sequence.

EQUIPMENT
- Blanket
- Toy
- Cloth
- Plastic bowl
- Hill
- Tape or rope
- Beanbag
- Articles of clothing
- Boxes or suitcases

KEY BENEFITS
- Concentration
- Stillness
- Working in teams
- Pacing

LANGUAGE FOCUS
fast, slow, stop

CRITICAL SAFEGUARDS
When asking children to do things quickly, ensure there are safe surfaces for them to fall onto.

TEACHING GEMS
• These activities are inspired by the classic fable of "The Tortoise and the Hare." Add this tale to your storytime so children can visualize the speedy hare and slow tortoise as they play.
• For "Tortoise Roll," have another adult (or an older sibling) lie on the floor and talk to baby while he's in the upside-down position. This adds stimulation to the activity while giving baby an even more dynamic understanding that there's more than one way to see the world.
• For games with verbal cues, such as "Slow-Fast-Stop," as the child learns to listen and respond to your verbal instructions, challenge his auditory and memory development by changing the cues (blow a whistle, use colors or numbers instead of words, and so forth). See page 27 for more ideas.

SARAH WHITING

ON THE MOVE	WATCH ME GROW	IN THE KNOW

Snugglers

FIRST SENSATIONS OF MOVEMENT. Even though infants don't yet have the power of independent mobility, when you move them, the brain is already picking up important information about balance—information it will need to steady them for crawling and, later, walking.

TORTOISE AND HARE WARM UP. Tell the story of Tortoise and Hare as you massage baby. Slow your voice and the massage as you introduce the tortoise; quicken the pace when you introduce the hare. (D 2–3 min.)

TORTOISE AND HARE GET READY TO RIDE. Lay baby on his back and pedal his feet like a bicycle. Pedal slowly like a tortoise and quickly like a hare. Sing the "Tortoise and Hare" song as you play. (D 1–2 min.)

TORTOISE AND HARE TAKE A BUMPY RIDE. Sit baby on your knee and bounce him very gently. Sing the "Tortoise" verse from the song as you slowly bounce baby; then quicken your pace as you sing the "Hare" verse. Always bounce very gently and watch for baby's reaction. Stop if he's not enjoying the ride. (D 1–2 min.)

Squigglers

ORIENTATION. Holding baby in different positions is great practice for the day when he'll need to figure out how to navigate his environment.

TORTOISE TIPS. Lay baby on the floor on a blanket and bundle his arms up together in the blanket so he's nice and snug. Now, gently roll him in circles so that he can feel the flatness of the floor on all sides of his back. Sing the "Tortoise" verse as you play. (D 2–3 min.)

HARE HOPS. Hold baby under his arms in front of you with his feet touching the ground. Sing the "Hare" verse, and very gently and slowly press him down a few inches so that his knees bend, then bring him back up slowly. Repeat several times for him to get the feel of the movement, then increase your pace to a gentle hopping motion. (D 2–3 min.)

TORTOISE ROLL. Sit and hold baby on your lap facing you. Place his favorite toy facing you on the floor. Hold baby securely around the shoulders and back. Sing the "Tortoise" verse and bend forward while you tip him back very slowly and carefully until his head is upside down. Hold for a few moments so he can examine his toy upside down. Come back to your sitting position. (R 3–5 times)

Scampers

YOUR VERY OWN WAY. When children are free to move around and react to their environment, they are not only getting where they want to go, they're developing confidence in their physical selves.

TORTOISE SHELL. As the child crawls around the floor, drape some cloth over his back. Encourage him to crawl out of it. Next, try putting a soft toy or an empty plastic bowl on his back (his "shell") to give him a different sense of himself as he crawls. (D 2–3 min.)

TORTOISE HOPS. Follow the child as he crawls around the room. Sing the "Tortoise and Hare" song. Following the rhythm of the song, every few paces pick up the child around the waist. Lift him a few inches off the ground, turn him around, and put him right back down so he can continue crawling. (D 2–3 min.)

CHASING THE HARE. Children just beginning to walk love nothing more than your encouragement. Get down on the floor and chase the child around. Catch him once in a while for a hug. Get in his way so he has to find his way past you. Pick him up, swing him around, then back to the floor and off he goes again! (D 5–10 min.)

Stompers

CONTROLLING SPEED is an important underpinning for coordinated, whole-body movement. But it's not as easy as it looks when you're still getting your balance.

TORTOISE AND HARE GO UP AND DOWN. On a small mound or hill, encourage the child to crawl very, very slowly up the hill, like the tortoise, and run down the hill fast, like the hare. Next, have him run up the hill as fast as he can and very, very slowly crawl back down. Sing the "Tortoise and Hare" song as you play. (D 2–3 min.)

SLOW-FAST-STOP. Prep children by explaining the Slow-Fast-Stop game: When you call out, "Slow," whatever they're doing, they have to slow down and go very, very slowly. When you call, "Fast," they have to speed up. And when you call out, "Stop," children have to stop. While they play, randomly call out the cues. Assist and remind children as needed. (D 5–10 min.)

FAST LANE. SLOW LANE. Use tape or rope to create two lanes side by side—a fast lane and a slow lane. Working with 1 child, have the child start in the slow lane and move very, very slowly. When you call out, "Fast," have him jump to the fast lane and run as fast as he can. Alternate between fast and slow to the end of the lanes. (R 2–3 times)

Scooters

SPEED SEQUENCES. Once children have mastered the ability to speed up and slow down at will, creating sequences with speed strengthens their control and balance while building cognitive and muscle memory.

TORTOISE AND HARE ROLL. Hare rolls fast. Tortoise rolls slow. Create a pattern for children to follow as they roll, such as "Hare-Tortoise-Tortoise-Hare." Reverse direction. (R 3–5 times with different patterns)

TORTOISE AND HARE PASS. Have the children form a circle, alternating tortoises and hares. Pass a beanbag around the circle using both hands—tortoises pass slowly, hares pass as fast as they can. Switch directions, then have children switch roles. (R 2–4 rounds) Next, have the tortoises get down on all fours and the hares crouch down. The tortoises then pass the beanbag slowly under their chest, while the hares jump up and crouch back down to pass it. Switch directions, then roles. (R 2–4 rounds)

THE TORTOISE AND HARE JIG. Together with the child make up a dance, alternating fast and slow movements. Have the child make up the fast steps while you make up the slow ones. Sing the "Tortoise and Hare" song as you practice your dance steps. (D 10–15 min.)

Skedaddlers

COMPLEX PHYSICAL PATTERNS rely on automated, foundational movements and a strong sense of internal balance and orientation.

THE TORTOISE RELAY. Divide the children into teams. Set up 2 racing lanes and put a pile of clothes (1 item for each child on the team) at the end of the lane. Give each team 1 small box or suitcase. When you say, "Go," the first player gets on all fours, his teammates put the suitcase on his back, and he must crawl to the end of the lane, put 1 item of clothing in the suitcase, and run back to pass it off to the next player. (R 2–3 times)

THE HARE RELAY. Divide the children into teams. Set up 2 racing lanes and put a pile of clothes (1 item for each child on the team) at the end of the lane. Give each team 1 small box or suitcase. When you say go, the first player puts the suitcase down in front of himself and jumps over it, then picks it up and puts it in front of himself again. He jumps over the suitcase in this fashion all the way to the end of the lane. He must put 1 item of clothing in the suitcase and run back to pass it off to the next player. (R 2–3 times)

HARE HEELS AND TORTOISE TOES. For this game, Tortoise walks on his heels (have the children practice) and Hare walks on his toes (have the children practice). Have the children line up and call out directions such as: "Hare heels forward, sideways, back, stop!" "Tortoise toes back, forward, side, step." When the children gain confidence, have them speed up their hare heels and slow down their tortoise toes! (D 5–10 min.)

SARAH WHITING

Tortoise and Hare:
On the Road Again
Dynamic Equilibrium: Managing Terrain

It's a beautiful morning, and Tortoise and Hare head out early. Up, up, up the mountain they go; then down, down, down they go on the other side. They cross the river through the thicket and into the forest where excitement is around every tree! Can you imagine the fast and slow adventures they'll find there?

EQUIPMENT

- Treasures from nature
- Sandbox
- Water
- Small cup
- Foam gymnastic wedge
- Textured surfaces (rug, bubble wrap, newspaper)
- 2" beam
- Basket
- Boxes
- Buckets
- Hoops
- Rope
- Plank
- Balls
- Net
- Drawing supplies
- Children's climbing equipment

KEY BENEFITS

- Body awareness
- Posture
- Balance
- Concentration
- Problem solving

LANGUAGE FOCUS

up, down, on, across, over, under

CRITICAL SAFEGUARDS

- **Babies:** Supervise closely so that babies do not put small objects such as stones, sticks, or pinecones in their mouths.
- **Older children:** Ensure natural materials (stones, sticks, pinecones) are well rounded and not too sharp.

- **All children:** Ensure adult supervision at all times when children are climbing; if possible, ensure adequate safety matting is in place.

TEACHING GEMS

- Navigating changing terrains is a powerful way to develop children's internal sense of balance. Doing so at different speeds adds to their growing capabilities. Use the tortoise and hare theme to prompt children to vary their pace. For instance, if a child is moving fast, call out, "Tortoise," as a signal for her to slow down. When you want to see her speed up, call out, "Hare."
- Use the song "Tortoise and Hare" (page 190) as often as you like during this activity sequence.

ON THE MOVE   WATCH ME GROW   IN THE KNOW

Snugglers

BODY MAPPING. Understanding the varying planes and terrain of the body is the starting point for independent movement.

BODY TERRAIN. Lay baby on the floor or a steady surface. Hold her hand open and guide it to explore the terrain of your body. Discover the softness of your hair, the slopes of your skin, the stubble of your beard, the tickle of your eyelashes, the warmth of your breath, and so on. Repeat with the sole of her bare foot. (D 2–3 min.)

NATURE'S TERRAIN. Take baby for a walk outside and collect a few treasures from the great outdoors, such as leaves, grass, and bark. Explore what they look like, feel like, smell like. What kinds of sounds can you make with your treasures? (D 10–15 min.)
Note: Be sure baby does not put anything in her mouth.

GUIDED TOUR. Lay baby on her tummy in your arms and give her an "aerial tour" of the room. Bring her high up in the air and hover low to the ground. "Fly" over the furniture so she sees what you see. Fly slowly at first, then vary your speed as you go. (D 2–3 min.)

Squigglers

NATURE WALKS provide baby with a fuller understanding of her world by introducing unique sensations—sights, sounds, smell, textures, and terrains.

HELLO, SANDBOX! Take baby outside and introduce the sandbox. (This activity also works well with an indoor sandbox on a rainy day.) Pour a little sand through your fingers and onto her arms and legs. Take off her shoes and socks and slowly dip her toes in the sand. If she's enjoying it, cover her feet with sand. Repeat with her hands (being sure baby does not put her fingers in her mouth during play). Add a little water and explore this new sensation: mud! (D 3–5 min.)

NATURE WALK. Take a long walk with baby in your arms. Point out and touch all the amazing aspects of nature—the trees, grass, flowers, uphill and downhill slopes, pathways between trees, etc. Collect treasures as you go and bring them back to your sandbox. Sit baby in the sandbox and together explore your treasures. Show baby how to build a mound of sand and decorate it with what you've found. (D 20–30 min.)

ADVENTURES IN SAND. Take off baby's shoes and socks and go for a crawl in the sand. (Again, be sure baby doesn't put her hands in her mouth during play.) Introduce a small cup for pouring sand. Add water to make mud. Make a small mound with the mud and show baby how to mash it down with her hands. Add other natural treasures (pinecones, leaves, flowers) for additional textural stimulation. (D 20–30 min.)

Scampers

CHANGING TERRAIN. Up until now, changes in terrain have been managed by you rather than the child. Now that she's moving on her own, she's employing her early senses of balance, intuition, and coordination to navigate.

SLOPES UP. Head outdoors and find a gentle slope or incline for the child to crawl up. (Indoors, lay down a foam wedge on the floor.) Support the child as she crawls up. Next, cover the slope or wedge with different textures (a piece of rug, bubble wrap, newspaper) to encourage her to grab hold as she crawls. (D 5–10 min.)

SLOPES DOWN. Repeat the "Slopes Up" game, only this time when the child gets to the top, support her to climb back down backward. Assist her to move her arms and legs in a backward fashion. Get outside and repeat on a gentle slope. (D 5-10 min.)

ROLLING HILLS AND VALLEYS. Lay the child on the floor and encourage or support her to roll from her back to her tummy and her tummy to her back. Roll slowly and roll fast. Next, encourage her to crawl up to the top of a foam wedge and then support her to roll very slowly back down. Head outdoors and repeat on a small mound or slope. (D 5–10 min.)

Stompers

EXPLORING UNEVEN SURFACES. The beginnings of understanding unpredictability come through the physical adventures of exploring the world as it presents itself: unevenly.

ONE LEG SHORTER. Lay out a 2" beam on the ground and support the child as she walks with 1 foot on the beam and the other on the ground in an up-down-up-down motion. Try it again, switching feet. Repeat, walking backward. Try it fast and slow too. Add height to the beam for added challenge. (R 3–5 times)

MY OWN STEPPING STONES. Grab a basket and take children for a nature walk. Gather materials to create your own stepping "stones"—such as stones of different sizes and shapes, leaves, bark, or sticks. Next, lay out your treasures on the grass to create a pathway. Support children to step only on the stepping stones. (D 20–30 min.)

THE LAND OF UNEVEN. Repeat "My Own Stepping Stones." This time, add other elements such as sturdy boxes, buckets, hoops, and ropes to create even more uneven surfaces. Add twists and turns, intersecting routes, sections where you go fast or slow, and so forth. If available, build the pathway up and down a gentle slope or incline. (D 20–30 min.)

Scooters

MAPPING YOUR ROUTE. The ups and downs of life begin by learning how to change your approach in the ups and downs of the playground.

QUICKSAND. Tortoise and Hare encounter a pool of quicksand! Can you help them get across? Together with the children, problem solve how to cross the sandbox without touching the sand. Have various materials available for their use, such as stepping stones, planks, and ropes. (D 10–20 min.)

DINOSAUR EGGS. Tortoise and Hare find a dinosaur nest. Can you help them get over the nest without stepping on the eggs? Lay out a shallow basket with balls in it (the nest) and various materials for children's use (planks, ropes, boxes). Strategize with the children to find all the ways over the nest, such as jumping, carrying each other, and building a bridge. *Note:* If you build a structure, be sure it's secure before they climb. (D 10–20 min.)

THE THICKET. Tortoise and Hare run into a prickly thicket. Can you help them find their way past it? String up a tennis net or some net mesh (the thicket) and work with the children to figure out how to get under or over the net. Challenge them to find all the ways they can navigate the net. For added challenge, have them hold hands as they go. (D 10–20 min.)

Skedaddlers

BIG TRIES AND BIG IDEAS. Imagination fosters new and exciting discoveries about one's own capabilities.

BANANAS. Tortoise and Hare are hungry. There are bananas up in the tree. How are they going to get them? Tie a yellow bandana around a climbing rope and work with the children to climb up high enough to touch the bandana. Support them as they climb up and down. If you don't have a climbing rope, explore other climbing methods, such as monkey bars or ladders. Monitor children closely. (D 10 min.)

CHOOSE YOUR OWN ADVENTURE. Tortoise and Hare are on the adventure of a lifetime! What happens? Encourage the children to draw a picture of what Tortoise and Hare are doing and share it with the group. Prompt discussion and demonstration. "What would you do if that happened?" Act out solutions. (D 20–30 min.)

TORTOISE AND HARE ADVENTURE. Now put it all together. Have the children create their *own* adventure and work with them to plan out a Land of Uneven obstacle course. Work together as a team to collect materials and equipment; decide the route and the rules of the game. Be sure to add elements of moving slow and fast like Tortoise and Hare. Then go on your adventure, one at a time, in pairs, or in teams. (D 2+ hours)

Wiggle Where?
Body Awareness: Body Design

SARAH WHITING

Wiggles are part of being a kid. But when you know how to put those wiggles to work, soon enough you'll be wiggling everywhere you go! So the question is, can you wiggle? See page 190 for lyrics to the song for this activity sequence, "Can You Wiggle?"

EQUIPMENT

- Mirror
- "Me" cards or dice (see page 190 for instructions)
- High-energy music
- *Optional:* Stuffed animal
- Camera and printer
- Scissors
- Beanbag
- Bucket
- Hoop
- Glue
- Stickers

KEY BENEFITS

- Spatial awareness
- Positioning
- Visual memory
- Stamina
- Fitness

LANGUAGE FOCUS

inside, outside, match

CRITICAL SAFEGUARDS

Ensure there is enough room for children to move around.

TEACHING GEMS

- At any age (including infancy), always tell the child what is going to happen before it happens. This shows respect for him (even if he can't understand your words yet), which builds trust between you, which reduces the chance for the child to startle or hesitate.
- Kissing games are fun for babies but most appropriate for parents and children. If kissing is inappropriate in your situation, try gentle patting or stroking, tickling (firm, not too light), butterfly (eyelash) kisses, or air-kissing. For more ideas, see the "Kissing Menu" on page 191.

ON THE MOVE	WATCH ME GROW	IN THE KNOW

Snugglers

AWAKENING TO THE BODY. Even the simplest movement and sensory experiences help infants learn the extent of their own bodies.

THE KISSING GAME. Lay the child on his back. (This is great for diaper time, when lots of skin is exposed.) Kiss, stroke, pat, or tickle baby in lots of different ways on his arms, legs, and tummy to create different sensations on his skin. (D 3–5 min.)

UPSIDE-DOWN KISSES. Slowly lean over baby so that he sees you upside down. Kiss or blow gently on his face, chest, tummy, knees, toes, and all the way back up. Next, kneel at baby's side and pat him beginning at his fingertips, up his arm, across his chest, and over to the other arm and fingers. (D 2–3 min.)

FLYING HELLOS. Lie down on the floor and hold up baby, supporting him under his arms. Fly baby to you and give him a big, silly "Hello!" Fly him around and bring him in for another landing. (D 2–3 min.)

Squigglers

MIRRORING. Babies take their cues from us—from how we move, how we speak, and how we express ourselves. And that all begins with studying our faces.

THE FACE GAME. Sit with baby resting against you as you both face the mirror. Take a tour of his face. Gently touch his eyes, ears, nose, mouth, cheek, and chin, narrating as you go. Next, turn baby toward you. Guide his hand to your face, narrating as you go. (D 3–5 min.)

FACE CARDS. Sit with baby facing you and assist him to select a "Face" card or roll the "Face" die. Show him the photo and move that part of your face in lots of different ways, talking about what you're doing. Watch to see if he mirrors your movements. Play again. (D 3–5 min.)

FACE TO FACE. Sit with baby facing you. Encourage him to choose a "Face" card or roll the die. Show him the photo and touch that part of your face. Encourage and assist him to mirror you, touching that part of his own face. Move that part of your face and encourage and assist him to touch your moving face as you talk about what you're doing. Play again. (D 3–5 min.)

Scampers

WHOLE-BODY DESIGN. Body design is an intuitive understanding of the different parts of the body and how they all work together.

THE BODY RAP. Put on some music and help the child choose a "Me" card or roll the die. Show the child the photo and then pat that part of his body to the beat of the music. Encourage and assist him to pat his own body or yours. Play again. If you wish, include his favorite stuffed animal and pat that part of soft toy's body, too. (D 2–3 min.)

THE BODY CHASE. Encourage and assist the child to throw the "Me" die or a "Me" card across the room. Chase after it together. Show him the photo, tap that part of his body, and put a sticker on it. Play again. (R 6 times)

THE BODY PUZZLE. Take a photograph of the child and print it out on cardstock. Cut the photo up into 6 pieces. Work with him to piece the puzzle together. Talk about where all the parts of his body go. (D 3–5 min.)

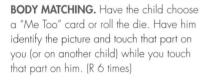

KNOWING THE DETAILS. The human body is an intricate design. Focus on helping the child get to know the details of his body.

BODY MATCHING. Have the child choose a "Me Too" card or roll the die. Have him identify the picture and touch that part on you (or on another child) while you touch that part on him. (R 6 times)

BODY DOUBLE. Have the child choose a "Me Too" card or roll the die. Have him identify the picture and touch that part of his body. Next, have him choose both a "Me" and a "Me Too" card (or roll both dice) and touch both parts of his body at once. (R 6 times)

BODY MOVES. Select a "Me" or "Me Too" card, or roll one of the die. Talk about the body part in the photo; then place a beanbag on the child so he can associate the feel of the beanbag with the name of the body part. Show him how to flick the beanbag off. Next, have him try to flick the beanbag into a bucket on the floor or to a partner for a silly game of catch. (R 6 times)

Scooters

MOVING PARTS. A great way to put a child's understanding of his body map into practice is to use his body for problem solving.

HOOPLA. Lay out a hoop on the floor for each child. Select a "Me" and a "Me Too" card (or roll both dice). Have the child put both of his own matching body parts inside the hoop, leaving the rest of his body outside of the hoop. Now do the reverse, leaving the matching parts outside the hoop and the rest of his body inside it. (R 3–5 times)

HOOPLA 2. Lay out lots of hoops on the floor, all touching each other. Select a "Me" card or roll the die, and have children put their matching body part in 1 hoop and stay in that position. Select a second card or roll the die again. Have children put the matching body part in another hoop. See how many different hoops they can fill with body parts! (D 3–5 min.)

BODY PARTY! Have the children stand in a big group all together. Select a "Me" card, or roll the die. Have each child match that body part with someone else (such as elbow to elbow). Holding that position, choose a "Me Too" card or roll the die, and have children match that body part with someone else (such as heel to heel). Continue playing until the positions break and giggling takes over! (D 3–5 min.)

Skedaddlers

THREE-DIMENSIONAL ME. Movement takes a lot of practice because of all the many different angles, shapes, planes, and directions that are possible when we move.

THE "CAN YOU WIGGLE?" SONG. Have children lie on their backs on the floor. Call out a body part and sing the "Can You Wiggle?" song, wiggling that part of the body to the song. Choose another body part and play again. (R 6 times) Repeat with children lying on their tummies, then standing up.

THE "CAN YOU WIGGLE?" DANCE. Put on some music and stand up straight. Select a "Me" or a "Me Too" card and a "Where" card (or roll the dice) and have children wiggle the matching body part in the direction indicated by the "Where" card. Wiggle to the beat and keep on wiggling; then play again with a different body part and direction. (D 2–3 min.)

THE "CAN YOU WIGGLE?" FINALE. Play "The 'Can You Wiggle?' Dance" again, only this time, have children keep adding a body part and direction until every part of them is wiggling every which way! (D 2–3 min.)

SARAH ALICE LEE

18
INTUITION

Getting to Know Me
Body Awareness: Body Mapping

Children are born with no understanding of their own body, which is why newborn arms and legs tend to flail about. Through movement, a child is using different parts of her body, and along the way, quite naturally develops an understanding of what her body is made up of, how it fits into her world, and eventually how to control it. See page 191 for simple songs to help children get to know their bodies and themselves: "Scrubbily-Bubbily-Tubbily" and "Getting to Know Me."

EQUIPMENT
- Sheer, soft scarves (light enough to float gently in the air) in a variety of colors
- String
- 2 chairs
- *Optional:* towel
- Basket

KEY BENEFITS
- Body awareness
- Fine-motor control
- Directionality
- Cooperation
- Critical thinking and problem solving

LANGUAGE FOCUS
around, through, over, under

CRITICAL SAFEGUARDS
- Be sure there's enough room for children to move around. Do not leave any child unattended with a scarf.
- Ensure the child never puts a scarf in her mouth or around her neck.
- In activities where the child has the scarf under her feet, support the child to avoid slipping.

TEACHING GEMS
- Try to incorporate diverse parts of the body (chin, ankles, backs of knees). The more details children learn, the better they will be able to map their bodies.
- Use bare feet and have as much bare skin exposed as possible to maximize the sensory experience.
- In group games, if a child doesn't like being touched by others, it's okay for her to say no and play these games on her own.

ON THE MOVE	WATCH ME GROW	IN THE KNOW

Snugglers

THE BEGINNINGS OF BODY AWARENESS. Taking a few minutes each day to focus baby's attention on her own body is a great start to helping her get to know her best learning tool—her own body.

GENTLE TOUCHES. Lay baby on her back and run a scarf over and around different parts of her body, talking to her about her feet, hands, legs, tummy, and so on as you go. (D 2–3 min.)

HELLO, FINGERS. HELLO, TOES. Weave a soft scarf like an accordion through baby's fingers and toes, then very slowly pull the scarf through to avoid tickling. (R 1 time for each hand and foot)

SCARF THREADING. Thread a soft scarf through baby's clothes (not her diaper) so the scarf is touching her skin. Thread it through 1 sleeve and out the other. Next, thread it down her shirt and out her pant leg. Slowly, gently pull the scarf through to give her a 360-degree sense of herself. (R 1 time)

Squigglers

WHERE DO I BEGIN AND END? Children learn to recognize their bodies from top to toe and from the inside out. Work these activities from the top to bottom, and from the baby's core out to her extremities.

SCRUBBILY-BUBBILY ANYTIME. Use a scarf and pretend to gently wash different parts of baby's body. (Of course, this game can be used at bath time, too.) Sing the "Scrubbily-Bubbily-Tubbily" song as you play. Start with baby's tummy and work outward: arms, elbows, wrists, fingers. (R 1 time)

PEEKABOO. Cover baby's knee with a scarf. "Oh, my! Where did your knee go?" Reach under the scarf and gently tap baby's knee. Lift the scarf and show her knee. Say, "There's your knee!" gently tapping the child's knee again. (R 2–3 times)

BABY WATERFALL. Tie several scarves or streamers to a string and attach the string to two chairs to create a "waterfall" for baby to crawl through. Take off baby's clothes so that the scarves tickle her whole body from head to toe. (D 3–5 min.)

ON THE MOVE	WATCH ME GROW	IN THE KNOW

Scampers

MY LOWER HALF. Developing a strong, intuitive sense of the lower half of the body is important in moving a child toward confident, independent walking.

TOE TO TOE. Get barefoot and lie on the floor toe to toe with the child. Press your feet together and "dance" in midair. Lead the activity until you sense the child moving on her own; then follow her movements wherever her feet take you. (D 2–3 min.)

ALL LEGS. Sit on the floor with your legs out in front and have the child sit in the same position on your legs. Thread the scarf through and around, in and out of both your legs and hers. Feel the tickle and talk about the scarf moving over, under, through, and around your legs. (D 2–3 min.)

SCOOTING SEALS. Have children get on all fours. Gently tie a scarf around the children's feet to create the seal's flippers, then have children crawl and bark like seals! Show them how to rear up and clap like a seal, too! (D 2–5 min.)

Stompers

ME IN 3-D. Because eyes are in the front of the body, generally we have a much stronger understanding of our front than our sides or back. That goes for children, too. Providing active experiences with the body in 3 dimensions strengthens children's overall sense of self, balance, and intuition as well as their emerging midline development.

THE "GETTING TO KNOW ME" SONG. Change up the lyrics of the classic "Head, Shoulders, Knees, and Toes" to explore all sides of the body. For additional challenge, have children try using the opposite hand to touch the opposite side of the body. (R 3 times per verse)

FLAPJACKS. Have children lie on floor; then have them flap their arms out to the side and slap them back to their sides. Repeat with the legs. Next, have them put both actions together. Now they're really flapping! (R 3 times)

SCRUBBILY-BUBBILY TOWEL TIME. Encourage children to wrap a scarf or towel around their backs and pretend to dry themselves. Sing the "Scrubbily-Bubbily-Tubbily" song while children "dry" all the back parts of their bodies—shoulders, bottom, knees, and so forth. *Note:* This is a great activity for bath time or pool time, too. (R 2–3 times)

Scooters

MY BODY. YOUR BODY. A sense of belonging and community begins when children understand their bodies are similar to other people's bodies.

SIMON SAYS: MY BODY. Have the children stand in a circle and play a game of "Simon Says" using body parts. "Simon says touch your nose." "Simon Says touch your heels." To add complexity, do 2 body parts at once: "Simon Says touch your nose *and* your heels." (D 2–5 min.)

SIMON SAYS: YOUR BODY. Pair up the children for another round of "Simon Says." This time, have them touch the part of the body on their partner. "Simon Says touch his nose." To start, have 1 child play while the partner stands still. To add challenge, have partners play simultaneously. (D 2–5 min.)

STUCK ON YOU. Have the children pair up. Begin by calling out a single body part, such as, "Hand." The children have to touch hands and *not* let go. Call out another body part, such as, "Knee," but tell the children they can't let go of their hands until their knees touch. As they master the game, call out 2 body parts to bring together at the same time. (D 3–5 min.)

Skedaddlers

LOOK WHAT I CAN DO! Body awareness is a key underpinning to using the body for more complex movements (and missions!).

SOMETHING UP MY SLEEVE. Hand out scarves to the children and have them hide the scarves inside their clothing. Talk about the different components of clothes, such as the neck openings, sleeves, and pant legs. When all the scarves are hidden, have the children pretend to be magicians, pulling the scarves through their clothes for an abracadabra show! (3–5 min.)

CHASING TAILS. Have children tuck a scarf into their clothing (waistband, sleeve, pant leg, and so on), but leave a short "tail" hanging out. Have them chase around and try to catch the tails! Repeat the game, putting the tail in another location for each round. (D 5–10 min.)

FLYING TWISTER. Give each child a different-colored scarf. Call out a body part and have children throw the scarves up in the air and catch their own scarf with that body part. Next, have the children pair up. Call out another body part and have children throw the scarves in the air, this time letting the scarves drop to the ground. Then have the partners pick up each of their scarves with that body part and drop them in a nearby basket. (D 5–10 min.)

Tunnel Trek
Spatial Awareness: Tunneling

Tunnels are full of mystery and adventure—and you never know where you'll end up! Let's go tunnel trekking and see what we can find.

EQUIPMENT
- Blanket
- Flashlight
- Book
- Boxes
- Toys
- *Optional:* ribbons
- Balls
- Tunnels (purchased or homemade)
- Squeaky toys
- Crinkly papers
- Pillows
- Beanbags
- Quest Chest
- Blindfold

KEY BENEFITS
- Spatial awareness
- Visual-spatial perception
- Stamina
- Problem solving
- Body control

LANGUAGE FOCUS
through, in, out

CRITICAL SAFEGUARDS
- Ensure baby's airways are always free during swaddling.
- Avoid using any sharp objects in the tunnel.

TEACHING GEMS
- Enclosed or constricted spaces such as tunnels give children real-world practice in fitting their body into space. This is their first exposure to spatial concepts. Use tunnels whenever you can throughout the day. For instance, place a tunnel in the doorway for spatially rich, superfun entrances and exits! Encourage children to go through tunnels at different speeds. The slower they go through, the better it is for the brain. The faster they go through, the more exhilarating it is.
- Long after children are walking, crawling can still have important developmental benefits. Tunnels come in handy to get kids back down on the floor and crawling, such as by creating small, low tunnels under tables or chairs or by setting up a blanket to tunnel under. Conversely, construct large tunnels from cardboard boxes or other materials for children to use large movement patterns like running, jumping, hopping, and skipping.
- Be sure to maintain supervision while children are in tunnels.

ON THE MOVE | WATCH ME GROW | IN THE KNOW

 Snugglers
THE FIRST INKLINGS OF SPACE. Getting accustomed to all the elbow room outside the womb takes a bit of time, so introduce the concept of space slowly and gently.

SWADDLE FOR TWO. Lie down and bring baby to your chest so you are tummy to tummy. Wrap a blanket snugly around both of you like a swaddle for both of you. Gently rock side to side as you sing to him. If swaddling is regulated in your area, wrap your arms around baby to hold him firmly to you and rock side to side as you sing. (D 5–10 min.)

SWADDLE ME. SWADDLE ME NOT. Start with baby fully swaddled. Hold him and rock gently. Maintain eye contact and continually talk or sing to baby as you loosen the swaddle a little bit at a time so he gets an increasing sense of elbow room. Again, if you need an alternative to swaddling, lay baby on the floor and wrap your hands around his torso to mimic the closeness of the womb. Very slowly move your hands away from baby to give him a gentle sensation of the new space around him. (D 5–10 min.)

TUMMY-TIME TALKS. Lay baby on the floor on his tummy and snuggle in next to him. Pull up a blanket over both of you to create a sense of enclosure. Take a flashlight and book under the blanket and read his favorite story. Talk and sing to make this a special time just for the two of you. (D 5–10 min.)

Squigglers

ME VS. SPACE. Children learn to understand the size and shape of their own body by comparing it to spaces of different sizes and shapes.

BABY BOXES. Get 3 different-sized cardboard boxes and cut off the tops. Encourage baby to get in each box for a few minutes to let him explore the space. Stay with him, talking or singing, and pick him up when he indicates he's had enough for now. (D 2–3 min. per box)

MORE BABY BOXES. Encourage baby to climb in and play in the different-sized boxes by hanging toys or ribbons inside them to entice him. Once you've tried all 3 sizes, turn the boxes on their sides and sit them right next to the child, encouraging him to explore the spaces from a different angle. (D 3–5 min.)

UNDERPASS. Present unique sensations of space by making yourself part of baby's movement path. For instance, as he's crawling, stand in front of him and encourage him to crawl through your legs. Roll a ball between your legs or dangle a favorite toy behind your knee. Get on all fours and entice baby to crawl under your tummy. (R 2–3 times)

Scampers

EXPLORING NEW SPACES. Tunnels create a personal passageway for understanding that space comes in different sizes: In large spaces, I'm small. In small spaces, I'm large!

MY FIRST TUNNEL. Introduce the tunnel by showing the child the entrance. Encourage him to explore. Place your hand into the tunnel. Then place his hands inside. Put a favorite toy in the middle of the tunnel for him to reach for. Go to the other end of the tunnel and beckon him to come to you. (D 3–5 min.)

PEEK-A-TUNNEL. Use the tunnel for a high-energy game of peekaboo. Start the child at one end. Encourage him to crawl through to you. Next, play the same game, but this time hide your eyes with your hands so the child can't see your eyes. Then, play again, this time peeking through the tunnel then hiding out of sight altogether. (D 3–5 min.)

CURVE IN THE TRACK. Create a curved tunnel so that the end of the tunnel isn't visible when the child enters. Encourage him to crawl through while you talk and sing so he feels connected to you by the sound of your voice. (R 2–3 times)

Stompers

TUNNEL TRICKS. Showing children how to use things in different ways inspires their imagination and ultimately their ability to transform "what is" into "what if?"

THE LOUD AND LUMPY TUNNEL. Fill the floor of the tunnel with soft toys, squeakers, crinkly papers, etc. Prop some pillows underneath the tunnel to create bumps in the road. After each pass through the tunnel, add more toys for the child to navigate. For instance, add a large, soft toy to partially block his way or a toy flute to toot. (D 3–5 min.)

TUNNEL THE LEADER. Set up multiple tunnels (or mix tunnels with open cardboard boxes to create a track). Lay the tunnels out in a pattern around the floor and play "Follow the Leader." Wherever the leader goes and however the leader moves (such as running, crawling, or jumping), the others have to follow. (D 5–10 min.)

THE TUNNEL CHALLENGE. Using the tunnel as a target, have the children try to roll or kick a ball through the tunnel and chase after it. The object is to switch all the children from 1 side of the tunnel to the other. (D 5–10 min.)

Scooters

SPACE EXPLORATION. Space feels different when you move through it in different ways.

ZOOEY TUNNEL. Encourage the child to move through the tunnel like different animals (bunnies hop, giraffes stand very tall, cats prowl, ponies prance). Have him make animal sounds as he goes. (D 3–5 min.)

THE SUPERZOOEY TUNNEL. Repeat the "Zooey Tunnel" game, only this time, do it backward. Next, have children try moving in pairs. How do monkeys tunnel while holding hands? How do kangaroos jump in pairs? (D 5–10 min.)

WORMLY WORMS IN THE TUNNEL. Have children wiggle like worms through the tunnel without using hands. Then wiggle through without using feet. Next, try wiggling through without hands or feet! Try all 3 wiggles on the tummy, then on the back. (D 3–5 min.)

Skedaddlers

THE TUNNEL PLAYSCAPE. Mastering movements inside a confined space gives children confidence to navigate the big wide world.

TWO-WAY TUNNEL. Have 2 children crawl through the tunnel from either end at the same time. Stand back and allow them to problem-solve how to pass each other inside the tunnel. Next, add 2 more children to create a traffic jam! (D 3–5 min.)

MEMORY TUNNEL. Put different-colored beanbags in the tunnel. Call out a color and have 1 child at a time go through and bring out that color. Next, call out 2 colors and repeat the game, 1 child at a time. Then, pair up children. Call out 2 colors and have them go through the tunnel together to find their colors. Continue adding beanbag colors for the children to tunnel in and find. For added challenge, have the children bring out the colors in the order in which you called them. (D 5–10 min.)

TUNNEL TREK. Have the child select 3–5 items out of the Quest Chest. Put them in the tunnel. Select 1 for the child to go find, but before he heads into the tunnel, blindfold him. This requires him to use all of his body intuition skills to negotiate the space and identify the object by its size, shape, and texture. *Note:* Do not blindfold a child or cover his eyes if he is not comfortable with this. (R 2–3 times)

Sardines in a Can
Understanding Size and Volume

There's nothing more fun than going someplace with all your friends. When we're on the move, we can pack ourselves like sardines! Can you squeeze in, too?

EQUIPMENT

- Toys (small, medium, and large)
- Stuffed animal
- Socks, hats, and mittens (of varying sizes)
- Laundry basket
- 3" plastic balls
- Hoops of varying sizes
- Plastic cups
- Water
- Sand
- Bucket or basin
- Plastic toy boat (bath toy)
- Tall container
- Shallow bowl
- Finger paint
- Paper
- Blanket
- *Optional:* feathers
- Chalk or tape
- Cardboard boxes (of varying size)
- Teddy bears or soft toys

KEY BENEFITS

- Understanding size
- Understanding volume
- Self-awareness
- Body awareness
- Strength management

LANGUAGE FOCUS

small, medium, large, long, tall, wide, too little, too much, just right

CRITICAL SAFEGUARDS

Never leave a child unattended in or around water. Supervise children at all times.

TEACHING GEMS

- Encourage holding things with varying pressure so children can explore the variances of volume, such as putting a sleeping bag into its sack or picking up leaves from the ground and putting them into a bag, then squashing them down to reduce the volume.
- Create your own measuring tape and spend the day or week measuring a variety of things wherever you go.

ON THE MOVE	WATCH ME GROW	IN THE KNOW

 ### Snugglers
EXPLORING SIZE. Spending time exploring things of different sizes gives baby a sense of her own size.

SMALL, MEDIUM, LARGE. Put a small toy in baby's hand for her to grasp. Next, give her a medium-sized toy. Then offer a large toy so she's grasping it with her fingertips. Talk to her about size differences. (D 2–3 min.)

YOU, TEDDY, AND ME. Hold baby's hand in yours and show her how the size of your hands differ. Then put a stuffed animal's paw in her hand and show her the size difference. Talk to her about the idea of small, smaller, and smallest. (D 2–3 min.)

HUG TIGHT. Hold baby in a hug, varying the pressure from very snug to gentle and loose. Next, hold baby's favorite stuffed animal against her tummy and wrap her arms around it. Assist her to hug the toy tight. Now pick up baby and toy together for a group hug. Give baby a different toy to hug for different sensations of size. (D 1–2 min.)

 ### Squigglers
GOLDILOCKS. Understanding the concepts of *too little, too much,* and *just right* begins with everyday play experiences.

THREE SOCKS. Gather 3 socks of varying sizes (adult, child, toy). Explore them with baby, putting different-sized socks on her feet and your own. Try this with hats and mittens, too. (D 3–5 min.)

BABY BALL PIT. Fill a laundry basket with 3" plastic balls and put baby in it to explore. Point out the balls falling out as you wiggle baby into place. Keep filling the basket with balls as she knocks them out. (D 3–5 min.)

HOOP CRAWL. Hold a hoop vertically in front of baby as she's crawling and encourage her to crawl through. Use different-sized hoops 1 at a time or several at a time to create a tunnel effect. (D 5–10 min.)

ON THE MOVE	WATCH ME GROW	IN THE KNOW

Scampers

POURING is a powerful learning tool for putting the concepts of size and volume right into little ones' hands.

POUR A LITTLE. POUR A LOT. Give the child a plastic cup and show her how to pour water. Have her try pouring a little at a time, gradually filling the cup to the top. Then have her overfill it so it spills out. Talk about "too little," "too much," and "just right" as you play. Try it with sand, too. (R 2–5 times)

WATERFALL POURING. With 2 plastic cups, children can explore pouring from 1 cup to the other. At first have the cups touching to help keep hands steady. Then, show them how to lift the pouring cup up and see the water falling a few inches into the empty cup. Try this with water, sand, and other materials. (D 5–10 min.)

DON'T SINK THE BOAT! Fill a basin with water and float a small toy boat in the water. Show the child how to dip her cup in the water to fill it. Pour water into the boat until it sinks. Next, encourage and assist the child to pour only a little water in the boat at a time so the boat doesn't sink. (R 3–5 times)

Stompers

MEASURING. Turn abstract concepts such as size, volume, and distance into tangible experiences for children.

WHAT DOES VOLUME LOOK LIKE? Fill a tall container with a pint of water. Now have the child pour the water into a shallow bowl. Find all kinds of containers and see how many you can fill with the same amount of water. (D 5–10 min.)

MEASURING HANDS AND FEET. Place a child's hand on top of yours and compare sizes. Next, you and the children all dip your hands into finger paint to create handprints. Compare sizes. Try this with his feet, or lie down and measure who has the longest body. (D 5–10 min.)

HOW FAR IS IT? Have the children lie head to foot to connect 1 point in the room or on the playground to another, such as from the door to the sandbox. Count how many children it takes to get to the sandbox. Next, have them lie shoulder to shoulder and count again. Discuss the difference. What other ways can children use their bodies to measure distance (for example, hand to hand or toe to toe). (D 10–20 min.)

Scooters

VOLUME VARIATION. Recognizing the changing dynamics of volume and space helps children understand the unpredictability of things.

MAKING THINGS SMALLER. Give a group of children a blanket to fold in half, then in half again. Have them continue to fold until they've made it as small as they can. Next, give them several sheets of paper. Have them fold 1 in half, 1 in quarters, 1 in eighths, and so forth. Lay out the folded papers alongside the original-sized paper and compare. (D 5–10 min.)

GROWING SAND. Scoop sand into 3 buckets so that 1 is a quarter full, one half full, and one full. With the children, compare the 3 buckets. Are they the same or different? What can we do to make them all the same? As children fill the buckets with scoops of sand, discuss and count how many scoops of sand are needed to fill each bucket. Repeat with water and practice pouring skills, or try other materials such as feathers. (D 5–10 min.)

GROWING SHAPES. With chalk or tape, make a large triangle on the floor and have 3 children lie down on the shape to form a triangle. Have the other children try to fit inside the triangle. Next, have 6 children form a triangle (2 children per side), and now see how many children can fit inside. Repeat with other shapes. (D 10–20 min.)

Skedaddlers

SPATIAL CONCEPTS. Planting the seeds of spatial reasoning happens when children use their bodies to fill space in different ways.

GROWING CIRCLES. With children in pairs, have 1 child stand still while the other child draws a circle around her partner's feet. Check the size of the circles. Now group children so that 2 stand side by side while a third child draws a circle around their feet. Compare the size of the circles to the earlier ones. Repeat with 3 children standing together, then 4, and so on, each time drawing a circle and stepping back to compare. Next, have all the children stand and squeeze together while you draw a circle around them. Then have them spread out as far as they can (still touching one another) and draw another circle. Discuss concepts of *more* and *less* as you compare the circles. (D 5–10 min.)

HOW BIG IS BIG? Find a large TV or refrigerator box and have the children measure it with their bodies. For instance, they can pace it off with their feet or hands and stretch their arms out to measure its width. They can lie down next to the box to measure its length and width. They can lie on top of each other to see how deep it is. What other ways can children discover to measure things with their bodies? (D 5–10 min.)

SARDINES IN A CAN. Put out boxes of varying sizes and challenge the children to think of different ways they could fit themselves inside. Let them explore individually. Next, bring out a large TV or refrigerator box and challenge them to figure out how to get all of the children in the box at the same time. Should they stand up? Lie down? Be partly in and partly out of the box? Stand back and give them time to problem-solve on their own. (D 10–15 min.)

Two Worms on a Plank

Strength Management: Pushing and Pulling

One day, Wormly Worm and Squirmly Worm set out to see who could inch their way down the plank the fastest. The plank was long, but they were strong and evenly matched, inching neck and neck down the plank. Then all of a sudden, somebody stepped on the end of the plank and they found themselves inching uphill! Can you show Wormly and Squirmly how to make their way up the plank?

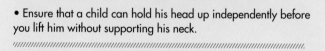

SARAH ALICE LEE

EQUIPMENT

- Soft toys (varying weights, sizes, and textures)
- Container to hold toys
- Basket or bucket
- Toy cars
- Ramps for toys
- Textured surfaces (rugs or bubble wrap)
- Rope
- Whiteboard
- Plank
- *Optional:* chalk or tape

KEY BENEFITS

- Force and resistance
- Understanding muscle strength
- Sense of self
- Teamwork

LANGUAGE FOCUS

across, along, up

CRITICAL SAFEGUARDS

- To ensure that a rope, plank, or other equipment can support a child's weight, always be sure it can support *your* weight.

- Ensure that a child can hold his head up independently before you lift him without supporting his neck.

TEACHING GEMS

An important part of developing children's intuition is experiences with weight, force, and resistance. Throughout the day find opportunities to explore weight concepts with everyday objects, and look for any opportunity for the child to experience his own weight in new ways.

ON THE MOVE	WATCH ME GROW	IN THE KNOW

 Snugglers

THE SENSATIONS OF MOVEMENT. Even though young babies aren't ready for deliberate movement, they are already gathering sensory information that will help them move on their own someday.

IN AND OUT. Lay baby on his back and slowly, gently bend his legs toward his chest and back out to his resting position. Push on the soles of his feet and feel him resist the pressure. Repeat with his arms, folding them in over his chest and back out. (D 1–2 min.)

BABY SIT-UPS. Lay baby on his back. Support him under his head, neck, and shoulders. Very slowly lift him up toward you to a supported, sitting position. Hold for a few moments, smiling and talking to him, then slowly lower him to his resting position. (D 1–2 min.)

BABY UP, UP, UP. Lie on the floor on your back with baby lying on top of you, on his tummy, so he faces you. Fully supporting him under his chest, slowly lift him up and back down so that his hands can touch and explore your face. Talk, sing, and maintain eye contact throughout the ride. (R 2–3 times)

Squigglers

PUT-AND-TAKE PLAY. The simple act of picking up and putting down objects gives baby important clues about managing himself and his environment.

PICK UP. PUT DOWN. Sit baby in your lap. Pile soft toys around the 2 of you and explore them with baby. Talk about the toys he picks up. Choose another toy and show it to him. Entice him to let go of 1 and pick up another, encouraging him to use both hands. Lift the toy high for him to reach for it. (D 5–10 min.)

REACH AND MOVE. Lay baby on his tummy on the floor and lie down facing him. Introduce several soft toys and watch to see which toy he reaches for. Once he grabs hold, tug on the toy (but don't take it away). This gives him a sense of resistance and encourages him to stretch and move toward you. (D 5–10 min.)

MY FIRST TOY BOX! Gather several soft toys and put them in a container on the floor. Sit baby on the floor next to the container and encourage him to explore. Cheer each time he reaches in and takes one. Continue to refill the container as he empties it so the game can continue, using toys of varying weights, sizes, and textures. (D 5–10 min.)

Scampers

KNOWING YOUR OWN STRENGTH. As children get vertical, they're experiencing new sensations of muscle strength and independence.

STEAL A KISS! Sit with the child on your lap facing you. Hold his hands. Pull him gently toward you, give him a kiss or an air-kiss, and slowly push him away. Make it fun and silly, repeating until he understands the game and starts to lean in on his own to "steal a kiss." As he takes over the lead, ever-so-gently add a little resistance when he's pushing toward you and pulling away from you. This gives him a sense of how to change his force and resistance. (D 2–3 min.)

RAMP UP. Crawling and pushing toy cars or trucks around the floor is a great way to develop the child's sense of intuition. Add textured surfaces such as rugs or bubble wrap to slow down his play and force him to push harder. Add ramps for the toys so that he has to push uphill. Go outside and play up and down a slight incline or hillside, in the sandbox, or in a mud puddle. (D 10–30 min.)

MY FIRST HANDSTAND. Start by showing the child how to walk like a monkey (put hands on the floor with your bottom in the air, walking on all fours with arms and legs extended). Give him lots of time and room to play and enjoy. When he's ready, have him stand in front of you facing away from you and plant his hands on the floor. Slowly lift his feet up off the ground as he supports himself on his hands. "Walk" his feet up your legs until he's upside down. Slowly walk his legs back down to the floor. (R 3–5 times)

Stompers

PHYSICAL GEOMETRY. Exploring different planes within their environment gives children a sense of the geometry of their world and how to navigate within it.

BUILD A ROAD. Use a line or rope on the floor for the child to follow. Have the child lie on his tummy, bending his elbows up with his palms on the floor tucked in close to his shoulders. Keeping his feet still, have him push up to a straight arm position, pull his body forward, then return to a resting position on his tummy. (D 2–3 min.)

BUILD A BRIDGE. Using a secure wall for support, have children explore ways to build a bridge with part or all of their body. For example, positions might include hands on the wall, 1 foot on the wall, sitting against the wall with knees bent, or leaning backward against the wall. Roll a toy car underneath a child's "bridge" to show the space he has created with his body. Then have half the children make bridges and the other half crawl under; repeat so everyone gets a turn. (D 3–5 min.)

BUILD A SKYSCRAPER. Start by having the child stand at the whiteboard and draw a box on the board. Next, prop a plank on a heavy book to create a slight incline. Supporting the child, have him walk up the plank and draw a box on top of the first box. Repeat, adding a little more height to the plank each time. See how tall you can build your skyscraper. (D 3–5 min.)

Scooters

NAVIGATING DEFINED SPACES. As children develop more coordination and body control, create new challenges by changing the playing field.

WORM ON A PLANK. Lay a plank on the floor and have the child crawl across on his belly. Next, have him wiggle across on his back. Then have him crawl across like a worm without using his arms. If he tips off the plank, he has to go back and start again. (3–5 min.)

TWO WORMS ON A PLANK. Lay down a long plank on the floor (or use chalk or tape to make a line on the floor). Have 2 children crawl across on their bellies to warm up. Next, have them lie down on their bellies in a line. Have the second child hold onto the first child's feet. Now have them navigate the plank together—the first child using his arms to pull and the second child using his feet to push. Repeat with children lying on their backs. (R 2–3 times)

UP THE PLANK. Incline a plank 2–3 inches off the ground. Have the child lie on his tummy and grip the sides, using his arms to pull himself up. (The feet should be as still as possible, or have him bend his knees to keep his feet out of the activity.) Raise the incline a few inches at a time for subsequent rounds. (R 3–5 times)

Skedaddlers

WEIGHT-BEARING ACTIVITIES directly develop upper-body strength while opening up new ways for the child to think about navigating space. These activities may be done indoors or out depending on your space and available equipment.

ROPE BRIDGE. Tie a rope to 2 sturdy posts so the rope spans horizontally across a smooth floor or other hard surface about 3 feet off the ground. Start by showing the child how to move along the rope hand-over-hand, both forward and backward, while walking alongside the rope. Next, have the child sit cross-legged on the floor under the rope. Have him pull himself along the rope hand-over-hand. Repeat going backward. (R 2–3 times)

PLANK AND ROPE. Incline a plank 2–3 inches off the ground. Secure a rope to a post, wall, or any other secure fixture. Run the rope vertically down the plank. Have the child lie on his belly and bend his knees so his feet are excluded from the activity. Standing by for support, have him use the rope hand-over-hand to pull himself up and down the plank. Repeat with him lying on his back. Raise the incline a few inches at a time to add challenge. Rest in between rounds as needed. (R 3–5 times)

RAPPELLING. Next, tie the rope to the top of a bar over a plank or an incline. Have the child use the rope to rappel (climb) up the plank holding tightly onto the rope. Allow a rest at the top, and then have him work backward to rappel back down. Assist and support at all times. Increase the degree of incline to add challenge. (R 5 times)

Jack and Jill
Strength Management:
Understanding Varying Weights

When Jack and Jill went up the hill, they discovered a pail of water was quite heavy. Maybe that's why Jack fell down and Jill tumbled down after him. Can you tell when something is heavy or light?

EQUIPMENT
- Balls of varying weights
- Bucket
- Various baby toys
- Push toy (carriage or wagon)
- 2 pails
- Water
- 2 tubs
- Paper
- Pebbles or stones
- Toy boat or plastic container
- Scarf
- Rope
- Hoops
- Various large and small objects
- Large cardboard box

KEY BENEFITS
- Strength management
- Teamwork
- Understanding weight concepts

LANGUAGE FOCUS
push, pull, light, heavy

CRITICAL SAFEGUARDS
- *Never* leave a child unattended in or around water. Supervise children at all times.
- Ensure the body weight in team events is evenly distributed.
- Never make the weights too much for the child to manage with moderate effort.
- Keep mixing up the weights so the child can physically feel the difference.

TEACHING GEMS
- When children learn to understand weight management, those skills can be transferred into many different life skills that require precise strength management. For instance, learning how to pour milk, how hard to push on the paper when writing, or even how tightly to hug a friend.
- Encourage children to be responsible and carry all their things (within reason of course).
- Many life skills require a child to learn about the idea of *too much, too little,* or *just right.* Playing and managing objects of different weight is a great way to give children tangible experiences with nuanced differences.

SARAH WHITING

ON THE MOVE

WATCH ME GROW

IN THE KNOW

 ### Snugglers
VARYING SENSATIONS heighten the sensory awareness and help fine-tune the brain's understanding of our sensory world.

PRESSURE MASSAGE. Lay baby on her back and massage her torso from top to bottom. Gradually increase pressure from light to firm. Repeat on her tummy. (D 2–3 min.)

PULSE MASSAGE. Lay baby on her back and massage her arms and legs. Create a pulsing sensation, gently pressing and releasing as you work down her arms and legs. (D 2–3 min.)

PUSHY PUSHY. Put your palm together with baby's palm. When she pushes on your hand, allow her to push you away with ease. Match her strength and gently push her hand back. Very gradually increase the amount of resistance so it's a little harder each time for her to push you away. Repeat with both hands and both feet. (D 2–3 min.)

Squigglers

CORE STRENGTH is an essential foundation to developing balance and independent movement.

PARACHUTE TILTS. Sit on the floor with baby between your legs facing away from you and leaning back against you. Gently tilt her to the side, supporting her around the chest and leaving her arms free. This should encourage the parachute reflex. Tilt to both sides. (R 1–3 times)

BUCKET BALL. Once baby is sitting independently, have her sit on the floor. Gather a selection of balls of varying weights and a pail or other container. Encourage baby to explore the balls to feel the different weights. Show her how to put the balls in the bucket or pail and take them back out. (D 5–10 min.)

HORSE RIDES. While baby is crawling around, place a lightweight object, such as a small teddy bear, on her back. If baby enjoys this game, gradually increase the weight she's carrying, using a different toy. Then show her how to rear up like a horse and drop the object, assisting her as needed. (D 3–5 min.)

Scampers

ARM AND LEG STRENGTH. Learning how and when to adjust muscle strength begins with everyday interactions with the environment.

MY FIRST PUSH-UPS. Support the child under the chest and hips with her hands on the floor. Hold her in that position and feel for her attempts to push against the floor. Gently lift and lower her as she pushes away. Repeat with her feet on the floor, lifting her up when she pushes away. (R 2–3 times)

MY FIRST WHEELBARROW. Place some of the child's favorite toys about 3" in front of her. With the child on all fours, lift her up under her thighs, supporting her under her chest and hips, insuring her back is straight and not bowed. Encourage her to walk forward with her hands, but do *not* push her. When she gets to the toys, lower her down so she can play. Over time, gradually increase the wheelbarrowing distance. (D 1–2 min.)

PUSH-AROUNDS. Introduce a push toy such as a carriage or wagon. Over time, introduce the idea of putting different things in the carriage. (Be sure they are of different weights.) This naturally adds weight and requires the child to vary her strength to push the carriage along. (D 5–10 min.)

Stompers

CARRYING. The simple act of carrying things gives the body and brain new movement experiences.

PARCEL POST. Create a small motory (obstacle course) around the room. Identify 3–5 stops along the way and have the child run the course. Then fill a pail with 3–5 toys. Challenge the child to make her way around the obstacle course, delivering 1 toy to each stop. Now go in reverse picking up parcels at each stop. (D 5–10 min.)

JACK AND JILL. To start, put a little water in a pail and challenge the children to take turns carrying it across the room with both hands. Repeat, having them carry it with the right hand and then the left. Gradually add more water to vary the weight. Head outside and repeat the activity on a slight hill or an incline. Try not to spill! (D 5–10 min.)

JACK AND JILL RACE. This is best done outside. Fill a large tub with water and set up an empty tub on the other side of the play area. Give the children each a pail. Show them how to fill their pail halfway with water. Then have them run to the other tub and empty their pail. The object of the game is to transfer all the water to the empty tub. Next, pair up the children. Have them fill their pail to the top and together return the water to the other tub. Try not to spill! (D 5–10 min.)

Scooters

COMPARING WEIGHTS. Exploring weight and tension builds a child's intuitive sense of herself and how to anticipate and negotiate the physics of our world.

WHAT'S HEAVIER? Fill 2 pails halfway, 1 with crumpled paper and 1 with water. Explore which is heavier. Next, have the child carry both pails (1 in each hand) and walk heel-to-toe along a line on the floor. Have her switch hands and walk the line again. Next, have the child choose what to put in pails and repeat the activity. (D 3–5 min.)

THAT SINKING FEELING. Have the children gather stones. Fill a sink or tub with water and float a small toy boat or plastic container. Have the children take turns adding 1 stone to the boat at a time. Encourage them to estimate how many more stones it will take to sink the boat! Repeat with other weighted objects, such as crayons or blocks. (D 2–3 min.)

ARM WRESTLING 101. Pair up 2 children and have them lie on the floor facing each other. Show them how to arm wrestle: clasp right hands and keep right elbows on the floor at all times. Have them tuck their left hand underneath their body so that it can't be used. (This is to be sure the match is even between the children and their excitement doesn't get the better of them.) Instruct them to keep every other part of the body still. Count, "1, 2, 3, go!" Repeat with the left arm. (D 5–10 seconds per round)

Skedaddlers

PROBLEM SOLVING. Giving children a task to achieve as a group creates opportunities for teamwork, leadership, strategizing, and problem solving.

UNEVEN TUG-OF-WAR. Loosely tie a scarf at the midpoint on a rope. Put a hoop on the floor to identify the center of the play area. Divide children into 2 teams. Start with 2 children on either side and the scarf over the center. Have them tug on the rope, trying to pull the scarf toward them. Next, add a player on 1 side of the rope. Tug again and discuss what happens. Now even up the teams and tug again. Explore what happens. (D 5–10 min.)

ARMFULS. Set up a motory (obstacle course) with 5 stations and a home base. Put 1 large object at each station, each object of differing weight (a ball, large box of feathers, bucket of blocks, and so on). The object of the game is to pick up all 5 objects and return to home base without dropping them. The children have to work out between them how to carry all 5 objects while negotiating the course. If children are struggling to manage all 5 objects at once, allow them to make multiple trips through the motory. (D 3–5 min.)

THE VERY BUSY BUS. Start by decorating a large cardboard box to be the bus. Next, work with the children to map out a bus route around the room. Encourage them to push the empty bus around the route to feel how light it is. Now have 1 child sit in the bus while the others push her around the bus route. Continue to add 1 passenger on each round until they can't push the bus anymore. (D 5–10 min.)

Game Day
Understanding Boundaries

The biggest day of all is Game Day, when everyone comes out to play their favorite games! What are your favorite games to play? See page 191 for lyrics to "Ring Around the Bull's-Eye," the song for this activity sequence.

EQUIPMENT
- Low obstacle (rolled-up towel or small pillow)
- Different-textured surfaces (newspaper, bubble wrap, towels, furry fabrics)
- Chairs
- *Optional:* blanket
- Stairs
- Toys
- Chalk or tape
- Blanket, sheet, or parachute
- Hoops
- Rope

KEY BENEFITS
- Spatial awareness
- Body awareness
- Temporal awareness
- Following rules
- Teamwork

LANGUAGE FOCUS
around, inside, outside

CRITICAL SAFEGUARDS
- When climbing stairs, always stay behind the child and support him as needed. *Never* leave a child unattended on or near stairs.

- When teaching a child to climb down stairs, always prompt and assist him to go down backward. When children are young, their heads are heavier than the rest of their body, so doing it this way is safer.

TEACHING GEMS
To play "Freeze Tag": Define the boundaries for the game and select 1 player to be "It." "It" will chase the other players. Other players run, trying to avoid being tagged. When "It" tags you, you have to freeze in place until 1 of 2 things happens: (1) you are "thawed out" by another player crawling through your legs *or* (2) all the players are frozen, the game ends, and a new person is chosen to be "It."

ON THE MOVE

WATCH ME GROW

IN THE KNOW

 ## Snugglers
MY FIRST BOUNDARIES. A child's understanding of the boundaries of space begins with understanding the boundaries of his body.

FACIAL FEATURES. Gently guide baby's hands around the contours of your face. Maintain eye contact and talk about the features he's touching. Next, guide his hands to touch his own face. Talk about his forehead, cheeks, chin, mouth, nose, and so forth. (D 1–2 min.)

THE ENDS OF ME. Slowly massage baby's hands 1 at a time, beginning at the wrists, palms, and backs of the hands. Massage each finger separately, slowly working down to the fingertip. Tap or kiss each finger when you get to the end. Repeat with the feet and toes. (D 2–3 min.)

BOUNCING OFF THE WALLS. Take baby's socks off and hold him facing away from you, holding his feet out in front of you. Tour the room, putting baby's feet on different surfaces such as the walls, furniture, pillows, and rugs. When you feel him push away, step back as though you're bouncing off the surface. (D 2–3 min.)

Squigglers

MOVING FREELY. With the onset of independent movement, babies naturally encounter boundaries. With boundaries come the beginnings of strategizing and problem solving.

FREE-RANGE FLOOR PLAY. Clear the floor of as many obstacles as you can to give baby wide-open spaces to move and explore. Start by sitting within reach of him. Gradually move yourself back a few feet at a time to entice him to come to you. Keeping a watchful eye, step out of sight, and see what he does on his own. (D 10–20 min.)

SOMETHING'S IN MY WAY! During "Free-Range Floor Play," introduce an obstacle between the 2 of you such as a rolled-up towel or small pillow. Entice baby to commando-crawl (belly-crawl) over the obstacle to get to you. Assist and support as needed. (D 10–20 min.)

FLOOR PLANS. Cover the entire floor with different-textured mats such as newspaper, bubble wrap, towels, and furry fabrics. Put baby down on all fours and explore the textures together. Step back a bit and encourage him to crawl to you. Reassure him if he hesitates to cross from one texture to the next. (D 10–20 min.)

Scampers

NAVIGATING BOUNDARIES. With independent movement comes an increased understanding of space and objects. **Note:** *Never* leave a child unattended on or near stairs.

BACK UP THE BUS. Line up table chairs in a row. If you'd like, cover them with a blanket to create a tunnel. Entice the child through the chairs, greeting him as he gets to the exit at the other end. Next, block the exit, encouraging him to crawl backward. (D 3–5 min.)

CLIMBING UP. Children often learn to climb *before* they can walk. When a child shows interest (pulling himself up and lifting his leg in an attempt to climb), introduce the stairs. Stand behind him for physical and moral support. Watch him work out how to lift his knee up on the first step and bring the rest of his body up. Support him around the waist for safety, but do not do the work for him. Cheer his attempts. Entice him to climb up farther by putting toys on next steps. (R 2–3 times each session.)

CLIMBING DOWN. Once the child begins climbing with ease, it's critical to train him how to get down safely. And that means climbing down *backward!* (Climbing down backward keeps the head above the body for balance.) For this, put him on the second step. Holding him securely under the chest, guide 1 knee down to the first step, then assist him to bring his other knee down. Repeat until he's back on the floor. (R 2–3 times each session)

Stompers

MODIFYING MOVEMENT. Impeding a child's movements with boundaries challenges him to move and control his body in new and different ways.

ON TRACK. With chalk or tape, make a long line on the floor or outdoor surface. Have the child follow the track, keeping 1 foot on the line at all times. Say, "Toot!" to go forward and, "Toot toot!" to go backward. For a group of children, have them keep 1 hand on the shoulder of the child in front of them. (D 2–3 min.)

OFF TRACK. Draw a curvy, twisted, overlapping line on the floor or outdoor surface—the more twists and turns the better. Have the child walk in a straight line to the other end of the play area while he *avoids* stepping on the track. Have him toot once to go forward and twice to go backward. For a group of children, have them keep 1 hand on the shoulder of the child in front of them. (D 2–3 min.)

DERAILED. When train cars go off the track, they roll! Draw a long, straight track on the floor. Then tell children to lie down at one end of the track with their fingers on the line above their heads. Explain that one "toot" of the train whistle means the children need to roll down the track, keeping their fingers on the track. Two "toots" mean to roll up the track. Three "toots" mean to stop rolling. Challenge children to roll as long as they can while listening for your cues. Encourage children to try to keep their arms straight and ankles together as they roll. (D 2–3 min.)

Scooters

RESPECTING BOUNDARIES. When children learn to respect boundaries in play, they're picking up clues about playing by the rules and respecting others.

MUSICAL BULL'S-EYE. Draw 3 circles to form a target on the floor or outdoor surface. Use different colors for the lines. Have the children hold hands and circle around the outside and sing the "Ring Around the Bull's-Eye" song. On the last line, call out the destination they all need to jump to together. Next time, have them try the game using different kinds of movements. (R 3–5 times)

JUMPING CHECKERS. Draw a giant black-and-white checkerboard on the floor or outdoor surface. (See the checkerboard diagram on page 191.) Have the children form teams. Have them line up on either side of the board facing each other. Using only the black squares, have them jump to the other side. When they meet in the middle, allow them to figure out how to navigate around one another without stepping on the white squares. Repeat using different kinds of movement. (D 5–10 min.)

CAT AND MOUSE. Have the children hold hands in a circle. Put 1 child in the middle of the circle (cat) and 1 child on the outside (mouse). The circle's goal is to stop the cat from reaching the mouse by blocking the cat from getting through the line. If the cat does get through, the circle lifts their hands to let the mouse inside. When the mouse is caught, she becomes the cat, the other child joins the circle, and a new mouse is chosen. (D 10–20 min.)

Skedaddlers

CHANGING BOUNDARIES. Life doesn't always come with defined boundaries, so play a game that gives children a chance to react to changing circumstances.

SHEEP ON THE LOOSE. Create a large play area and show the children its boundaries. Make 1 corner the corral. Divide the children into 2 teams—the Sheep and the Farmers. Give the Farmers 1 large blanket, sheet, or parachute to hold taut between them. (This is their moving fence.) When you say go, the Sheep scatter, staying in bounds. The Farmers need to figure out how to work together, using their moving fence to get all the Sheep into the corral. Round 2: switch positions. (D 5–10 min.)

DODGEHOOP. Give each child a hoop and have them line up on either side of a running lane. Select 1 child to run the lane. As the child runs, the players on the sidelines roll their hoop to try to catch the runner. The runner has to watch out for all the oncoming hoops and try to dodge them. If the hoop catches (touches) the runner, that hoopster becomes the new runner. (D 10–20 min.)

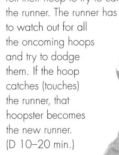

SHRINK TAG. Outline a large playing field with yellow rope and invite the children to play a traditional game of "Freeze Tag." Next, try "Shrink Tag": In this version there is no "thawing"; the round ends when all the players are frozen. At that point, redraw the boundaries around the frozen players (shrinking the play area), choose a new person to be "It," and start again. (D 15–30 min.)

Steposaur Steps
Directionality

The Steposaurs are having a hard time figuring out which way to step. Sometimes Frontosaurus-Backosaurus goes backward when she means to go forward and forward when she means to go backward. Inosaurus is always out of bounds. Outosaurus is always in trouble. And never, ever get next to Nextatops when he decides to sit down. Can you help the Steposaurs step in the right direction?

EQUIPMENT
- Rattle and other baby toys
- Soft toy car
- Pipe cleaner
- Feathers or foam balls
- Streamers
- Ball
- Fabric
- Cardboard boxes
- Towels
- Gym mats
- Stretchy Lycra
- Fabric or rope for tails
- Dot stickers

KEY BENEFITS
- Directionality
- Problem solving
- Developing object permanence

LANGUAGE FOCUS
in, out, front, behind, between, through, under, over, around

CRITICAL SAFEGUARDS
- When covering a child, always give the child an easy out if she doesn't like to be confined.
- Use gym mats whenever there is an instance where a child could tip or roll onto a hard surface.

TEACHING GEMS
- Language + Experience = Understanding. Always talk about and comment on the child's position and direction so she can hear the language that is associated with the movement.
- Sometimes ask the child what she is doing so she can verbalize her position.

SARAH WHITING

ON THE MOVE WATCH ME GROW IN THE KNOW

 Snugglers

POSITION. Young babies need to learn about themselves before they can understand their world. Learning about position in relation to their own body is an important first step.

INOSAURUS. OUTOSAURUS. Gently open baby's hand and place the handle of her rattle *in* her hand. Tell baby the rattle is *in* her hand. Now open her fingers and gently release the toy, telling her it is now *out*. Repeat with the other hand. Repeat with other toys and textures. (D 1–2 min.)

FRONTOSAURUS-BACKOSAURUS GOES FOR A RIDE. Lay baby on her back. Using a soft toy car with soft wheels that spin easily, gently roll it up the front of her body and talk about *front*. Put baby on her tummy and roll the truck down the back of her body from top to toe; talk about her *back*. (R 3–5 times)

BETWEENOSAURUS FINGERS. Open baby's hands and extend her fingers. Place a soft pipe cleaner on her palms and rub them together. Explain that the pipe cleaner is *between* her hands. Repeat with the soles of her feet. (R 2–3 times)

Squigglers

OBJECT PERMANENCE. Babies are just learning that when things disappear from sight, they still exist. Using games that explore concepts such as *up* and *in* give babies tangible experiences with what is and is not in sight.

INOSAURUS POND. Fill a container with feathers or another soft, tactile material such as foam balls. Hold and support baby on your knee. Dip her foot *in* and *out* of the container. Show baby as you dip her foot *in* and cover it completely. Ask, "Where is your foot?" Pull it *out* and show baby where it is. Try with her knees, hands, and elbows, too. (D 2–3 min.)

THROUGHAPOD WATERFALL. Hold baby upright against your body. Tape or tie some streamers to a doorway and together go *through* the waterfall. Turn around and repeat. Sit baby down facing the waterfall and go through it by yourself. Now play a game of Throughapod Peekaboo! Encourage baby to commando-crawl (belly-crawl) through to you. (D 3–5 min.)

UNDERDACTYL WINGS. Roll a ball gently toward baby. As it's rolling, throw a piece of fabric over the ball. Surprise! Ask, "Where did the ball go?" Get on the floor with baby and explore the material, crawling *under* the fabric to find it! (R 3–5 times)

Scampers

PHYSICALIZATION. Physicalizing directional language helps a young child "feel" the words.

INOSAURUS CRATER BOUNCE. Place several cardboard boxes around the floor. Supporting the child under her arms, slowly lift her up then place her *in* a box. Lift her *out* and onto the floor. Repeat, bouncing from box to box, talking about when she is *in* and *out* of the craters. (D 3–5 min.)

OVERDACTYL MOUNTAIN. Roll up several towels lengthwise and place gym mats over the top to make a bumpy pathway. Encourage the child to climb *over* the mountain and down the other side. (D 3–5 min.)

AROUNDARAPTOR WRAP. Gently wrap the individual parts of the child's body (leg, arm, torso) with a long piece of stretchy Lycra material. As you wrap, talk about going *around* her leg. Culminate in wrapping the child so her arms and legs are inside. Unwrap. (D 3–5 min.)

Stompers

UNDERSTANDING MY DIMENSIONS. The very simple concept of *behind* dimensionalizes children's understanding of themselves in a 3-D world.

BEHINDADON WAGS HER TAIL. Tuck a scarf or rope into the back of children's trousers. Get down on all fours with them and show them how to wag their tails. Wag fast. Wag slow. Wag big. Wag small. Encourage them to look back to see their tails wagging. (D 2–3 min.)

BEHINDADON CAN'T FIND HER TAIL! Tuck a scarf or rope into the back of children's trousers and have them stand. Recite the "Behindadon" rhyme (page 191), spinning 3 times to the left, then 3 times to the right, then looking behind to find their tails. (R 2–3 times)

UPSIDEDOWNADON. Tuck in or tie a scarf or rope at the back of each child's trousers or around children's waists. Pair up children, standing back to back. Have 1 child bend down, look between her legs, and pull the other's tail. When the other child's tail is pulled, she bends down and grabs her tail back! Repeat, starting with the other child. Then change partners and play again. (R 3–5 times)

Scooters

LINING UP seems so simple, yet it gives young children deep and tangible understandings of their bodies in relation to others. Add directional language for high-impact, conceptual learning.

STEPOSAURUS LINEUP. Practice all the different ways you can line up along a rope on the floor. For instance, all facing front, all facing back, alternating facing front and back. Line up shoulder to shoulder, elbow to elbow, fingertip to fingertip. Line up like frogs and leap over one another. Line up like a tunnel with legs spread wide and have each child crawl through. (D 3–5 min.)

STEPOSAURUS STEPS. For a fun problem-solving game, give each child the name of another child in the group. Have all children line up along a rope on the floor. When you say go, each child has to work out how to get directly in *front* of the assigned other child in the line. Repeat with *back*. Then have them line up shoulder to shoulder and work out how to get *next to* the other child. (D 3–5 min.)

BETWEENOSAURUS REX. Have 2 children stand shoulder to shoulder and lean into each other (but not use their hands). Have a third child squeeze between them. Continue until all of the children have squeezed in and the 2 original children are on the ends of the line. Repeat with children standing 1 behind the other. (D 2–3 min.)

Skedaddlers

DYNAMIC TEAMWORK requires knowing how your body works and reacting to how others move. Not only does this give children a better sense of themselves, it gives them important clues for managing social situations.

CONNECTOSAURUS. Put dot stickers randomly around the room on the floor. Have the children line up on 1 of the dots. Have them put their hand on the shoulder of the child in front of them and keep it there at all times. Together as a team, have them work out how to connect all the dots with their line. Repeat with children linking arms like Nextatops (see "Nextatops" activity). (D 5–10 min.)

NEXTATOPS. Have 2 children stand shoulder to shoulder and link arms. Show them how to walk like Nextatops—at the same time, each swings her right foot out to the right. (The player on the left side will be crossing her right foot in front of her partner.) Then swing their left feet out to the left. (The player on the right side will cross her left foot in front of her partner.) Have them cross the room, pick up an object you mention (such as a red ball), and return it. For added challenge, add more children to create a wide-wider-widest walking Nextatops! (D 5–10 min.)

FRONTOSAURUS-BACKOSAURUS. Put children in pairs, standing back to back and linking arms. Have them decide between themselves who is Frontosaurus and who is Backosaurus. Call out, "Frontosaurus," and the front child takes the lead. Call out "Backosaurus," and the back child takes the lead. Next, give them tasks to accomplish together, such as "go across the room, pick up the red ball, and bring it back." (D 5–10 min.)

Ultimate Tug-of-War
Upper-Body Strength

It's time for the Ultimate Tug-of-War! Come on—we need all the tuggers we can get!

EQUIPMENT
- Pillow
- Fitness ball
- Freestanding and fixed mirrors
- Flashlight
- Blanket
- 2 chairs
- Stretchy fabric or other fabric
- Balloon in a balloon bag, soft foam ball, feather, or other toy
- Bar from which a child can hang
- Rope

KEY BENEFITS
- Stamina
- Flexibility
- Neck and upper-body strength

LANGUAGE FOCUS
up, over

CRITICAL SAFEGUARDS
- **Babies:** Use baby-safe mirrors whenever possible, particularly when baby is crawling on top of the mirror. Adult supervision is required at all times when working with mirrors.
- **Older children:** The umbrella move is tricky. Manage this activity 1 child at a time so you can assist and support as needed.
- In many settings, balloon activities are not appropriate for children under age 5, so we have suggested alternative materials. Supervise children at all times while playing with or blowing up balloons. For added safety, use balloon bags to cover the balloons.

TEACHING GEMS
In the early months, short amounts of time on the tummy provide one way to help babies develop strength in the neck and upper body. However, some children may not enjoy being in this position. Be guided by the child and stop the activity if he appears agitated or uncomfortable.

ON THE MOVE   WATCH ME GROW   IN THE KNOW

 ### Snugglers
NECK STRENGTH at birth isn't enough for baby to control his head on his own. This is why it's imperative you take extra care to support baby's head and neck at all times.

NECK AND SHOULDER MASSAGE. Lay baby on his back on a flat surface. Support his head and neck with 1 hand while massaging with the other. Gently massage from the back of his head to behind his ears, down the back of his neck, across the collarbone, and down his shoulders. (D 2–3 min.)

EYE TO EYE. Lay baby on the floor. Position him on his tummy with a thin pillow under his chest so that his upper body is slightly elevated. Lie in front of him with your chin on the floor so you are eye to eye. Talk and sing while you encourage him to reach toward you. (D 2–3 min.)

UPSY BABY. Lay baby on his back on a fitness ball and hold him securely for support. Tilt the ball forward very slowly so baby is in a vertical position, then rock him back to horizontal. Next, hold the ball still with your knees and assist baby to lift his upper body off the ball toward you. Cheer his efforts with a big hug. (D 2–3 min.)

Squigglers

SUSTAINED HEAD CONTROL. As neck strength develops, baby will soon be able to maintain control of his head, which is an essential precursor to crawling. Once he's on the move, crawling is a natural way to continue strengthening his neck, shoulders, and upper-body muscles.

DANCING IN THE MIRROR. Put baby on the floor on his tummy in front of a mirror. Stand or kneel behind him so that he can see you in the mirror. Now dance, sing, and make funny faces to encourage baby to lift his head and watch you (and himself) in the mirror. (D 2–3 min.)

BABY IN THE MIRROR. Put baby on the floor on his tummy. Get on the floor in front of him with a hand mirror. Encourage him to commando-crawl (belly-crawl) toward you so that he can see himself crawling. Inch back to extend the play. (D 3–5 min.)

HALL OF MIRRORS. Place a variety of different-sized mirrors around the floor. Position them so that baby can see himself as he crawls around the room. Have some positioned vertically and others lying on the floor to create a baby-sized hall of mirrors. (D 5–10 min.)

Scampers

PUSHING AND PULLING are natural ways to develop upper-body strength through the course of everyday play.

LIGHT CHASER. Encourage the child to crawl as much as possible by enticing him with fun games. Dim the lights a little and shine a flashlight on the floor to attract him to chase the light. (D 2–5 min.)

TUG TUGS. On a smooth floor, lay the child on his tummy on top of a blanket. Be sure there's room to slide around. Have the child hold 1 end of the blanket and very slowly pull him along the floor. Also try it with a stretchy fabric or another material that gives the child a different gripping and tugging experience. (R 2–3 times)

1-2-3 WHEE! With 2 adults, each holding the child by the elbow, forearm, and hand, lift him and give him a swing. Whee! Encourage him to lift his body as high as he can. *Note:* Make sure to support the child's elbows, forearms, and hands to protect young developing arm joints. (R 3–5 times)

Stompers

UNDERSTANDING THE DYNAMICS OF FORCE requires many different experiences with manipulating objects of different weights.

SEAL STRETCHES. Have the child lie on the floor on his tummy. Have him touch his nose to the floor, then push up with his hands stretching his nose as high to the sky as he can. (Keep feet still on the floor.) Dangle a balloon bag, soft foam ball, feather, or other toy over his nose and encourage him to stretch even more to tap the balloon! (R 2–3 times)

SEAL SOCCER. Show the child how to bat the balloon (or other soft, lightweight toy) with his nose—no hands or feet allowed. Choose a goal or target area and try to nose the balloon into the goal. Set a timer and see how many goals he can get in a set amount of time (1, 2, 3 min.). (D 5–10 min.)

SEAL CATCH. Have the child hold his arms straight out in front at shoulder height with hands facing palm out (wrists touching) to create seal flippers. Encourage him to catch a balloon or soft foam ball with his flippers. Then try batting the toy with 1 flipper then the other. Now try a game of "Seal Catch." (D 3–5 min.)

 ## Scooters

DISCOVERING "UP." Pulling yourself up helps children develop muscle strength while learning the concept of *up*.

HANG 10. Have the child hang from a bar with both hands using the cortical grip (4 fingers over the bar, thumb under, locking the fingers for a secure grip). Assist and support as needed. Begin counting and see how long he can hold on. Have or help him write down his score on a card. After some rest, have him try again to see if he can improve his score. Stop when there is no more improvement and try again another day. (R 3–5 tries)

HANG 20. Using the cortical grip (see "Hang 10") have the child hang from a bar with both hands. Standing at his side, assist and support as needed. Next, encourage and support him to lift 1 knee to his chest. Repeat with the other knee. Now ask him to "march" in midair. Next, have him lift 1 leg out straight in front and hold for a count of 5. Then the other. Then both together. *Note:* He should avoid swinging. (R 3–5 tries)

STRAIGHT ARMS. Have the child stand between 2 chairs that are facing each other. (Be sure the chairs are on a carpet or other nonslip surface.) Have him put his hands on the chair seats. Show him how to lock his elbows and, when he's ready, tuck his feet underneath him so he's holding his body weight with only his arms. Repeat with the child sitting on the floor with his feet stretched out in front of him, elbows locked with palms pressing on the floor. Have him lift his body with his heels on the floor. Repeat, having him lift his body while holding his feet off the ground. (R 3–5 tries)

 ## Skedaddlers

POWER PLAYGROUND MOVES. Using classic play patterns as a starting point, encourage children to experiment with their power potential.

THE UMBRELLA. Start by crab-walking around the room to warm up. (Children sit on the floor with hands behind them, then lift up their bottoms and walk like a crab.) Then have them create the umbrella (bridge) position: Children lie on their backs on the floor and place their hands palms down by their ears with fingers pointing toward the feet. Then they press both feet firmly on the floor and lift their bodies. Support and assist children as needed to create and hold for 3–5 seconds, then rest. (R 3–5 times)

BUMP IN THE ROAD. One on one with the child or with pairs of children, give each child a turn to wheelbarrow around the room. (The child walks on his hands while you hold his raised legs and support him as needed under the hips and chest to avoid bowing.) Stop for a short rest then try again, only this time, each time you call out, "Bump in the road!" the wheelbarrow has to stop and do 1–5 pushups before continuing. (R 1–2 times)

ULTIMATE TUG-OF-WAR. Create teams and introduce a traditional tug-of-war game. Change it up as the children play. For instance, tug with only right hands, then left. Tug with one foot off the ground. Tug with the rope overhead or at their feet. Tug sitting down, lying on tummies or backs. What other ways can children tug? (R 2–3 rounds)

On the Road to Cartwheeling
Developing Core Strength

It's a big day—the Cartwheel Carnival, when everyone and everything is spinning and twirling and flipping! Are you ready for the Cartwheel Carnival?

EQUIPMENT
- Feather or other soft object
- Board
- Large cardboard cylinder
- Ball
- Rope
- Adhesive dots
- Bench
- Cartwheel training mat
- Pillows
- Baby swing

KEY BENEFITS
- Body rhythm
- Temporal awareness
- Balance
- Midline development

LANGUAGE FOCUS
side to side, upside down, over, right, left

CRITICAL SAFEGUARDS
- Support the child on both sides of her body, especially around her waist.
- Ensure the child feels comfortable being upside down.

TEACHING GEMS
- When attempting cartwheels or any complex movement, be sure to allow the child to lead with the side of the body that is most comfortable for her.

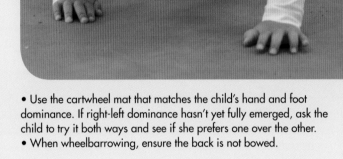

- Use the cartwheel mat that matches the child's hand and foot dominance. If right-left dominance hasn't yet fully emerged, ask the child to try it both ways and see if she prefers one over the other.
- When wheelbarrowing, ensure the back is not bowed.

ON THE MOVE　　　**WATCH ME GROW**　　　**IN THE KNOW**

 Snugglers
REPETITIVE MOVEMENT PATTERNS are comforting to young children while giving them a growing sense of mastery over their daily routine.

TICKLEWHEEL. Lay baby on her back with her hands and feet exposed. Use a soft feather or other gentle texture and tickle her hands and feet using the cartwheel sequence—right hand, left hand, left foot, right foot. Repeat counterclockwise. (R 3–5 times)

CARTWHEEL CLAPS. Lay baby on her back. Bring her right hand to her center, then bring her left hand up to meet it. *Clap!* Repeat with her feet, bringing her left foot to center then meeting it with her right. *Clap!* Repeat counterclockwise. (R 3–5 times)

SWING AND TAP. Sit down and lay baby in your arms slightly facing you, supporting her head with your hands and her body with your forearms. Gently glide baby back and forth away from you and back toward you. As you do, blow on baby's hands and feet in the cartwheel sequence—right hand, left hand, left foot, right foot. Repeat counterclockwise. (R 3–5 times)

Squigglers

SIDES. Mastering complex body movements like cartwheeling begins with a fully realized understanding of one's own body, including the sides of the body.

TICK TOCK. Hold baby upright, supporting her by the waist and upper body. Recite "Hickory Dickory Dock" (see page 191 for the words to this nursery rhyme) and tip her body like the hands of a clock, 1 gentle "tick" at a time, to the 1:00 position. Repeat in the other direction to the 11:00 position. Repeat again with baby facing away from you. (D 2–3 min.)

TIMBER! Surround baby with pillows. Slowly tip her backward and encourage her to sit back up. Next, tip her to her right side, then left. *Note:* Only do this with a child who has mastered independent sitting. (R 2–3 times)

WIBBLE WOBBLE. Make a "wobble board" out of a flat piece of board on top of a strong cardboard tube. Sit baby on the top while supporting her around the waist. Continue to support her as you gently tip and roll her side to side. (D 2–3 min.)

Scampers

WEIGHT TRANSFER. Learning to balance and control the transfer of one's own weight is all part of developing the rhythm needed for more complex movements later on.

ROCKING RIDE. Sit on the floor with your legs straight out in front of you. Sit the child on your knees, straddling her legs on either side of yours. Rock side to side so her feet touch the floor. Feel for her pushing off the floor and respond to this with a bigger rocking motion. (D 2–3 min.)

ROCKING DANCE. Stand the child on your feet. Hold her hands out to the side like a windmill. Gently rock side to side so she can experience the sense of transferring her weight. Slowly turn in circles as you rock. Take a few small steps backward and forward while maintaining a steady pace of side-to-side rocking. (D 2–3 min.)

MY FIRST KICKBALL. Have the child stand. Support her around the waist for balance and assist her to put 1 foot on a ball and kick it. Repeat several times, encouraging the child to try it on her own. Repeat with the other foot. (D 2–3 min.)

Stompers

MOTOR PLANNING. Learning to move the individual parts of the body in an organized sequence underpins all complex movement.

SIDEWAYS MONKEY WALKING. Put a rope on the floor. Have the child bend over the rope with her hands on the floor and her legs straight. Have her move sideways along the rope, stepping the hands to the right first (right hand followed by left hand), then feet (right foot followed by left foot). *Note:* You may need to assist the child to hold her hands or feet still while the other parts move. Repeat in both directions. (R 2–3 times)

SPIDER CRAWL. Have the child stand facing the wall and put the back of her right hand on the wall. Keeping that hand stuck to the wall like a spider, have her turn and step to the left so that her body is now facing away from the wall. Next, have her stick the back of her left hand to the wall and turn again (bringing her right hand around) so she's back to facing the wall with her right hand on it. Encourage the child to try walking the length of the wall or all the way around the room, always keeping 1 hand stuck to the wall! (D 3–5 min.)

WALL WALKING. Have the child stand in front of a secure wall facing away from the wall. Then have her bend over and put her hands on the floor. Assist and support her as she "walks" her feet backward up the wall. Encourage her to stretch as high as she can until her legs are straight and she is upside down. Now guide her to walk back down the wall and stand up. (R 3–5 times)

Scooters

UPSIDEDOWNEDNESS. A child's sense of balance and uprightness can only be mastered when she explores all different kinds of orientations with her body.

HAND WALKING. Start by warming up with a few minutes of wheelbarrowing. (The child walks on her hands while you hold her raised legs and support her as needed under the hips and chest to avoid bowing.) Next, assist the child to walk her feet up your body so that she's at a 45-degree angle to you. Supporting her around the ankles at all times, encourage her to walk forward on her hands. Continue the supported play, gradually having her move her feet further up your body until she is completely upside down and walking on her hands. (D 2–3 min. at a time)

LILYPAD LEAPFROG. Lay out dots in a straight line, and have the children line up behind the first dot. One by one, have all the children jump 2-footed along the spots and run back around to get in line again. Next, have the first child jump on the first dot and crouch down. The next child leapfrogs over the first and crouches down. Continue until all the children have leapfrogged all the way across and are back in line. (D 5–10 min.)

BUDDING BRONCO. Have the child stand to the side of a low bench and put her palms down in the middle of the bench. Assist her to kick her legs up in the air and back down to the same side of the bench. When she's ready, encourage her to try it on her own, kicking as high as she can. Next, assist her to kick her legs up in the air and back down to the other side of the bench (cartwheel style); support her at the waist. Again, when she's ready, encourage her to try it on her own, kicking as high as she can. (R 3–5 tries)

Skedaddlers

VISUALIZATION. Use visualization techniques to teach complex movement patterns. For instance, encourage children to use their active imaginations to picture themselves doing the activity before they start. "What does it look like to ride a bucking bronco?"

BUCKING BRONCO. Repeat "Budding Bronco," only this time the child can have both hands on the ground. Have her crouch down and put her palms on the floor. Encourage her to kick both legs in the air and return to her starting position. Support as needed, encouraging her to kick higher and higher to a near-handstand position. (R 3–5 tries) Once the child begins to master the movement, encourage her to kick and turn in midair, landing to the left or right of her starting position.

CART ROLL. Repeat "Bucking Bronco," only this time, grab hold of the child's legs as she kicks up. Support her by the calves and ankles and hold her in a handstand position for a few moments. Then, very gently, assist the child to bend her elbows to lower her body; hold her as she rolls forward out of the position back to the ground. (R 3–5 times)

SUPPORTED CARTWHEEL. Repeat "Cart Roll," only this time, while the child is in the supported handstand position, tip her legs to the left and then to the right so she can feel the shift of her weight. Assist her to bend her right elbow and gently tip her legs to the right. Have her bend her knees to land feetfirst off to the side. Repeat, going to the left. (R 3–5 times)

Grabbypillar
Hand Strength

Grabbypillar and his friends love to go every which way. They go up. And they go down. They go right. And they go left. And they're often seen going round and round just for the fun of it. They go and go all day long and they never get tired. That's because Grabbypillar and his friends each have 100 legs! That's a lot of legs! Problem is, they can never seem to agree on which way to go together, and that means lots of legs going every which way all at once. Can you help sort out all those legs and get Grabby and his friends going together? (See pages 191–192 for song lyrics for this activity sequence.)

EQUIPMENT
- Long sock
- Homemade Grabbypillar (see Teaching GEMs)
- Soft foam balls
- Zippered jacket or sweatshirt
- Pillowcase
- Play dough
- Nimble sticks (see page 49)
- Rope

KEY BENEFITS
- Finger and hand manipulative skills
- Finger and hand strength
- Finger and hand dexterity

LANGUAGE FOCUS
up, down

CRITICAL SAFEGUARDS
- Adult supervision is required at all times.
- Be sure the play dough and nimble sticks are nontoxic.

TEACHING GEMS
- **Babies:** Watch for the movement messages the child is showing you: check that he is able to place the palm of his hand on the ground and that he is not making a fist with his hand or is unable to uncurl his fingers fully. If you do see this, hand and foot massage will likely help release the reflexes for more deliberate movement.
- **All children:** Provide opportunities for children to experience and explore their upper-body strength both in the activities here and in other natural play patterns such as push or pull toys and supervised climbing.
- To make your homemade Grabbypillar, fill a sock with a few other socks and tie the end to create a soft, squishy critter. Make sure the sock is not evenly stuffed so it gives the hands a variety of experiences.

MOVING SMART

ON THE MOVE   WATCH ME GROW   IN THE KNOW

 ### Snugglers
I AM POWERFUL. Encouraging independent movement right from the start fosters an early sense of self and self-esteem, while working to release the primitive reflexes.

FINGERS AND TOES. Sit comfortably and lay baby on your knees facing you. Maintain eye contact. Firmly but gently massage the palm of each hand individually. Gently uncurl all of his fingers together, then 1 at a time. Next, remove his socks and massage his foot. Gently play with the toes, uncurling all his toes, then 1 at a time. (D 3–5 min.)

TUG OF LOVE. Take a long sock and tie a knot in the toe. Gently uncurl baby's fingers and put the knot on baby's palm. When he grasps the sock, gently tug on it several times. This stimulates the palmar (grasp) reflex and provides the fingers a first sensation of give-and-take. (D 1–2 min.)

GRABBYPILLAR. Make a homemade Grabbypillar (see "Teaching Gems"). Encourage baby to explore Grabbypillar with both hands. Move Grabbypillar slightly out of reach (such as just over his head or just to the side of him) to encourage baby to reach for it. (D 3–5 min.)

Squigglers

PUSHING AND PULLING helps build muscle strength and stamina in the upper body, which lays the necessary groundwork for developing hand and finger fitness.

GRABBYPILLAR CRAWL. On a smooth surface, lay baby on his tummy. Hold 1 end of Grabbypillar while encouraging baby to hold the other end with 1 or both hands. Tug gently, but don't pull, holding Grabbypillar steady to see if the child can pull his whole body forward. (D 1–2 min.)

GRABBYPILLAR OPPOSITES. Sit opposite baby and join hands. Slowly push baby's right hand back while pulling his left hand forward. Repeat in the opposite direction. Next, gently pull baby's right hand up in the air while moving his left hand down. Repeat in the opposite direction. (D 2–3 min.)

GRABBYPILLAR ROWBOAT. Sit behind the child and hold hands. Rock back and forth, "rowing" with your arms. Next, sit opposite the child, hold hands, and rock back and forth, guiding the child to rock toward you when you rock back and rock backward when you rock toward him. To finish, gently rock the child all the way back and then slowly pull him close for a great big hug. (D 2–3 min.)

Scampers

DELIBERATE GRIP. From the earliest days, little ones have a very strong grip, fostered by the palmar (grasp) reflex. As that reflex releases, more deliberate control of the hands is possible.

GRABBYGRIP. Fill a sock with soft foam balls all the way up to the top. Give the child the sock and encourage him to squeeze. Watch the balls come flying out. Encourage him to retrieve the balls and play again! (R 3–5 times)

GRABBYZIP. Put on a jacket or sweatshirt with a large zipper. Sit with the child in your lap and show him how the zipper works. Assist him to try to zip it up and down, then encourage him to try it on his own. Go on a coat hunt and find other zippers to try. (D 3–5 min.)

GRABBY ON THE FLY. Lay a pillowcase on the floor and put a soft foam ball in the center. Encourage the child to hold 2 corners of the pillowcase while you hold the other corners so it is taut. Gently lift your end and roll the ball toward the child. Next, lift it quickly so the ball flies in the air. Encourage him to follow your lead and get the ball flying high. (R 2–3 times)

Stompers

THE POWER OF "SQUISH." Strengthening the core and upper-body muscles along with the arms, wrists, hands, and fingers are all necessary underpinnings for the refined hand movements children need someday to write.

HOW CATERPILLARS KNEAD DOUGH. Put 4 wads of play dough on the floor. Barefoot, have the child step on 1 wad with 1 foot, then on the second wad with the other foot. Next, have him lean forward to squish the other 2 wads with his hands. Let him work the dough, squishing it through all the fingers and toes. (D 3–5 min.)

GRABBY SQUISH. Have the child sit on the floor with his elbows out to the side at shoulder height, then squish a wad of dough between his hands as hard as he can. *Aargh!* Next, have him bend his knees out to the side and put play dough between the feet, squishing the dough as hard as he can with his feet. *Aargh!* Now have him do both at the same time! (D 2–5 min.)

DOUBLE GRABBY SQUISH. Pair up children and have them face each other to play "Grabby Squish" as a team. Squish the dough with 1 hand, then the other, then both. *Aargh!* Have them meet their right hands together, then their left hands. *Aargh!* Next, have them step back, press both hands together, and lean into each other, squishing with all their might! *Aargh! Aargh!* Have them sit and try it with bare feet! (D 1–3 min.)

Scooters

HAND STRENGTH AND MANIPULATIVE SKILLS GO HAND IN HAND. While building muscle strength, the fingers are also building stamina, dexterity, agility, and nimbleness!

GRABBYPILLAR WENT CLIMBING. Have each child hold a nimble stick with 1 hand and walk the fingers of the other hand up to the top of the stick and back down. Repeat with the other hand. Next, sing the "Grabbypillar Went Climbing" song as the hands go up and back down. (R 2 times)

ROLY-POLY GRABBYPILLAR. Lay 2 nimble sticks in front of children and show them how to roll the sticks forward and back. Have them roll the sticks with both hands at once, then roll with just the right hand, then the left. Sing the "Grabbypillar Went Rolling" song while exploring other ways to roll the nimble sticks (up and down inclines, over their own bodies, down the wall). (D 2–4 min.)

GRABBY TWINS. Show children how to "climb" the nimble sticks hand over hand all the way up and then back down. Then sing "Grabbypillar Went Climbing." When the children are well practiced at the hand-over-hand motion, string a rope across 2 chairs and have them practice walking their hands across the rope first to the left, then to the right. (D 2–5 min.)

Skedaddlers

AUTOMATING PRECISE FINGER MOVEMENTS requires many different experiences through both everyday play and dedicated fingerplay activities.

GRABBY TWINS AT PLAY. Have children start by climbing the right hand up and down a nimble stick while the left hand is still. Then, on a horizontal surface, have them roll a nimble stick back and forth with the left hand. Now put the 2 together—right hand climbing, left hand rolling. Reverse. Sing "The Grabby Twins Went Out to Play" as children play. (D 2–3 min.)

GRABBY UP AND DOWN. Have children start by walking the fingers up and down a nimble stick, first the right hand, then the left. Then with 2 nimble sticks, have them walk the fingers up and down at the same time. Next, they can hold 1 nimble stick at the top and the other at the bottom. Race the fingers up and down in opposition to each other. Sing "The Grabby Twins Went Up and Down." (D 2–3 min.)

GRABBY OVER AND OVER. Repeat the previous activity, only each time the hand reaches the end of the nimble stick, children flip the stick over and keep going up. Repeat in the opposite direction going down, down, down! Sing "The Grabby Twins Went Up and Down" as you play. (D 2–3 min.)

SARAH ALICE LEE

Don't Drop Fidgety Fox
Knowing Your Own Strength

Fidgety Fox is in a pickle. She's been invited to the Barefoot Ball. Now, Fidgety loves going barefoot, but when she does, her toes tickle. When her toes tickle, she giggles. And when she giggles, she snorts! No one's going to want to dance with a barefoot, tickle-toed, snorty little fox! Can you help Fidgety Fox get to the ball without touching her ticklish toes to the ground?

EQUIPMENT

- Soft scarf
- Soft toy
- Baby-friendly objects of varying weights
- Upbeat music
- Beanbags
- Straight wooden ladder 6'–8' long
- Car tire
- Rope
- Blindfold
- Gym mats

KEY BENEFITS

- Teamwork
- Problem solving
- Stamina
- Perseverance
- Strength management

LANGUAGE FOCUS

under, between, around

CRITICAL SAFEGUARDS

- Adult supervision and support is required whenever a child is off the ground.
- Decide with the children a trigger word to signal if they want to stop these or any other activities.

TEACHING GEMS

- See page 192 for ideas for "Don't Drop Fidgety Fox" games.
- For ladder activities, crossing a ladder that is lying on the ground is trickier than it looks. And there's no one right way to achieve it. Support and encourage the child as she makes her way across. Give her cues such as, "I wonder what would happen if you moved your foot to the next rung?" Affirm her progress with specific cues, such as, "I like the way you move 1 hand then the other."

ON THE MOVE	WATCH ME GROW	IN THE KNOW

Snugglers

AGILITY AND FLEXIBILITY begin with experiencing a wide variety of movement patterns.

THIS LITTLE PIGGY WENT TO MARKET. Recite the classic "This Little Piggy" nursery rhyme and wiggle baby's fingers. Repeat with the toes. Then, repeat wiggling both her fingers and toes, first on the right, then on the left. *Note:* See page 192 for words to the nursery rhyme. If you wish, substitute a different animal, such as "this little mousy." (D 2–5 min.)

FOOT TUGS. Hold baby's foot and gently wrap a soft scarf around it; give it a soft tug to stretch baby's leg out straight. Repeat with the other foot, then both feet together. Watch baby's toes curl up with delight and notice the beginnings of her pulling back against the scarf. (D 2 min.)

SCARF TUG. Roll up a soft scarf so that it resembles a sausage. Sit on the floor with the child facing you. Encourage her to hold 1 end of the scarf and play a gentle tugging game. When she tugs back, exaggerate your reaction by leaning forward to her and giving her an air-kiss! (D 2–3 min.)

ON THE MOVE	WATCH ME GROW	IN THE KNOW

 Squigglers
BODY CONTROL. Understanding your own strength begins very early.

PASS THE PARCEL. Hold baby firmly around the waist and hand her to another adult in various ways, such as a sandwich pass (both of you hug baby as you hand her off), passing her over your shoulder, or passing her through your legs. (D 2–5 min.)

PASS THE PARCEL 2. Sit on the floor in an L shape with baby sitting on your knees facing you. Show her a soft toy; pass it to her and have her pass it back to you. Show her fun ways to pass it between you, such as passing it around your back, passing it around baby's back and over to her, tossing it, or catching it. (R 2 times)

PASS THE PARCEL 3. Lay out objects of varying weights on the floor in front of baby. Sit opposite her and encourage her to pick up a parcel and pass it you. Continue passing it back to her in different ways (from up high, from down low, or from the side) so that she's mirroring your movements. (R 3 times)

 Scampers
BUILDING STAMINA. High-energy, continuous, repetitive movement helps children develop stamina.

DO THE STOMP. Hold the child in your arms, facing away from you. Lean her against your body and support her under her bottom and legs. Turn on some upbeat music with a heavy beat and stomp around the room so she can feel the beat. Hold out her feet and tap them against the wall or furniture so she feels like she's dancing, too! (D 2–3 min.)

DO THE CAN-CAN. Hold the child in your arms, facing away from you. Lean her against your body and support her under her bottom and legs. Turn on some upbeat music and dance, kicking your legs in the air. Hold out her feet and circle her legs in the air like the can-can! (D 2–3 min.)

DO THE COSSACK. Hold the child in your arms, facing away from you. Lean her against your body and support her under her bottom and legs. Turn on some upbeat music and dance. Hold out her feet so she is kicking them in the air! On the downbeat, bring the child down to the ground so that her feet touch the floor and her knees bend, then bounce her back up for more dancing! (D 2–3 min.)

 Stompers
EMOTIONAL DEVELOPMENT AND CONTROL. Opportunities for little ones to push through what they think are their limits readies them for new challenges.

LADDER CRAWL. Lay a ladder on the floor. Support the child around the waist and have her crawl across it without touching the ground. Next, securely prop up 1 end of the ladder approximately 6" off the ground. Continuing to support the child around the waist, have her climb up the ladder and back down. (R 3 times)

LADDER RELAY. Divide children into 2 groups at either end of a ladder that is lying on the floor. One at a time, have each child crawl across the ladder with a beanbag on her back, without touching the floor or dropping the beanbag. When the child gets to the other side, have her pass the beanbag to the next child, who will take it back across the ladder. Support children around the waist as needed. Repeat with the ladder securely inclined about 6" off the ground on 1 end. (D 5–10 min.)

LIFT AND ROLL. Lay a car tire on the floor. Encourage and support the child to squat down, put her hands under the tire, and lift it up into a vertical, rolling position. Next, have her push the tire so it rolls. Mark how far she got the tire to roll. Try again to see if she can extend the distance. (R 1–3 times)

 Scooters
KNOWING MY OWN STRENGTH. Testing the strength of others helps you discover your own strength.

BOUNCING FIDGETY FOX. Pair up children facing each other. Have them hold hands and jump on each beat together: jump, jump, jump, snort! (R 5 times) Repeat, only this time, on each beat: jump, jump, jump, belly bump! Note: Ensure that children have their chins up and held back from one another. (R 5 times)

PUSHY FIDGETY FOX. Pair up children facing each other with their hands clasped behind them. Have them lean into each other so that their left shoulders are touching. Count down 3, 2, 1, then push into each other. Encourage them to push until someone snorts to stop the game. Take a rest and try again with the right shoulders. (R 2–3 times)

SUMO FIDGETY FOX. Lay a rope on the floor. Pair up children facing one another, each on the opposite side the rope. Have them put their palms together and count down 3, 2, 1, then push into each other as hard as they can until 1 steps over the rope or snorts to call an end to the game. (R 2 times)

Skedaddlers

RESPECT FOR OTHERS. Physical team building encourages self-respect and respect for others.

PIGGYBACK RIDES. Teach children the traditional piggyback ride. Encourage them to work as a team by giving them simple goals. For example, cross the room while piggybacking, pick up a ball, and return it. For added challenge, blindfold the carrier and have the rider direct her with verbal instructions. Repeat, switching positions. (D 3–5 min.)

PYRAMID FIDGETY FOX. Lay gym mats on the floor and create teams of 3. Have the children select 2 to get down on the mat on all fours, shoulder to shoulder. Have the third child climb up and kneel on their backs, distributing her weight evenly between the 2. (Support as needed.) Count to see how long they can hold this position. Take a rest. Next, have them create their pyramid again and try to crawl a few steps forward, then back. Be sure the child on top is holding on securely to the others' shirts. Repeat, changing positions so that everyone gets a turn to be top fox. (D 5–10 min.)

DON'T DROP FIDGETY FOX! Select one child to be Fidgety Fox. The rest of the group's job is to work out how to get Fidgety from 1 end of the play area to the other without letting her touch the ground—snorting as they go! Explore ways to carry Fidgety, assisting and supporting as needed for safety. (See list of suggestions on page 192.) Switch Fidgeties and try another method. (D 2–3 min.)

SARAH WHITING

Escape from the Zoo
Building Stamina

Uh-oh. The animals at the zoo have escaped! Poor Zookeeper Catchem just can't catch them! The monkeys swing too quickly. The zebras run too fast. The giraffes are too tall! The kangaroos bounce too high! Can you show Zookeeper Catchem how to move like the animals so he can catch them?

EQUIPMENT

- Bubble solution and wand
- Tissue paper
- Blocks
- Plastic bottles and pebbles to fill them
- Water
- Food coloring
- Glitter
- Ticking clock or timer
- Bell
- Soft chair
- Slide
- Hoops
- Rope
- 2 chairs
- Beanbags

KEY BENEFITS

- Stamina
- Strength
- Agility
- Flexibility

LANGUAGE FOCUS

up, down, in

CRITICAL SAFEGUARDS

- When using bubbles with babies, take care not to get the bubbles too close to the child's face, mouth, nose, and eyes.
- Ensure that there is enough room to move in big ways.
- Whenever possible, play these games outdoors for more space.

TEACHING GEMS

- High-energy play is the easiest, most natural way for children to develop the strength, fitness, and stamina they need. Use these or any other high-energy games the children like to play, adding a twist by having them move like different animals.
- Be sure to try the different ways to crawl and walk described in "There's More to Crawling and Walking Than Meets the Eye" (pages 192–193).

ON THE MOVE	WATCH ME GROW	IN THE KNOW

Snugglers

GENTLE REPETITION. Repeating activities for babies gives them a sense of the duration of time.

RASPBERRIES. Lay baby on his back so he can see you. Place your lips against your own hand and make silly raspberry sounds (pfft). Next, hold up his hand and make raspberries on his hand. As he grows accustomed to the game, make raspberries on his arms, tummy, legs, and feet. (R 1–3 times)

BUBBLE WATCHING. Lay baby on his back. Blow bubbles in front of baby's field of vision, which is about the length of his own arm. Point to the bubbles. Talk about how bubbles float. Pop the bubbles for a big surprise. (D 3–5 min.)

BUBBLE CHASE. Lay baby on his back. Blow bubbles in front of him and encourage him to reach for them. Next, blow bubbles to his right side and encourage him to reach. Repeat on his left side. (D 3–5 min.)

Squigglers

DO-IT-YOURSELFING. Whenever a child can do something for himself, he's naturally building stamina in his muscles.

RIP IT UP. Lay a piece of soft paper (such as tissue) on the floor. Lie down with baby on the paper and show him how to rip the paper. Start slowly and quietly, gradually building up speed and excitement as you rip. Step away once he has the idea. (D 3–5 min.)

BUILD AND SMASH. Work with baby to build a tower of blocks. Knock it down as many ways as you can think—with your hands, feet, head, and so forth. Step away once he has the idea. (D 5–10 min.)

BABY BOWLING. Fill 6 empty plastic bottles halfway with pebbles. If you can, use different-colored pebbles. Seal tightly and stand the bottles on the floor like bowling pins. Encourage baby to crawl through the bottles, knocking them down as he crawls. Reset the pins and play again . . . and again! (D 5–10 min.)

Scampers

AGAIN! AGAIN! Not only is repetition a great way to foster learning—it also builds physical, intellectual, and emotional stamina. Lean into what interests the child and embrace his desire for repetition with enthusiasm.

ROLLING RAINBOWS. Fill several plastic bottles with water, food coloring, and glitter. Seal tightly. Encourage the child to explore the bottles. Roll bottles to him and encourage him to roll them back. Stand the bottles up and knock them down. Try stacking the bottles. Follow the child's lead and repeat whatever he likes to do. (D 3–5+ min.)

ROLLOVERS. Work with the child to show him different ways to roll. For instance, lay the child on his back and tilt his hips to encourage him to roll to his tummy. Next, tilt his shoulders or cross his legs to encourage his roll. Repeat to the left and right. Next, assist him to roll 360 degrees to the left then to the right. (D 3–5+ min.)

SOUND HUNT. Hide a ticking clock or timer and together, go look for the sound. Encourage the child to move any way he likes—walking, crawling, rolling, or any other silly way of moving. Follow his lead. Cheer and ring a bell when you find the sound! (D 3–5+ min.) Repeat as often as he likes.

Stompers

VERTICALITY. Anytime you defy gravity, you're challenging the body and brain to do more than it's done before. That's called stamina!

MONKEYS ON THE MOUNTAIN. Sitting on a soft chair and supporting the child at all times, have him climb up your body all the way to the top, pat you on your head, and climb back down. When he shows confidence in the game, try the game standing. (D 1–2 min.)

MONKEYS ON THE SLIDE. Assist child to climb up the slide, turn himself around, and slide back down. Repeat as often as he likes. Next, have him climb up the slide, turn himself around, and lie on his belly (head up, feet toward the ground), holding onto the sides as he inches his way back down. Repeat as often as he likes. (D 5–10 min.)

KANGAROO JUMPS. Kangaroos can jump really high! Dangle something over the child and have him jump straight up to touch it. Raise it up and have him jump again until he touches it. Continue to make the target higher and higher. (D 3–5 min.)

Scooters

TEAM GAMES. When kids run together, they push each other to go farther.

ESCAPE FROM THE ZOO. Uh-oh! The animals have escaped! Use a large area outside and encourage the children to run and scream for as long and as loud as they can. Next, assign a Zookeeper for a frenetic game of tag. If the Zookeeper tags you, you go back to the zoo. Rest for a few minutes, then encourage children to show you how different animals run free! (D 5–10 min.)

RUNAWAY HOOPS. The seal's hoops are on the loose, too! Roll a hoop and encourage the children to chase and catch it. Next, set up a race lane. Roll the hoop and have the children race the hoop to the end of the lane to catch it. Then show the children how to roll a hoop for themselves. As they gain confidence, have them roll hoops up and down inclines. (D 5–10 min.)

RUNAWAY RIVER. The animals need to cross the river without getting their feet wet. Lay out 10 hoops to act as stepping stones. Have children step through all the hoops without touching them. Next, have them show you how different animals (ducks, monkeys, bears, kangaroos) would navigate the hoops. If you step on a hoop, you have to try again. As the children gain confidence, space out the hoops to create a longer course. (D 5–10 min.)

Skedaddlers

PHYSICAL PERSEVERANCE yields mental toughness. Create games that test children's ability to move in different ways over a distance.

RUNAWAY LIMBO. Tie a rope to 2 chairs or have 2 children hold the rope taut. Put on some music and limbo under the rope. Next, lower the rope and limbo again! Then try doing the limbo as different animals would. (D 5–10 min.)

RUNAWAY RELAY. Have the children choose 4 animals to run a race. Form teams of 4 and have them decide among themselves who will play the different animals. Give each team a beanbag (to serve as a relay baton) and do a relay race. For the next round, add a Zookeeper. If the Zookeeper tags you, you have to freeze and count to 5 before continuing. (D 5–10 min.)

BACK TO THE ZOO. After a fun day on the loose, it's time for the animals to go home for dinner. Create an obstacle course. Form the children in a conga line. Have the entire conga line run the obstacle course, each child keeping 1 hand on the child in front of him at all times. Encourage the children to work as a team to solve the obstacles. Next, have the children select animals and run the course moving like those animals, each person always somehow staying in touch with the child in front of him.

Let's Go to Hopscotch Camp
Whole-Body Development: Jumping and Hopping

Hopscotch isn't just a game, it's a way of getting around. Imagine if every sidewalk were a hopscotch board. How would you get from here to there? It's time to go to Hopscotch Camp!

EQUIPMENT
- Beanbags
- Blanket
- Squeaky toy
- Adhesive dots of different colors
- Pillow
- Music
- Chalk or tape
- Bell

KEY BENEFITS
- Stamina and fitness
- Agility
- Homolateral midline development

LANGUAGE FOCUS
in, out, around, on

CRITICAL SAFEGUARDS
Support the child when jumping on uneven surfaces.

TEACHING GEMS
• Use a beanbag rather than a stone for hopscotch. Beanbags don't bounce or roll, lessening potential frustration.

• Try to do as much of this activity as possible with bare feet and legs to provide more sensory messaging for the child.
• When learning to do any specific skill, such as the "Learning to Hop Up and Down" activity, do not rush the process. Allow plenty of time for the child to master each step with confidence so that she can do the movement automatically (without thinking about it). Then move on to the next step in the learning process. *Note:* When a child is learning to hop, focus on learning to hop with the dominant foot first. When that is automated, switch to the other foot and start again from the beginning.
• See the layout and rules for hopscotch on pages 193–194. Size the hopscotch squares for the size of the children. Remember, new hoppers have little feet and short legs. Also try changing the shape of the hopscotch board, such as making the board circular.

ON THE MOVE   WATCH ME GROW   IN THE KNOW

Snugglers
REFLEXIVE MOVEMENT. The push-away reflex assists baby through the birthing canal. After birth, the reflex works to strengthen leg muscles in preparation for independent movement.

FOOT MASSAGE. Lay baby on the floor on her back. Hold her bare foot up at 90 degrees. With your thumb, stroke firmly down the foot from the big toe pad to the heel. Next, create a pulsing sensation, squeezing in and out as you massage. (D 1–2 min.)

FOOT TAPS. Repeat the "Foot Massage" activity, only this time tap firmly down the foot. Next, hold baby's feet facing one another and "clap" her toes together. Hold baby's ankles and rub the soles of her feet together. Avoid tickling. (D 1–2 min.)

PUSH-AWAY TIME. Lay a blanket on the floor and put baby on her tummy. Hold your hand firmly against the soles of baby's feet. If the push-away reflex is still active, she will reflexively push away from your hand and move herself forward. (D 1–2 min.)

Squigglers
FOOT AND LEG AWARENESS. Independent movement is facilitated by baby's emerging awareness of her whole body—right down to her toes!

PLAYING FOOTSIE. Lay baby on her back and hold a bell above her feet. Show her how to kick the bell to make it ring. Encourage her to kick at the bell as much as she likes. (D 2–3 min.)

FROG LEGS. Lay baby on her back and show her ways her knees move. Pull her knees in close to her chest. Keeping knees bent, open her knees out to the side. Bring 1 knee back to center, then the other. (D 2–3 min.)

UPSIDE-DOWN BIKE RIDING. Lay baby on her back and help her "pedal" her legs as if riding a bicycle. Pedal forward and backward, both legs alternating, then 1 leg at a time, then both legs together. (D 2–3 min.)

Scampers

FOOT AND LEG DEVELOPMENT. Strengthening the muscles, tendons, and ligaments in the lower body prepares little ones for going vertical.

UPSIDE-DOWN DANCING. Put on some music and lay the child on the floor with her feet in the air. Assist her to "dance" upside down. Use her full range of motion, including knee and ankle flexing, hip rotations, and scissor kicks. (D 2–3 min.)

PICKUPS. To encourage deep knee bends, put a few small toys at the child's feet and encourage her to crouch down for them. Assist by holding her at the waist to keep her steady. (D 3–5 min.)

ROCKET SHIP LAUNCH. Hold the child under her arms. Encourage her to crouch down. Bob up and down as you count, "5, 4, 3, 2, 1, blastoff!" On the word *blastoff*, lift her high in the air. Whee! (R 2–3 times)

Stompers

DEFYING GRAVITY. Balance, coordination, and leg strength come together in big new ways when children start testing their ability (and courage) to leave the ground.

PILLOW JUMPING. Place a squeaky toy under a pillow and stand the child on the pillow. Holding her under her arms, encourage her to jump up and down, using the pillow to give her more spring (and squeak). (D 2–3 min.)

JUMPING SPOTS. Spread out adhesive dots of different colors on the floor, using multiples of the same color. Put on some upbeat music. Call out a color and have the children find and jump on that color, continuing to jump to the beat until all the children have found a colored dot. Repeat with another color. (D 3–5 min.)

JUMPING LINES. With chalk or tape, make a straight line on the floor. Have the children line up at the beginning of the tape. Have them straddle the tape and jump forward to the end. Next, encourage them to jump with both feet together on the tape. Add curves and turns to the tape to encourage them to steer their jumps. (D 3–5 min.)

Scooters

HOPPING. Learning to hop is one of the most sophisticated midline activities for the human body, involving refined balance, coordination, and control.

THE JUMPALONG. Lay out a path of dots and lines on the floor that includes straight parts, curves, turns, and zigzags. Have the children play follow the leader. The leader follows the path, jumping 3 times on each dot, then jumping forward along the line. (D 3–5 min.)

LEARNING TO HOP UP AND DOWN. Have children hold onto something stable and stand on 1 foot. Next, still holding on for balance, have them hop on the grounded foot while the other foot is kept off the ground. Repeat using the other foot. When the children are ready, have them let go and try hopping in place on their own. (R 2–3 times)

JUMP AND HOP. Start by having children alternate 2-footed jumping and 1-footed hopping in place: jump, hop on the right foot, jump, hop on the left foot. Repeat until children can do the pattern with ease. Next, call out a random pattern (jump, jump, hop, hop, jump) and have them repeat the pattern. (D 3–5 min.)

Skedaddlers

COMBINATION SKILLS. Simple as it appears, hopscotch demands mastery of many physical skills and the ability to combine those skills in multiple ways.

THE HOPALONG. Start by having the children hop on 1 foot in place. Repeat on the other foot. Next, draw or mark a line in front of the children and have them hop forward to the line. Repeat as often as needed until they can hop forward with ease. Repeat on the other foot. Then, lay out a short path on the floor and have the children play follow the leader, hopping along the path (3–5 hops to start). (D 5–10 min.)

THE JUMP TWIST. Start by having children jump as high in the air as they can. Next, demonstrate how they can change position while in midair by twisting the torso as they jump. Challenge children to jump and twist their bodies 90 degrees to the right, then to the left. Then see if they can jump and turn 180 degrees to face backward. (D 3–5 min.)

HOPSCOTCH! Introduce the fundamentals of the game (see the game rules on pages 193–194). Be sure to have children switch the hopping foot after each game so they get a well-balanced experience. Have fun! (R 2+ games)

Mixed-Up Motories
Whole-Body Coordination:
Overcoming Obstacles

There's more than one way to get from here to there, but watch out for those mixed-up motories. They are sure to trip you up! Imagine having to walk a balance beam, swing on a rope, burrow through a tunnel, jump 3 times, and spin around—all just to cross the room!

EQUIPMENT
- Stroller
- Various equipment and materials for making an obstacle course (see Teaching GEMs)
- Foam wedge
- Toy
- Plank
- Pool noodles
- Different-sized containers (sturdy enough for children to stand on)
- Ropes
- Log
- Monkey bars
- Blindfold

KEY BENEFITS
- Stamina
- Endurance
- Muscle tone
- Fitness
- Positive self-image

LANGUAGE FOCUS
high, low, over, under, through

CRITICAL SAFEGUARDS
Adult supervision is required at all times for all of these high-energy activities. In particular, provide physical support when children are working with equipment they are not familiar with, or any equipment that elevates them off the ground, regardless of their experience level.

TEACHING GEMS
- Motories (obstacle courses) can be set up indoors or out depending on the space required and weather restrictions. Be sure to include directional arrows to indicate which way to go.
- Your motory toolkit can be made up of things you already have on hand, such as: balance beam; planks; tunnels; ropes to walk along, jump over, or crawl under; cones to define running patterns; pails (filled) to carry a distance; taped or drawn pathways for running, hopping, jumping; stepping stones; target games (with balls or beanbags); hoops; pool noodles and other foam toys; large, fixed playground equipment; and anything else you have on hand that children enjoy playing with.
- Be sure when you're selecting elements to create a balance of kinetic benefits. Use the Kinetic Scale as your guide, and try to ensure that you have elements that will challenge children's senses, balance, intuition, power, coordination, and control.

SARAH WHITING

ON THE MOVE | **WATCH ME GROW** | **IN THE KNOW**

Snugglers
MODELING POSITIVE MOVEMENT. Sustained movement makes people feel good. Model positive movement for baby, even from the youngest age.

STROLLER STRIDES. Place baby in his stroller and look for (or set up) a mini obstacle course to navigate. Takes turns to the right and left and 360 degrees. Walk briskly and talk to baby about being on the go! (R daily)

STROLLER STRIDES 2. This time add more twists and turns to your route, and vary your speed from slow to fast. Talk and sing to baby as you go, being sure to talk about the things you both see every day and new points of interest. (R daily)

OUR FIRST MOTORY. Hug baby tightly to your chest. Walk briskly around your mini obstacle course. Try different ways of moving, too—walk sideways or backward, dance with baby in your arms, etc. (R daily)

Squigglers

PRE-PLAYGROUND PLAY. Babies are too little for big-kid equipment, of course, but with your help, there are lots of benefits to giving them a sneak peek at what they'll be able to do someday.

UP THE SLIDE, BABY STYLE. Place baby on his tummy on a foam wedge with his head above his feet. Place a toy at the end of the wedge to encourage him to crawl toward it. Put your hands behind his feet to give him something to push against and encourage him to crawl uphill. (R 2–3 times)

DOWN THE SLIDE, BABY STYLE. Secure a smooth plank on a slight incline (3–4 inches off the ground). Sit baby at the top of the plank, firmly supporting him around his waist at all times. Very slowly slide baby down the plank. Whee! As baby gets comfortable with the ride, go a little faster. (R 3–5 times)

MY FIRST MOTORY. Repeat "Down the Slide, Baby Style." This time, put a cardboard box or play tunnel near the end of the plank. After you've slid baby down the plank, put him on all fours and encourage him to crawl through the tunnel. Strive to make this a seamless movement pattern, continuing straight off the plank into the tunnel. (R 2–3 times)

Scampers

VARIED MOVEMENT. Giving children lots of different movement experiences prepares the foundations for more advanced, complex movements later on.

USE YOUR NOODLE. Put a favorite toy on the floor and be sure the child sees it. Then pile a bunch of pool noodles over it so he can't see the toy anymore. Encourage him to dig through the noodles to find his prize. (D 2–3 min.)

CHICKEN NOODLE SOUP. Lay out several noodles, as many as you have, placing them randomly in a confined area. Encourage the child to make his way over, under, around, and through this giant bowl of noodle soup. (D 5 min.)

MOTORY MADE OF NOODLES. Create a motory out of noodles. For instance, place them on the ground to create shapes, numbers, or letters and have the child explore them. Stand the noodles up and get him to knock them over. Roll them around the floor and encourage him to chase after them. (D 5 min.)

Stompers

MAKE YOUR OWN MOTORY. When children are part of creating playful challenges, they are more engaged in conquering them. From this point forward, encourage children to participate in setting up the play parameters.

MAKE YOUR OWN STEPPING STONES. Together with children, gather different-sized containers sturdy enough to stand on. Create a stepping-stone path. Support children around the waist as they step across the stepping stones. Add more stones and create curves and turns in the path for extra challenge. (R 3–5 times)

MAKE YOUR OWN BALANCE BEAM. With children, head outside with a rope and search for a fallen log. (If you don't have ready access to logs, use an alternative, such as a plank, that the children can imagine as a log. The important thing for this activity is for the children to do the work of creating their own playscape.) Tie the rope around the log and together, drag it back to your play area. As a team, continue to hunt for and collect logs and decide together how to lay them out. Now support the children as they learn to walk the logs and discover all the ways you can play with a log! (D 20–30 min.)

MY OWN MOTORY. Work with children to map out their own motory, giving them pride of authorship in the play. For this activity, the goal is to create a course with equipment and play concepts they already know. The challenge comes in how they transition from one element to the next. (See list of ideas in the Teaching GEMs.) (D 20–30 min.)

Scooters

CONTINUOUS MOVEMENT. Motories challenge children to change how they move at every turn, which builds overall coordination and body control.

FLIP WORMS. String several ropes across the room, securing them to table legs about 12" off the ground. Have children lie on their tummies and wiggle like worms under the ropes. Have them repeat, this time wiggling on their backs. Go again, wiggling on tummies, only this time at the halfway mark, call out, "Flip." They have to flip over onto their backs and continue to wiggle. (R 3–5 times)

ROPE CLIMBING. Tie a rope securely to the monkey bars. Supporting the child at the waist, have him climb the rope as far up as he can. Lift him back down. Take a rest. Practice climbing up until he's comfortable with the movements, then add climbing back down the rope, too. *Note:* When climbing the rope, the child's hand position needs to be with the thumb on top of the hand during the hand-over-hand grip. The legs should wrap around the rope to lock in a secure grip. While supporting himself with his legs (and your assistance), he moves his hands up, then shimmies his feet up and back into a locked, secure grip around the rope. (R 3–5 times)

MIXED-UP MOTORIES. Create a circuit of 5 challenges and have the children take turns running the course. Observe and assess which of the challenges the children have mastered. When they're ready, replace that challenge with a new one and run the course again. (R 3–5 rounds)

Skedaddlers

SOCIAL DYNAMICS. Giving children opportunities to explore what they can do on their own, or with a partner or team, gives them different experiences with concepts of motivation.

PERSONAL BESTS (PBs). Work with children to set up their favorite motory challenges. Have each child run the course, and time them. Mark their times on their own PB charts (see page 28). Each time they run the course, also mark their time with a stick to show children their progress. (R 2–3 times)

DOUBLE-TROUBLE MOTORY. Pair up the children and have them run the course together. On the next round, blindfold 1 child and have the other guide his partner safely through the course. Stand by for support at all times. Swap the blindfold and repeat. (R 1 time each)

TEAM BESTS (TBs). Group the children into teams and have them run the course together. Mark their times on their TB chart (see page 28). Point out that the *total team time* is what matters, so it's important to help each other along the way. After each round, discuss how they did and work with them to form strategies for improving their time. (R 3–5 rounds)

SARAH WHITING

Pop Go the Bubbles
Flexibility and Agility

It never rains when you're having fun. But it bubbles a lot! And when bubbles come out to play, the fun starts popping everywhere! Catch 'em! Pop 'em! Dodge 'em! What else can you do with bubbles?

EQUIPMENT
- Soft music
- Bubble machine or gun
- Bubble solution
- Bubble wands
- Flyswatters
- Cardboard tube or plastic spoon
- Straws or ice-cream sticks
- Rope
- Spots

KEY BENEFITS
- Eye-everything coordination
- Agility
- Eye tracking
- Eye fitness

LANGUAGE FOCUS
through, into, off

CRITICAL SAFEGUARDS
- When using bubbles with babies, take care not to get the bubbles too close to the child's face, mouth, nose, and eyes.
- Never float the bubbles directly over children's eyes, and keep bubble mixture away from children's mouths.
- Store bubble mix in a secure container.

TEACHING GEMS
- Unless otherwise stated, create masses of bubbles using a bubble machine or bubble gun.
- For a homemade bubble recipe, see page 194.

ON THE MOVE	WATCH ME GROW	IN THE KNOW

 ### Snugglers
QUIET TIME doesn't have to be inactive for baby. Floating bubbles create a spectacle for new eyes and a chance to try out those fingers and toes.

BUBBLES IN THE AIR. Lay baby on her back on the floor. Put on some soft, "floaty" music. Stand behind her head and blow bubbles around her so she watches the bubbles without interruption. (D 2–3 min.)

KICK THAT BUBBLE. Lay baby on her back on the floor with her socks and shoes off. Blow bubbles around her. Lift 1 of baby's feet and hold it to pop the bubbles with her toes. Repeat with the other leg and with arms. (D 2–3 min.)

POP GO THE BUBBLES. Lay baby on her tummy and blow bubbles around her so she tracks their movement with her eyes. Encourage her to reach for the bubbles. Each time she pops one, make a funny sound (pop! tink! poof!). (D 2–3 min.)

 ### Squigglers
DYNAMIC TRACKING. Eye tracking while still prepares the eyes for the day they will need to move while the body is in motion—the beginnings of eye-everything coordination.

BUBBLE CLAP. Sit baby between your legs on the floor. Have someone blow bubbles around you. Take baby's hands in yours and together clap the bubbles good-bye! Each time you clap a bubble, make a funny sound (pop! tink! poof!). (D 2–3 min.)

SWAT THAT BUBBLE. Sit baby between your legs on the floor. Have someone blow bubbles around you. Together hold a fly-swatter and, as the bubbles fly by, hit, flick, and pop the bubbles. Each time you swat a bubble, make a funny sound (pop! tink! poof!). (D 2–3 min.)

BUBBLE CHASE. While baby is crawling around the floor, blow bubbles for her to chase. Use a bubble machine or fan to stir up even more fun! Each time she pops a bubble, make a funny sound (pop! tink! poof!). (D 2–3 min.)

| ON THE MOVE | WATCH ME GROW | IN THE KNOW |

 ### Scampers
EFFICIENT ENERGY. Children need power to help the body deliver efficiency of movement.

BUBBLE SHAPES. Kneel in front of the child. Blow bubbles around her through different shapes and sizes of bubble wands. Blow the bubbles just out of her reach to encourage her to chase after them. (D 2–3 min.)

BUBBLE BAT. Sit the child on the floor and give her a cardboard tube or plastic spoon. Blow bubbles around her and encourage her to bat at the bubbles in the air. Have her try the bat with each hand and with both hands together. (D 2–3 min.)

MY FIRST BUBBLES. Show the child how to blow into the bubble wand to make her own bubbles. (Explain that the bubble wand is like a birthday candle. Take a deep breath and blow really hard!) Watch to see where they go. Blow bubbles up and down, to the left, and to the right. (D 3–5 min.)

 ### Stompers
FLEXIBILITY. When children use parts of their body in unusual ways, it challenges them to stretch both their bodies and their minds.

BUBBLE CATCH. Call out a part of the body (such as the elbow) and have children touch their elbows. Next, turn on the bubble machine and have children catch the bubbles with their elbows. Repeat with the other elbow and with different parts of the body. (D 3–5 min.)

THUMBS UP. As the bubbles float, call out a finger (thumb, pointer finger, pinkie). Have the children pop bubbles with just that finger. Try 1 hand, then the other. For added challenge, have the children take off socks and shoes and try it with different toes. (D 3–5 min.)

BASKETBUBBLE. Have the child stretch out her arms and join her hands together to make a basket. See how many bubbles she can have pass through her basket without popping them. For added challenge, have her make a basket with just her hands. (D 3–5 min.)

 ### Scooters
SLOW MOVEMENTS. When things move slowly, it gives the eyes time to keep up and the body time to organize.

BUBBLE MONSTER! Have each child stand in 1 spot and not move from it. Ask the children to show you how a Bubble Monster stomps and clomps really loudly: *Stomp! Clomp! Stomp!* Now really *slowly* (and loudly): *Stomp! Clomp! Stomp!* Now blow bubbles toward the children and have them stomp and clomp as slowly and as loudly as they can! Repeat, stomping and clomping as fast and quietly as they can. (D 2–3 min.)

BUBBLE MAGNET. Give children plastic straws and show them how to catch bubbles with a straw. Challenge them to catch a bubble any way they can. Next, see if they can catch one on the end of the straw, in the middle of the straw, and even on the tip of the straw. Be gentle and steady. (D 5–10 min.)

BUBBLE KARATE. Have children balance on 1 foot and hold that position. Blow the bubbles toward them. Have them try, while balancing, to kick the bubbles in slow motion. Have them try to stay on 1 foot as long as they can, and then switch to the other foot. (D 5–10 min.)

 ### Skedaddlers
AGILITY is the ability to move the body quickly and nimbly; it grows body confidence.

WHALE SPOUT. Have children spread out so there's room to move. Blow bubbles into the air and tell children to try to keep the bubbles in the air as long as they can. Show children how to do this by chasing the bubbles and blowing them back up into the air before they pop. (D 3–5 min.)

JACK BE NIMBLE. Lay out a rope in a circle and have children take turns standing inside it. Blow bubbles into the circle and have children jump over the bubbles before the bubbles touch the ground. Set the timer for 10 seconds. Count how many bubbles children can jump over. (R 3–5 times)

DODGEBUBBLE. Lay out a rope in a circle and have the child stand inside it. Staying inside the rope, blow a bubble toward her and have her dodge the bubble. Add more bubbles for added challenge and excitement. For a group game, have all the children dodging the bubbles and each other! (D 5–10 min.)

Crawlimals
Coordinated Movement: Crawling for All Ages

Watch out! Here come the Crawlimals, the craziest creatures you've ever met. Crawlimals are one part something and one part something else. And just when you think you've figured them out, they pull a switcheroo—and now they're something else!

EQUIPMENT

- Toys
- Sheet
- Chair or table
- Rope
- Bucket
- Beanbags
- Adhesive dots
- Music
- Timer
- Animal cards
- Hats

KEY BENEFITS

- Teamwork
- Problem solving
- Midline development
- Stamina

LANGUAGE FOCUS

all directional language (in, out, up, down, and so on)

CRITICAL SAFEGUARDS

Ensure the crawling space for children is free from hazards.

TEACHING GEMS

- Whenever possible, do activities barefooted. This aids in body awareness.
- Song lyrics are on pages 194–195. For detailed information and ideas related to crawling, see "There's More to Crawling and Walking Than Meets the Eye," pages 192–193.

SARAH ALICE LEE

ON THE MOVE   **WATCH ME GROW**   **IN THE KNOW**

 Snugglers
PRECRAWLING. A child's brain needs to experience lateral and opposition movements in preparation for the child's learning to move independently.

MOVING SONG: INCHY INCHWORM. Lay baby on his back on the floor or another firm surface. As you sing "Inchy Inchworm: Up and Down," hold his legs around his ankles and lift them up and down gently. Next, lift 1 leg up and down, then the other. Repeat with the arms. (D 2–3 min.)

MOVING SONG: CHIRPY BLUEBIRD. Lay baby on his back on the floor or another firm surface. As you sing "Chirpy Bluebird: In and Out," hold his legs around his ankles and gently bend his knees into his body and then straighten again. Now do this with 1 leg, then the other. Repeat with the arms. (D 2–3 min.)

MOVING SONG: FUNNY LITTLE MONKEY. Lay baby on his back on the floor or another firm surface. As you sing "Funny Little Monkey: Tangled Up," hold his right ankle and left wrist. Gently lift them up at the same time to meet, then bring them back to the ground. Repeat several times, then swap sides. (D 2–3 min.)

Squigglers

DIMENSIONALIZED MOVEMENT. Rolling from his back to his tummy is baby's first independent understanding of the 3-dimensionality of his own body.

MOVING SONG: LITTLE GREEN FROG. Lay baby on his tummy on the floor. As you sing "Little Green Frog: Out and Back," hold his ankles and gently open and close his legs. Now try moving 1 leg at a time while gently holding the other leg still. Then, push baby's legs gently up and out so his knees bend into frog legs! Repeat with the arms. Repeat with baby lying on his back. (D 2–3 min.)

MOVING SONG: LITTLE CHICKADEE. Lay baby on his tummy on the floor. As you sing "Little Chickadee: Side to Side," hold his ankles and gently move his legs from side to side. Now move 1 leg at a time out to the side while gently holding the other leg still. Cross the moving leg over the top of the stationary leg. Repeat with baby lying on his back. (D 2–3 min.)

MOVING SONG: LITTLE GREY HARE. Sit on the floor with your legs together and sit baby on your legs facing you. Tap the front and back of his body as you sing "Little Grey Hare: Front and Back." Next, sing the song again, lifting and turning him front to back. (D 2–3 min.)

Scampers

THE CRAWLING IMPERATIVE. Once children master being vertical, they tend to want to walk rather than crawl. But crawling is a powerful movement pattern for brain development. Entice children back to the floor with attractive, fun crawling enhancement activities.

MOVING SONG: BIG OLD BEAR. Sit the child on the floor and sit facing him singing "Big Old Bear: To the Right." Each time you sing "right," tickle his right knee. Repeat the song, this time sitting to his right a few feet away. Entice him to turn his body to the right and crawl to you. Repeat to the left with the "Big Old Whale: To the Left" lyrics. (D 2–3 min.)

MOVING SONG: SILLY LITTLE PUPPY. Sit on the floor with the child and entice him to chase a favorite toy around your body as you sing "Silly Little Puppy: Round and Round." Hold the toy out of reach and slowly move it away so he follows it. Bring it around your back (always keeping it within his field of vision) so that he circles all the way around you. Repeat in the other direction. (D 2–3 min.)

MOVING SONG: BOLD LITTLE MOLE. Attach a sheet to a chair or table about 12" above the ground. Hold the other end taut. Put several toys at 1 end to attract the child and encourage him to crawl under the sheet. Keep the sheet very low so he gets a sense of being enclosed by it. Sing "Bold Little Mole: Down and Under" so he knows you're there. Flutter the sheet from time to time. (D 2–3 min.)

Stompers

ADAPTIVE MOVEMENTS. As little ones master the mechanics of human movement, they can begin to transfer that knowledge into new forms of physical expression.

CRAWLIMALS. Show children how to crawl like an animal. Pick one they haven't tried before. Now, make a road using 2 parallel pieces of rope or draw 2 long parallel lines on the floor. Encourage children to crawl forward between the lines, turn around, and come back. Next, have them try crawling backward between the lines. (D 3–5 min.)

CRAWLIMALS ROAD CREW. Make a curvy road with the rope and place a bucket at the end. Place several beanbags along the road. Encourage a child to crawl to pick up a beanbag, place it under his chin, then crawl to the end and drop it in the bucket. Repeat with other children until the road is clear. Repeat trying different ways of crawling. Try it backward, too. (D 3–5 min.)

CRAWLIMALS ADVENTURES. Introduce an animal (such as an elephant) as a focus for the day. Explore the unique qualities of elephants—how big they are, what they sound like, where they live. Next, show children how to move like an elephant, and challenge them to move like that throughout the day. Now go on elephant adventures, indoors and out. Retell your adventures with stories, drawings, and songs. (R on and off throughout the day)

Scooters

IMAGINATIVE MOVEMENTS. Embodying different characteristics of another person or creature gives children the motivation to move in ways they haven't necessarily thought of before.

MUSICAL CRAWLIMALS. A fun version of musical chairs, lay out dots in a circle (one fewer than the number of children). Have the children pick an animal (such as an elephant) to move like, then start the music. When the music stops, each of the elephants has to find a dot. The one without a dot remains in the game, continues to move like an elephant, and chooses the next animal for the others to play. Continue until everyone is a different animal. (D 10–15 min.)

CRAWLIMALS CRAWLADES. Sit the children in a circle. Have 1 child go to the center and move and sound like an animal of his choice (such as an elephant). The others have to guess what animal he is. When they've guessed, everyone gets up and moves in a circle like an elephant. The child who was in the middle chooses the next child to go to the center of the circle, and the play begins again. (D 10–15 min.)

CRAWLIMALS CRAWLATHON. Explain the concept of a marathon—a very long run with lots of people. Then tell children they are going to do a "crawlathon" throughout the day. Start by allowing them to crawl as they see fit, setting the rule that they must have at least 1 knee on the ground. Then set a timer for every 30 min. (or any time frame that works for you and your group). Each time the timer sounds, call out a different crawling animal for children to be! (R on and off throughout the day)

Skedaddlers

CRAWLING IN DIFFERENT COMBINATIONS. Crawling allows the body to experiment with complex movements, which builds whole-body coordination.

MY FIRST MIXIMALS. Put a variety of animal cards or pictures of different animals in a hat. Pair up the children and have each pair draw 1 card from the hat. Work with them to figure out how to use both their bodies to move as that 1 animal. For instance, 1 child could be the front legs of the animal, and the other the back legs. With a group of children, they can all play simultaneously or make a silly charades game out of it. (D 5–10 min.)

MIXIMALS. Put pictures of different animals in 2 different hats: the Top Hat and the Bottom Hat. Start by having each child pick from the Top Hat and move just their arms like that animal (such as a bird). Next, have children select from the Bottom Hat and move their legs like that animal (such as a cow). Now have them put both together, for example flapping their arms like a bird while ambling like a cow. Be sure each child names his unique "miximal." ("I'm a birdamoo.") (D 10–15 min.)

MIXIMAL MIXUP. Repeat the "Miximals" activity, this time having children add other features to their unique miximal. For instance, what does a birdamoo sound like? What games do birdamoos like to play? What happens when a birdamoo and a puppyfrog meet? Next, have the children choose a partner and exchange "parts"— for instance, the birdamoo becomes a birdafrog, or the puppyfrog becomes a puppymoo. (D 20–30 min.)

The 3-Legged Triple-Toed Triopsicle!
Midline Development: Homolaterality

Imagine what it would be like to be a 3-legged triple-toed triopsicle. . . . What could you do if you had 3 feet and 3 knees—and 20 toes, 20 fingers, 4 eyes, 4 ears, and 2 heads!

SARAH WHITING

EQUIPMENT
- Pot or drum
- Wooden spoon or drumstick
- Pillows
- Soft scarf
- Streamers
- Hoops
- Bell
- Chalk

KEY BENEFITS
- Homolaterality
- Body rhythm
- Coordinated movement
- Body control
- Directionality

LANGUAGE FOCUS
left, right, top, bottom, front, back

CRITICAL SAFEGUARDS
- Read the moves and assist children when needed.
- Ensure that activities done lying down are on a flat surface.

- Encourage children to take off their shoes for a more secure foot grip.

TEACHING GEMS
- You may notice that for children whose midlines are not yet fully developed, complex movement patterns may be challenging. For instance, if you move a young baby's arm out to the side, her head may move as well.
- When children need to turn left and right, make it easier for them by putting a mark on their right hand and foot. Tell them that the marked hands and feet are on the right side of their body and the side with no marks is the left.

ON THE MOVE **WATCH ME GROW** **IN THE KNOW**

Snugglers

ISOLATING SIDES of baby's body gives her clues to how her body is constructed.

ONE-SIDED MASSAGE. Massage 1 side of baby's body at a time. Start at the top of her head and work down the right side of her body all the way to her toes. Repeat on the left side. Next time, massage baby's upper body, then her lower body. (D 2–3 min.)

HALF-A-ROBICS. Similar to "One-Sided Massage," this time lift baby's right arm and right leg up in the air at the same time while leaving the left side still. Repeat on the left side. Next, lift baby's arms up in the air then back down. Repeat with the legs. (D 2–3 min.)

SIDE ROLLS. With baby's hands by her sides and her legs together, gently roll her onto one side of her body and hold her there for 5 seconds. Then roll her back to the center for 5 seconds, then to the other side and hold 5 seconds. (R 3 times)

Squigglers

BILATERAL MOVEMENT occurs when baby uses the hand that is closest to what she wants. Left- or right-handedness is still in the process of emerging.

1, 2, 3, CLAP! Lay baby on a flat surface on her back, so that she can see you. Bring the palms of her hands almost together and count 1, 2, 3, and then, on the fourth beat, clap the hands. Try this with the feet. Watch to see baby start to do this on her own and assist when needed. Sing a favorite song to keep the beat as you play. (D 3–5 min.)

ONE-SIDED RHYTHM TAP. Turn baby over on her tummy. Bend her left foot up in the air and tap her toes and the bottom of her foot. Gently tap up her leg, along her left side, and up and down her left side. Repeat on the right. Sing a favorite song to keep the beat as you play. (D 2–3 min.)

UNICYCLING. Lay baby on her back and lift just her right leg in the air. Pedal the right leg like a 1-sided bicycle. Repeat with the left leg. (D 2–3 min.)

Scampers

MOVING PARTS. Moving her body 1 side at a time helps the child move toward understanding that her body has 2 sides and that each side can move and do different things at the same time.

DRUM RIGHT. DRUM LEFT. Collect a pot and wooden spoon or a drum and drumstick. Sit the child in front of the drum and encourage her to play. Next, hold the drum to her right to encourage her to drum with her right hand. Repeat on the left. (D 3–5 min.)

TOWER GO BOOM! Work together with the child to build a tower of pillows. Encourage her to crawl over it to knock it over. *Boom!* Next, build the tower taller and assist her to stand and knock it over. *Boom!* Next time, assist her to kick the tower and then crawl through the pillows. *Boom!* (D 3–5 min.)

AIRPLANE PROPELLER. Have the child sit opposite you and join her ankles together with a soft scarf. Lift her legs together and circle them around like a propeller on a plane, first to the right and then to the left. Try other movement patterns (up and down, zigzag) and make shapes such as triangles, squares, and figure eights. (D 3–5 min.)

Stompers

HOMOLATERAL MOVEMENT, the ability to move 1 part of the body while keeping the other parts still, is a signal that sophisticated, whole-body movement is emerging.

SEAL DIVING. Have children lie on the floor on their tummies with arms tucked to their sides. Encourage them to lift their heads and upper bodies off the ground and hold for 5 seconds. Next, have them lift only their legs as far off the floor as they can and hold for 5 seconds. Everyone barks like seals! (D 2–3 min.)

PARACHUTE JUMPER. Have children lie on the floor on their tummies with arms out to the sides. Encourage them to lift their heads, arms, and legs off the floor, balancing on their tummies. Hold for 5 seconds. Then have them tuck their arms to their sides and try it again. (D 2–3 min.)

CIRCLING CIRCLES. Have children lie on a smooth, slippery floor on their left sides and use their right feet and legs to move their bodies in circles. Have them repeat, lying on the right side and using their left feet to circle in the opposite direction. (D 2–3 min.)

Scooters

HOMOLATERAL OPPOSITION. The key to mastering 1-sided movement—homolaterality—is to practice keeping 1 part still while the opposite part moves.

ONE-SIDED MARCHING. Have children stand. Keeping right arms and legs still, have them "march" their left arm and leg up and down while standing in place. Next, tell them to use the left foot to turn their body in a tight circle (still keeping the right side still). Repeat, using right arms and legs to march. When they get really good at this, march backward. (D 2–3 min.)

AIR TRAFFIC CONTROLLER DANCE. Group children in pairs. Set up a goal and have 1 child (the controller) stand beside it. Give her a streamer for each hand. Have another child (the airplane) stand several paces back. The controller directs the airplane with 1 hand moving and the other still—pointing to the left and right to guide the airplane to the gate. Swap roles. (D 3–5 min.) *Note:* As the children get familiar with the game, add silly hand signals. For instance, twirl the streamer and the airplane has to spin around.

FROGGIESCOTCH! Set up 6 hoops in a straight line on the floor. One by one, have children jump like a frog through all the hoops, trying not to touch them. Have children be sure to land hands first in the hoop, then jump both feet into that same hoop before continuing to the next hoop. (R 2–3 times)

Skedaddlers

COMPLEX MOVEMENT PATTERNS. Sophisticated movements like hopping require an intuitive physical understanding of homolaterality.

HOP AROUND THE CLOCK. Have the children hop in a circle. When the clock strikes 1 (ring a bell), they hop on the right foot. When the clock strikes again, they switch to the left foot. Work around the clock to 12. Next, add arm movements. For instance, when hopping on the right foot, have children lift their right arm in the air. (D 5–10 min.)

LEFT-TURN HOP. Draw a grid pattern on the floor or pavement to simulate streets. Give each child a starting point and a destination to get to. The children will hop along the streets to get to their destination but are only allowed to turn left to get where they're going. Stand back and see if they can work out how to hop from 1 end of the play area to another by turning only left. Repeat with children turning only right. (D 5–10 min.)

THE 3-LEGGED TRIPLE-TOED TRIOPSICLE! Pair children of similar size and tie 1 leg each together to create a 3-legged racer. Have the children move around to get used to the opportunities and limitations this partnership creates. Next, create a start and finish line. Have each pair take turns running as fast as they can while you time them. Repeat to see if they can beat their best time. Next, add curves and turns to the course to add challenge. (D 10–20 min.)

Crocodile Flop
Midline Development: Laterality

Have you ever noticed that crocodiles have very short legs? Short legs are great for keeping close to the ground. But what happens when you have short legs and you want to move around a lot? Well, you might flop a lot. You might stomp a lot. And if you're a very clever crocodile, you might dance a lot, too! Shall we try moving like a crocodile?

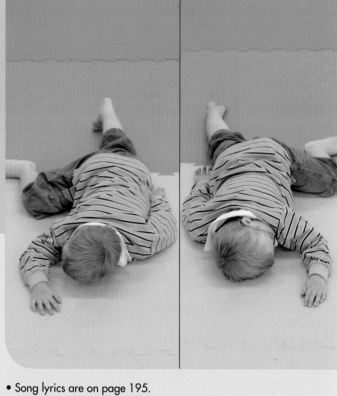

EQUIPMENT
- Sock puppet
- Red socks
- Blue socks

KEY BENEFITS
- Midline development
- Eye-hand coordination
- Eye-foot coordination
- Rhythm and timing

LANGUAGE FOCUS
left, right

CRITICAL SAFEGUARDS
Ensure there is enough space for the children to carry out this activity without bumping into one another.

TEACHING GEMS
- While left and right are important directional concepts, knowing left and right is also a critical life skill. See pages 38–39 for ideas on teaching left and right.

- Song lyrics are on page 195.
- You may need to adjust your speed depending on the movement messages the child is showing you. Slowing down gives him time to concentrate and allows the brain to better absorb the physical sensations.
- So much of this activity involves the left and right sides of the body. To assist children in seeing and understanding the difference between the 2 sides of their body, place a sticker on 1 hand, or use 2 different stickers, 1 for each hand. This can also be accomplished with different-colored socks.

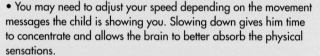

SARAH ALICE LEE

ON THE MOVE **WATCH ME GROW** **IN THE KNOW**

Snugglers

INTEGRATING THE FENCING REFLEX. The fencing reflex is designed to assist baby's journey through the birth canal. It creates a reflexive relationship between the head and arms—when baby turns his head to the right, the right arm stretches out and the left arm folds in. After birth, it's necessary for the child to integrate this reflex in order to make way for independent crawling and walking in the future.

CHEEK SPEAK. Lay baby on the floor on his back and gently turn his head to the right. You'll likely see his right arm stretch out and his left arm fold in automatically. This is the fencing reflex at work. Lie next to baby's turned head and put your cheek down on the floor so you're eye to eye. Talk to him and maintain eye contact. Repeat on the left side. (D 1–3 min.)

CLOUD WATCHING. In a shady spot outdoors or on the floor indoors, enjoy time with baby by lying down, putting him on your tummy face up. Holding him securely with your left hand, gently bring his right hand out to the side. Note that he may move his head to the right involuntarily. Repeat to the left. (R 2–3 times) Next, turn baby on his tummy so you're lying tummy to tummy and repeat the activity. (R 2–3 times)

CROCODILE SCALES. Lay baby on his back on the floor. Give him a massage, tapping your fingertips down his tummy, legs, and arms as if you were counting his crocodile scales. Repeat with baby on his tummy. Next, massage the crocodile scales on the right side of his body. Then the left. This technique gives baby a unique tactile sense of his whole body, which is important for getting up and going on his own. (D 2–3 min.)

Squigglers

BABY CROCODILE STEPS. A baby getting ready to crawl needs to spend time moving his arms and legs together and in opposition. Many of the primitive reflexes are still active, though, making that difficult to do without a little help from you.

CROCOROBICS. Lay baby on the floor and gently hold his hips still while assisting him to twist his torso first to the right and then to the left. Repeat, keeping his torso still and tipping his hips to the side, crossing 1 leg over the other. (R 2 times) Have a break and encourage him to reach out and grab his toes with his fingers. When his hands and feet meet, he's learning the full extent of his body. Next, try some more "Crocorobics." (D 2–4 min.)

CROC ROCK-AND-ROLL. Once baby is up on all fours, stimulate this position by giving him a "Crocodile Scales" massage down his back, the back of his legs, and his feet. When you get to his crocodile toes, encourage baby to lie flat on his tummy and roll over to his back. Encourage him to return to all fours in order to give him lots of practice in that position. And crocodiles love tummy rubs, so be sure to give him a "Crocodile Scales" massage on his tummy, too. (R 3–5 times)

CROC-AT-A-TIME. Simple as it may seem, moving 1 part of the body at a time is tricky for little ones, so take this slow and applaud all of baby's efforts! Have him sit in front of you facing a mirror. Assist him to bend both arms out to the side in strongman position (bent at the elbow), then back down. Next, assist him to bend both knees up, then back down. Now experiment. Bend 1 arm out, then the other. Bend 1 knee out, then the other. Try alternating left and right, arms and legs, 1 at a time. Encourage him to repeat the movements on his own. (D 2–5 min.)

Scampers

EMERGING MIDLINES. With a child's midlines beginning to emerge, it's time to start giving him a sense of full-body coordination. But don't expect success on the first or even the tenth try here; instead, watch to see if the movements get easier, more fluid, and more within his control over time. Assist as needed.

CROC-A-DOODLE-DO! The crocodile just woke up, but where is he? Put a sock puppet on your hand, go to the child's left, and shout out "Croc-a-doodle-do!" to encourage him to turn his head to the left. Repeat on the right. The goal here is to encourage neck and shoulder strength through simple side-to-side neck movements, which also assist in integrating the fencing reflex. (R 2–3 times)

CROC SOCKS! Find 2 pairs of different-colored socks, such as red and blue. Put the red socks on the child's right hand and right foot. Put the blue socks on his left hand and foot. Now play a matching game, encouraging him to touch the 2 red socks together and the 2 blue socks together. Next, swap the socks on his hands and help him match the colors again, this time across his body. (D 2–5 min.)

CROC SOCK UPS! Use the red socks on the child's hands and blue socks on his feet for this one. Encourage the child to crawl around and roar like a crocodile! Assist the child in lifting his red "foot" (hand) up off the ground without falling out of the all-fours position. Then lift the other red "foot." Now repeat with the blue feet. (R 2–3 times)

Stompers

EXPLORING HALF THE BODY. The midlines define the halves of the body—left and right, top and bottom, and front and back.

SLOW HELLO. The goal here is to move only 1 part of the body at a time very slowly. Sit on the floor with the child sitting between your legs for support. Have the child adopt the strongman arm position with his legs out straight in front of him throughout the activity. Try various movements to wave hello to the crocodile: (1) Slowly turn just the child's head to the right, roar, "Hello!" and bring his head back to center. (R 3 times) (2) Slowly extend the right forearm out to the side, wiggle his fingers, roar, "Hello!" and return to center. (R 3 times) (3) Slowly lift up the right knee, wiggle the toes, roar, "Hello!" and return to the floor. (R 3 times) Repeat all actions to the left.

MORE SLOW HELLOS. Sit on the floor with the child sitting between your legs for support. Repeat the "Slow Hello" activity to warm up, then use these same movements in an alternating pattern. (1) Right arm, left arm, right arm, left arm. (2) Right knee, left knee, right knee, left knee. Remember that the goal is to isolate each movement, keeping the rest of the body still while moving very slowly. And be sure to wave and roar, "Hello!" each time. Crocodiles like it when folks are friendly! (R 3 times)

CROC STRETCH. Crocodiles love to lie in the sun and stretch out. Have children lie on their backs on the floor, with arms down by the sides and legs straight. Tell them they are going to move slowly, like a crocodile. Then have them do 3 movements at the same time: turn the head to the right, move the right arm up into the strongman position, and bend the right knee out to the right. (Remind them to keep the left side still while they do this.) Once in position, they can wiggle their fingers and toes and roar, "Hello!" Have them return to the center and try it to the left. (R 3 times)

Scooters

MIDLINE + BALANCE. Midline development unlocks the ability to move the whole body with seamless coordination, but that can only happen when a child's balance can support him.

CROCSICLES! Standing for this next set introduces the added challenge of balance. (1) Have children stand with the arms in airplane position and lift the right knee, then the left. Work up to a slow march, alternating left and right. (2) Repeat the movement with the arms in the strongman position, forcing the core muscles to work harder to maintain balance. (3) With arms in airplane position, children lift their right knee and yell out, "Crocsicle!" Have the children freeze and hold that position for 2–5 seconds. Repeat to the left. (4) With arms in the strongman position, have children lift the right knee, yell out, "Crocsicle!" and hold for 2–5 seconds. Repeat with the left. (D 2–3 min.)

CROCNASTICS! Have children stand with the arms in strongman position and lift the right knee up and touch it with the right elbow. Repeat on the left. (R 3 times) Next, have them lift the right knee up and touch it with the left elbow. Repeat on the other side. (R 3 times) Then have them try alternating right and left, building up some speed. To add challenge, yell out "Crocsicle!" and have the children try to hold the position they're in for 1–3 seconds.

CROC NINJA! Crocodiles have some serious ninja moves. Have children begin by standing with feet together and strongman arms. (1) With the left side of the body still, they turn the head to the right, extend the right arm out and leg out to the right (with the toe touching the floor). Return to center and repeat on the other side. (2) Speed up the movement alternating from left to right. (3) Repeat, adding a ninja-style jump (and a fierce crocodile roar) to transition from left to right. (R each step 3–5 times)

Skedaddlers

LEFT AND RIGHT come into physical and conceptual focus for kids through midline development.

CROCODILE FLOP. Have children lie on their tummies with their arms at the sides and legs straight. Tell them to turn their head to the right, strongman the right arm, bend the right knee out to the right, and freeze like "crocsicles" for 2 seconds. Return to center and repeat on the other side. As children develop fluidity in their movements, add a crocodile roar each time they switch. Once the movements appear fluid, select from the "Crocodile Flop" song lyrics (page 195) to change the pace. (R 2–3 times)

CROC LEFT AND RIGHT. First, have children lie on their backs and repeat the movements from the "Crocodile Flop" activity. Next, put a sticker on each child's right hand to distinguish it from the left. Call out, "Croc right," and encourage children to "crocodile flop" to the right so they can see the sticker. Then call out, "Croc left," and have them crocodile flop to the other side. Then sing the "Crocodiles Left and Right" lyrics (page 195) and have children repeat the movements to the pace of the music. For more silly fun, children can make different animal sounds each time they switch sides. (R 2–3 times)

CROSS-CROC. Begin by having children lie on their tummies. Tell them to turn their head to the right, strongman arm the right arm, and bend the left knee out to the left. Repeat on the other side (head to the left, left strong arm, right knee bent). These positions challenge the body and brain to manage tricky opposition moves simultaneously. Next, sing the "Flopping Crocs" lyrics (page 195) to encourage the child to move to the pace of the music. Before they roar each time, they switch sides. (R 2–3 times)

The Beanbaggles Brigade
Midline Development: Cross-Laterality

The Beanbaggles have come out to play. Trouble is, they don't know how to play any games. Can you show the Beanbaggles how to play?

EQUIPMENT
- Beanbags
- Pillowcase
- Basket
- Music

KEY BENEFITS
- Temporal awareness
- Body rhythm
- Reasoning
- Eye-hand coordination
- Eye fitness

LANGUAGE FOCUS
over, across, behind

CRITICAL SAFEGUARDS
Automaticity of movement is achieved at different times for different children, so be sure to go slowly and take your time. If the child struggles, step back 1 or 2 progressions until she is more comfortable and confident with the movements.

TEACHING GEMS
- When working in pairs passing the beanbag, have children keep their head still and track their own beanbag.
- When children reach across their midlines, insure they keep their torso straight so that just their arms or legs move. (Often children will turn or twist into awkward positions or postures to avoid crossing the midline.) If a child is struggling with cross-lateral movements, break it down for the child and assist as needed to cross 1 arm or 1 leg at a time.
- Encourage cross-pattern movement wherever possible.

ON THE MOVE   WATCH ME GROW   IN THE KNOW

 Snugglers
NATURAL INTERACTIONS. For infants, free time on the floor supports and fosters their natural development.

BEANBAG SENSORY MAT. Place beanbags inside a pillowcase and put it on the floor to create a unique sensory mat. Lay baby on her back and play with her while she rests on the unusual surface. (D 2–3 min.)

MEET THE BEANBAGGLES. Lay baby on the floor and offer her a beanbag. Encourage her to grasp it and explore it with her fingers. Help her squish it in her fingers to feel the unique texture. (D 2–3 min.)

ROLL OVER, BEANBAGGLES. Place the "Beanbag Sensory Mat" on the floor and lay baby on it. Place her horizontally on her tummy so she has room to roll. Assist her to roll over and feel and hear the beanbags crinkle and crunch underneath her. Try rolling her from front to back and back to front, too. (D 3–5 min.)

147

Squigglers

EARLY COORDINATION. Understanding how all of the parts of our body move together or independently begins when children start to move for themselves.

BEANBAGGLE GRAB. Lay baby on her back and hold a beanbag above her shoulder so she can see it. Encourage her to reach and twist for the beanbag with her opposite hand across her body, which encourages reaching, stretching, and rolling. (D 2–3 min.)

THE BEANBAGGLE PILE-UP. While sitting, pile a bunch of beanbags in front of baby. Cover her legs with them so she feels the weight. Uncover her knee and tickle it. "Peekaboo!" Encourage baby to pick up the beanbags or kick them away with her legs, then stretch to reach the ones that have fallen off the pile. (D 3–5 min.)

BEANBAGGLES SHUTTLE. Sit baby on the floor and place 6 beanbags in a basket in front of her. Encourage her to reach in for them. Next, place an empty basket next to the first basket so baby can move the beanbags from 1 basket to the other. From time to time, switch the 2 baskets to encourage the use of both the right and left hands. (D 3–5 min.)

Scampers

LATERAL MOVEMENTS are the steppingstones to full-body coordination and highly sophisticated, cross-lateral movement patterns.

BEANBAGGLES TWIST. Lay the child on her back on the floor. Put a beanbag on either side of her. Gently lift her right leg over her left and touch or kick the beanbag with the right leg. Repeat on the other side. Have the child barefoot if possible. (D 2–3 min.)

BEANBAGGLES STRETCH-UPS! Lay the child on her back and lift both of her hands up in the air. Bring 1 hand back down by her side while leaving the other up in the air. Repeat on the other side. Next, give her one beanbag to hold in her right hand. Repeat the activity, leaving the right hand up as you bring the left hand down. Repeat with the left. (D 3–5 min.)

BEANBAGGLES SCISSORS. Assist the child to cross her right arm over her left arm. Repeat in the other direction (left over right). Turn on some music and repeat these scissor movements to the beat. (It will likely take some time to automate these movements, so continue to assist as needed to avoid frustration. Rest when she needs to.) To change things up, give her 2 beanbags to hold—one in each hand—and repeat the game. Next, take 1 beanbag away and have the child hold the other in her right hand to play. Repeat with the left hand. (D 2–3 min.)

Stompers

INTRODUCING CROSS-LATERAL MOVEMENT. Cross-lateral movements don't come naturally to children at first. Introducing some simple opportunities for cross-patterned movements through play gives them a feel for what will come later on.

BEANBAGGLES CROSSING. Have the child sit on the floor. Put a pile of beanbags on her right side and an empty basket on her left. Assist her to cross her left hand over her body to pick up a beanbag and put it in the bucket. Repeat using the right hand. For a group of children, have them sit in a circle, picking up and dropping the beanbags on the floor beside them for the next child to pick up. Be sure they are all using only one hand at a time and that they are crossing over their bodies each time. (D 3–5 min.)

BEANBAGGLES PICKUP. Repeat the "Beanbaggles Crossing" game, only this time have the child use a set of plastic tongs to pick up the beanbags for extra challenge and to strengthen the pincer grip. For a group of children, pass out tongs to each child and repeat as described in "Beanbaggles Crossing." (D 3–5 min.)

COUNTING BEANBAGGLES. Repeat "Beanbaggles Pickup," only this time ask the child to count aloud as she safely escorts the Beanbaggles into the basket. For a group of children, pass out tongs to each child and repeat as described in "Beanbaggles Pickup." Have the children count in unison. (D 3–5 min.)

Scooters

PARTNER PATTERNS. Working with a partner gives children different perspectives and experiences with their own coordination.

BEANBAGGLES GO FLYING. Pair up 2 children and have them face each other with their arms in the basketweave position (children cross their arms and hold onto each other's wrists to form a basket). Place a beanbag on their hands and have them work together to figure out how to throw it up in the air as high and far as they can without letting go of each other. Next, try the game again, only this time, see if they can catch the beanbag together, too.
(D 3–5 min.)

BEANBAGGLES HANDOFF. Have the child stand and hold a beanbag in her left hand with her arms in genie position (both arms held out to the sides at shoulder height with forearms and palms up). Tell the child to stretch both hands to the front and bring them to the middle, handing off (switching) the beanbag from the left to the right hand. Repeat going the other way. For added challenge, try the handoff behind the back, behind the head, and under 1 knee.
(R 3 times in each direction)

BEANBAGGLES HAND-TO-HAND. Pair up 2 children; explain that one is Player 1 and the other is Player 2. Have them face each other with their arms in the genie position. Put one beanbag into Player 1's right hand. Have her pass it directly across to Player 2's left hand. Player 2 hands it off to her own right hand and passes it back to Player 1's left hand. This creates a circular passing movement. Go the other way. Next, have the children try passing across the body (right hand to right hand, left hand to left hand). (D 3–5 min.)

Skedaddlers

TEAM MOVES. Organizing the body to move how and where we want it to is tricky enough, but children must learn to move in coordination with others, too.

BEANBAGGLES-GO-ROUND. Have children sit in a circle facing the middle and pass 1 beanbag around the circle, counterclockwise. Have them reach across their body to receive with their right hand, switch the beanbag to their left hand, and reach across their body again to pass it off with their left hand. Repeat in a clockwise direction, having children receive with their left hand, switch the beanbag to their right hand, and reach across their body to pass it off with their right hand. Try this with eyes closed, too. (D 3–5 min.)

BEANBAGGLES GO BACKWARD. Have children sit in a circle facing the middle. Warm up with 1 round of "Beanbaggles-Go-Round." Play the next round in the same way, only this time have the children pass the beanbag behind their backs.
(D 3–5 min.)

THE BEANBAGGLES BRIGADE. Have children sit in a circle. Warm up with 1 round of "Beanbaggles-Go-Round." Then begin to introduce 1 additional beanbag each time they complete a round until you have 1 beanbag per child going around the circle. As children play, randomly call out "Change" to change direction. And see if they can keep the brigade going while standing up and sitting back down. Don't drop the Beanbaggles! (D 3–5 min.)

Farmer Gates
Complex Coordinated Movement

It's a busy day on the farm. Can you help the farmer move the sheep and the cows in and out of the barn?

EQUIPMENT
- Soft toy
- Squeaky toy
- Mirror
- Chair
- Ball
- Music

KEY BENEFITS
- Midline development
- Body awareness
- Coordination
- Laterality

LANGUAGE FOCUS
open, close, left, right

CRITICAL SAFEGUARDS
Ensure the floor is free from hazards when moving around with children.

TEACHING GEMS
- When directing children left and right, have an arrow pointing in the direction you want the children to move toward. When facing children, remember to show the opposite direction to what you call so children see it correctly.
- Help children visualize left and right by marking the sides of the body with different-colored stickers, such as red on the left and blue on the right.
- When children are opening and closing arms and legs together, look out for a motor overflow. Motor overflow is a natural, involuntary occurrence signaling that the midlines haven't fully matured and the brain is having difficulty with complex movement patterns. For instance, you may see the mouth mirroring the movement or the tongue sticking out. Or you may see another part of the body moving even when it's not involved in the required activity (such as both shoulders hunching at the same time or the left hand copying what the right hand is doing.) When you see this happening, simplify the activity. Start by isolating independent movements—just the arm or just the foot—until the movement pattern appears fluid, easy, and automatic for the child. Then add a second movement to build up to more complex movement patterns.

ON THE MOVE   WATCH ME GROW   IN THE KNOW

 Snugglers
MOVEMENT CUES. Feeling what it is like to have different parts of the body move in sync and in opposition helps program baby's brain for complex movement.

GOOD MORNING, FARM! Lay baby on his back. Lean over him and offer him your fingers to grasp. Say, "Good morning, sheep!" Very slowly and gently, bring his arms out to the side, then back to center. Now let's wake up the cows. Place your fingers on baby's ankles and gently push his legs apart and back together. "Good morning, cows!" (R 3–5 times each)

COWS AND SHEEP ON THE MOVE. Lay baby on his back. Gently move his right hand and left leg out to the side then back to center. Repeat with the other side. (R 3–5 times each)

SHEEP AND COW CROSSING. Lay baby on his back. Gently move his arms out to the side and back to the center, then cross the right hand over the left and return it to center. Repeat, this time crossing the left over the right. Repeat with the legs. (R 3–5 times each)

Squigglers

ON THE ROAD TO CRAWLING. Putting baby in a position where he can see, feel, and move his arms and legs in different ways prepares him for the more complex movement patterns to come.

DOUBLE DOORS. Stand holding baby against your chest facing out. Stand opposite another adult and baby. Put on some music and tap the babies' toes together. Line up the soles of their feet so they are gently pushing against each other. In that position, swing babies' legs out to the side with their feet still touching and return to center. Try it with 1 leg at a time, too. (R 3–5 times)

CATCH THE STRAY. Sit on the floor with baby between your legs. Open your legs and assist baby to open his. Place a soft toy (a cow if you've got one) between baby's legs. Together, close your legs and baby's, corralling the toy. ("Moo!") Then open the legs and let the cow loose. (R 3–5 times)

SQUEAKY GATE. Sit on the floor with baby between your legs. Place a squeaky toy under your leg. Now open baby's arms to the side and back to center. Squeak the toy with your leg as they close. *Squeak!* Repeat with baby's legs. *Squeak!* Then try the right arm and left leg simultaneously. *Squeak!* Repeat on the other side. (R 3–5 times each)

Scampers

TWO-SIDEDNESS. Exploring movements using 1 or both sides of the body works to develop the brain's full understanding of the body's many dimensions.

THE SPRING IS BROKEN. Sit on the floor with the child between your legs. Hold his hands and slowly open the arms to the side, then quickly spring them back to a clap in the center. Next, keeping the right arm stretched out in front, open only the left arm out to the side and spring back to a clap. Repeat to the right. Then repeat the same pattern with the legs. (R 3–5 times each)

THE LATCH IS BROKEN. Kneel behind baby while you both look into a mirror. Repeat "The Spring Is Broken" game, only this time bring the arms out quickly to the side and slowly back to center. Repeat with the legs. (R 3–5 times each)

HIGH GATES. Sit in a chair and stand the child on your feet, supporting him carefully around the waist. Open and close your legs slowly so his open and close with yours. Now open just your right leg to the side. Then the left. (R 3–5 times)

Stompers

LEFT AND RIGHT. Children learn to establish an understanding of left and right when they move their body and hear the language of direction at the same time.

CATCH THE STRAY 2. Sit the child facing you on the floor with each of your legs in the open position. Roll a ball toward him and encourage him to catch it with his legs. Work with him to trap the ball by closing his legs around it. (D 3–5 min.)

SHEEPDOGGING. Have the child stand opposite you. Tell him he's a sheepdog, and it's his job to catch the sheep (the ball). Roll a ball along the ground and encourage him to stop it any way he can. As he gains confidence with the game, have him try to stop the sheep with his feet, hands, knees, elbows, and so forth. (D 3–5 min.)

SLEEPY GATES. Have the child lie on his back on the floor. Explain that his arms and legs are like gates that can open and close. Kneel behind his head and explain that the object is to open and close whichever gate you call out and tap. Have him move both arms out to the side and back down (imagine the arms of a snow angel). Repeat with the legs. Then do both at the same time. Next, have him open just the right gates (right arm and right leg). Then the left. Be sure to give the child both a verbal and physical cue throughout the play. Do this activity slowly and quietly so he has time to absorb the sensations of isolated movement. (D 3–5 min.)

 ## Scooters

COORDINATED TEAMWORK. Working with others challenges children to coordinate their movements in dynamic context with others.

WHICH GATE? Have the child lie on his back on the floor. Kneel behind his head and explain that the object is to open and close whichever gate you tap. Start with 1 gate at a time and create random combinations, then try 2 gates at once. Now try it sitting up, which gives the brain an experience of a different orientation for these complex movements. Pair up children, having 1 child play the role of the tapper. Switch roles after a few minutes. (D 2–3 min.)

THROUGH THE GATES. Turn on some upbeat music. Have 2 children form a gateway by joining hands above their heads. The others form a line and go through the gates. As the line leader goes through the gates he joins up with the end of the line to keep the game going. Whenever the music stops, the gates close (arms drop to waist level), and the next 2 children in line become the gatekeepers. For more fun, have the children move in different ways through the gates (hop, jump, heel-to-toe walk). (D 2–3 min.)

THE REALLY BIG GATE. Have children hold hands and form 2 lines facing each other. Tell the children at one end to reach across and hold hands as well. (They are the gate's hinge!) On your cue, the children step backward to create a single, straight line (an open gate). Now reverse the process and close our really big gate, with the 2 children standing firm as the hinge. (R 3–5 times)

 ## Skedaddlers

When the midlines have been fully established and the concept of left and right is internalized, moving in a well-coordinated manner becomes easier and easier.

MOO AND BAA. Have children sit on the floor with their arms out in front of them. Tell them that their arms are the sheep gates and their legs are the cow gates. When you say, "Moo," children open both cow gates and keep them open until you moo again. When you say, "Baa," they open both sheep gates and keep them open until you baa again). (D 2–3 min.)

QUACK GATES. Repeat the "Moo and Baa" game to warm up. Then explain that a duck has come into the barnyard, and things are now going every which way! Each time you quack, the children must close and open their gates at the same time. (For instance, open the cow gates while closing the sheep gates.) Have them stop and hold that position (legs open, arms closed) for a few moments, then reverse the simultaneous movement—cow gates (legs) closing as sheep gates (arms) are opening. Work up to a pace at which children can do this fluidly. (D 3–5 min.)

ALL MIXED UP. Repeat "Moo and Baa" and "Quack Gates" as warm-ups, with legs as cow gates and arms as sheep gates. Then, explain that the cows and sheep are all mixed together in the same field, and children need to move them. First, have children open and close the left sheep gate and the right cow gate simultaneously. Then do the reverse, opening and closing the right sheep gate and left cow gate. Now really mix it up. Have children keep the right sheep gate open while they open the left cow gate and close the left sheep gate. Continue, having fun with all the possible combinations! (D 3–5 min.)

Put Your Tap Shoes On
Body Rhythm

The Quackities love dancing—especially tap dancing! It's so much fun to hear the tap-tap-tap in rhythm to the beat-beat-beat of the music. And when they really get going, look at them flap-flap-flap! What do you imagine it's like to be a tap-tap-tapping, flap-flap-flapping Quackity?

EQUIPMENT
- Small plastic bottles with secure lids
- Stones, rice, or beads
- Coins
- Glue
- Music
- Shoes
- Chalk or tape
- Rope
- Beanbags
- Bucket stilts
- Equipment for obstacle course
- Stickers

KEY BENEFITS
- Body rhythm
- Balance
- Body awareness
- Beat and rhythm exploration
- Midline development

LANGUAGE FOCUS
along, light, soft

CRITICAL SAFEGUARDS
- Coins are a choking hazard. Supervise children closely when coins are in use.
- Use a durable glue to secure the coins to the "Shake and Tap" shakers and to the toes and heels of shoes.

TEACHING GEMS
- Song lyrics and rhymes are on pages 195–196.
- **Beat:** Think of *beat* as the master timekeeper for a musical piece. It is the constant pulse that runs throughout the music.

- **Rhythm:** *Rhythm* is the actual pacing of the note values. Rhythm tells the story of the music. For example, the rhythm for the "Quackity Tap" song is *da-da-da-DAH*.
- To make "Shake and Tap" shakers, half-fill some small empty plastic bottles with stones, rice, or beads. Secure the tops firmly and glue a coin underneath each bottle.
- To make tap shoes, securely glue a penny to the heel and toe of children's shoes.
- To make bucket stilts, drill two holes in the bottoms of 2 identical plastic buckets. Thread rope through the holes to make handles. Knot the rope to secure it in the holes, making sure that the rope handles are the same length on each stilt. Children stand with 1 foot on each overturned bucket bottom and hold the ropes tightly as they walk.

ON THE MOVE

WATCH ME GROW

IN THE KNOW

Snugglers
BEAT COMES NATURALLY. Babies are accustomed to the steady beat of their mother's heart. In the early years, sound combined with touch builds on that innate knowledge.

BEAT AND RHYTHM MASSAGE. Lay baby on the floor and get close to her. Sing "Quackity Tap" or your favorite song and very gently use your fingertips to tap the steady beat of the song down baby's arms, tummy, and legs. Next time, tap out the rhythm. (D 2–3 min.)

PFFT MASSAGE. Hum "Quackity Tap" or your favorite silly song while blowing raspberries on baby's skin, "*pfft*ing" to the beat. Move in patterns—for instance, from head to toe, from her tummy out to her fingertips, or in circles. Next time, "*pfft*" to the rhythm. (D 2–3 min.)

FIVE LITTLE DUCKS. Sit baby in your lap and recite the classic "Five Little Ducks" nursery rhyme (see page 196). As the 5 ducks go out to play, walk your fingers to the beat up and over her tummy and out of sight. When only 4 come back, walk 4 fingers up and over her tummy back to where you started. Repeat, going up and down her legs or arms. (D 2–3 min.)

Squigglers

MUSICAL BEAT AND RHYTHM help baby get in sync with you and her environment.

QUACKITY TAP. Hold baby securely in your lap facing you. Sing "Quackity Tap" or your favorite song while gently bouncing her to the beat. Sing "Quackity Flap" and flap baby's arms out to the side to the beat. Repeat, using the rhythm of the song. (D 2–3 min.)

QUACKITY CLAP. Sit baby on your lap facing you. Sing "Quackity Snap" and march your knees up and down to the beat. Next, hold baby's hands and sing "Quackity Clap," clapping her hands together on the beat. Repeat using the rhythm of the song. (D 2–3 min.)

THE QUACKITIES. Sit baby on your knee. Sing all 5 of the Quackities songs. "Quackity Tap": Hold baby's feet and sing at a fast pace, marching her legs to the beat. "Quackity Flap": Hold baby's arms out and flap. "Quackity Snap": Slow down the beat a bit, and rock baby back and forth. "Quackity Clap": Hold her hands and clap to the beat. "Quackity Nap": Slow the beat way down, rocking baby to the beat as you sing. (D 2–3 min.)

Scampers

BEAT AND RHYTHM. While beat creates a sense of unity between the child and her world, rhythm opens the door to her own unique interpretation.

SHAKE AND TAP. Give the child 1 "Shake and Tap" shaker for each hand. Put on some music and tap and shake—up high, down low, fast, and slow. (D 2–3 min.)

THE TAP-TOGETHER TAP. Sit the child opposite you. Hold 1 "Shake and Tap" shaker and give the other to the child. Tap the bottoms of the bottles together (coin to coin). Put on some music and tap away! Tap up high, down low, to the side, fast, slow, etc. (D 2–3 min.)

TAP TIME. Tape and shake all over the room. Put on some music and groove to the beat, using your "Shake and Tap" shakers. Encourage the child to explore tapping in her own way. Tap bottles together, tap on the floor, on the walls, and so on. Make as much noise as you like while exploring beat and rhythm! (D 3–5 min.)

Stompers

SOUND-MAKING MOVEMENT. Using as many senses as possible gives children comprehensive messages about how to use their bodies.

TAP SHOES. Find a smooth, hard floor for this game. Have or help children put on their tap shoes. Turn on some high-energy music and encourage children to discover the sounds they can make with their feet. Make up a dance and practice it loudly! (D 5–10 min.)

A CHORUS LINE. Have the children put on their tap shoes and stand in a line. Put on some high-energy music and show them how to stomp or jump to the beat. Encourage them to listen to themselves all tapping at the same time. For advanced play, have half the children jump on the first beat, the other half jump on the second beat (jump-listen-jump-listen). (D 3–5 min.)

THE HEEL-TOE TAP. With chalk or tape, make a line on a smooth, hard floor surface as a visual guide. Have the children put on their tap shoes. Put on some high-energy music and have them walk the length of the line listening for their taps. Next, have them tiptoe down the line, listening for the differences. Next, have them walk on their heels. For advanced play, have them walk heel-to-toe, being sure to make deliberate steps to hear their taps. (D 5–10 min.)

Scooters

LAYERING CHALLENGES. Automated movements such as walking become the springboard for acquiring new physical capabilities.

TIGHTROPE WALKING. Lay a rope on the floor in a straight line to act as your tightrope. Explore all the ways to walk a tightrope (heel-to-toe, tippy-toes, heel walking, sideways, backward, twirling, arms out, arms at the sides, holding hands with a partner), trying to stay on the rope at all times. Now turn on some music and walk the tightrope to the beat. (D 5–10 min.)

PERFECT POSTURE. Place a beanbag on each child's head. Using airplane arm wings, have them walk the tightrope one by one trying to stay on the rope while keeping the beanbag on their head. Encourage children to look up and focus on you as they walk the tightrope. Next, turn on some slow-tempo music and have them try to walk the tightrope to the beat, first without the beanbag and then with it on their heads. (R 3–5 times)

STILT WALKING. Show children how to walk on bucket stilts. Then, one by one, have them straddle the tightrope, walk the length, turn, and walk back. Next, have them try walking backward. Then turn on some music and have children dance their way on stilts down the line to the beat! For advanced play, assist children to crosswalk over the rope. (D 5–10 min.)

Skedaddlers

GETTING IN SYNC. Learning to develop your own body rhythm becomes more complex when others are involved.

MUSICAL MOTORY. Set up an obstacle course (see page 134) and put on some music. Have the child run the course. When the music stops, she has to freeze wherever she is and only begin again when the music starts. Great for pairs or teams as well. Change up the course and play again. (D 2–3 min. per round)

DOUBLE DRUMMER. Pair up children. Have them stand facing each other. Put on some music and call out a body part (such as shoulder). Each child has to gently tap the shoulder of her partner to the beat of the music. Call out another body part (such as knee). While continuing to tap the shoulder, children also have to tap their partner's knee. Continue to call out body parts in a row and have the "drummers" try to keep up with the beat of your callouts. (D 3–5 min.)

TRIPLE DRUMMER. Repeat the "Double Drummer" game, only this time with 3 children facing one another. Put stickers on their left hands so they remember left from right. Put on some music and call out a body part and direction (such as shoulder-left and elbow-right.) As the drummers drum to the beat of the song, continue calling out new instructions. (D 3–5 min.)

Food Fight
Judging External Distance and Timing

It's dinnertime and Mama Bird's babies are waiting in the nest. And they are hungry! As Mama Bird flies overhead, the babies are all excited. *Peep! Peep!* Mama Bird better time things just right or the babies will start a fight!

EQUIPMENT

- Objects to make mobiles
- Bubbles
- Music
- Feathers
- Plastic spoons or flyswatters
- Hoops
- Beanbags
- Rope
- Chair
- Swing
- Balls
- Sturdy boxes or other barriers

KEY BENEFITS

- Timing
- Judging distance
- Temporal awareness
- Decision making
- Eye-hand-foot coordination

LANGUAGE FOCUS

stop, go, now

CRITICAL SAFEGUARDS

- Adult supervision is required for all play and games with mobiles, bubbles, and feathers to ensure that they do not go in a child's mouth or eyes.
- Handheld mobiles require adult supervision at all times.

SARAH WHITING

TEACHING GEMS

To make your own handheld mobile, tie ribbons to child-safe shiny objects, then tie the ribbons to a dowel or stick so they dangle.

ON THE MOVE	WATCH ME GROW	IN THE KNOW

 ### Snugglers
EARLY EYE MUSCLE DEVELOPMENT builds the tools the child will need later for eye-hand coordination.

LOOK! SHINY OBJECTS. Lay baby on his back and dangle a handheld mobile approximately his arm's-length distance from his eyes. Slowly twirl the mobile around, stopping at each shiny object to encourage his eyes to fixate. (D 1–2 min.)

TOUCH! SHINY OBJECTS. Lay baby on his back and dangle a handheld mobile above him, just out of his reach. Twirl it so he can focus on each object. Move it down closer to him so he can reach for the objects. Pull it away slowly so his eyes have time to practice focal range. (D 2–3 min.)

SHINY OBJECTS EVERYWHERE. Lay baby on his back and dangle a handheld mobile above him to attract his eyes. Slowly move it to his left and watch to see his eyes follow. Move it slowly side to side and up and down to allow his eyes full range of motion. If he's tipping himself as he follows, encourage or assist him to roll over. (D 2–3 min.)

Squigglers

BUBBLE WATCHING. Indoors or out, bubbles are ideal for early eye tracking. They glisten and glide slowly, allowing the eyes to keep up. Later, they move at just the right pace for little crawlers and walkers to catch.

BUBBLE WATCHING. Lay baby on the floor on his back and blow bubbles within his field of vision. Watch to see his eyes and hands track with them. Repeat, laying baby on his tummy. This is great outside on the grass, too. (D 3–5 min.)

BUBBLE CATCH. Sit baby on the floor and sit down facing him. Blow bubbles toward the floor, then up above his head. Blow bubbles to his left and right. Get behind him and blow bubbles over his shoulders. As he begins to reach and move for them, stand back and blow bubbles to him so he gets the sense of an object in motion moving toward him. (D 2–3 min.)

BUBBLE SPLAT. With baby sitting on the floor, blow bubbles out of his reach to encourage him to crawl after them and "splat" them. Blow bubbles within his reach. Show him how to clap the bubbles to splat them. Then, catch a bubble on your hand and encourage him to splat it! High five! *Note:* Be sure to wipe baby's hands after the activity to avoid getting soap in his mouth. (D 2–3 min.)

Scampers

FEATHERS FLYING. Like bubbles, feathers move at a child's pace, making tracking, chasing, and catching within their reach.

FEATHER FLOAT AND CATCH. Sit the child on the floor. Put on some music with a slow beat and sit with him. Place feathers on different parts of his body and blow them up in the air. Encourage him to crawl or pull up to catch them. Put feathers on yourself and repeat the game. (D 3–5 min.)

FEATHER PIE. Sit with the child on the floor and give him a plastic spoon or flyswatter. Put a large pile of feathers in front of him and start mixing up your "feather pie." See how high you can get the feathers to fly. (D 3–5 min.)

FEATHER DUSTER. Sit with the child on your lap or on the floor so that he can see you. Hold a feather up for him to see, then slowly bring it close. "Dust" his nose, cheeks, forehead, ears, neck, and hands. Next, give him the feather and encourage him to "dust" himself—and you. (D 3–5 min.)

Stompers

TIMING IS EVERYTHING. Learning to judge when and how to react does more than build the body. It's preparing the brain with important cues for anticipation, estimation, and prediction.

ROLL AND CHASE. Show the children how a hoop rolls. Then roll it for them and have them take turns chasing after it. If a child catches it, have everyone call out, "Boom!" Next, work with the children to show them how to roll a hoop for themselves. Once they've mastered it, have them pair up and take turns rolling and chasing. "Boom! Boom!" (D 10–15 min.)

HERE COMES MAMA BIRD! Give the child a beanbag. Lay a hoop on the floor in front of him. Explain that the hoop is the baby bird in its nest waiting for Mama Bird to arrive home with worms for dinner. Show him how to drop the beanbag into the hoop. Next, slowly slide the hoop from side to side in front of him, keeping your pace even and slow. Explain that when you say, "Peep," he should drop the beanbag (the worm) into the hoop. (R 5–10 times)

JUMP THE NEST. Tie one end of a rope to a chair. Put the chair in the middle of the play area. Have children form a circle around the chair. Tie the other end of the rope to your own ankle. Circle around the group slowly like Mama Bird. As the rope comes their way, they have to step on it. Gradually increase your pace in accordance with children's ability to gauge the timing. (D 3–5 min.)

Scooters

PENDULUM PLAY. Giving children experiences with the slow, steady, predictable pace of a playground swing gives them a chance to practice their timing while in motion, without having to think about moving their bodies, too.

LUNCHTIME. Place a hoop on the ground under a playground swing. Help the child lie on his tummy on the swing so he's facing the hoop. Give him a beanbag to hold. When he's ready, gently swing the child front and back. Keep your pace even and slow. Explain that when you say, "Peep!" he should drop the beanbag into the hoop. (R 3–5 times)

SNACK TIME. Repeat "Lunchtime," only this time place 2–3 different-colored hoops under the swing (fruits, vegetables, and yummy worms for the baby birds). Give the child 1 beanbag and call out a color to aim for. Keep your pace even and slow. Explain that when you say, "Peep!" he should drop the beanbag into that colored hoop. Encourage him to try it without your cue. (R 3–5 times)

DINNERTIME. Repeat the "Snack Time" game, only this time place 3 different colored hoops under the swing and give the child 3 beanbags in colors that match the hoop colors. Keep your pace even and slow. Pick a color and explain that when you say, "Peep!" he should drop that colored beanbag into that colored hoop. Encourage him to try it without your cue. (R 3–5 times)

Skedaddlers

JUDGING DISTANCE AND TIMING. Temporal awareness lays the groundwork for analysis, anticipation, and prediction.

OUT TO LUNCH. Define a play area and scatter 8 balls of the same color around the space. Have the children stand outside the play area and give each child a different-colored ball. The object of the game is for children to roll their ball into 1 of the other balls, trying to knock it out of the play area. Each time a child hits a ball, shout out, "Peep!" (D 5–10 min.)

LUNCH LINE. Mark off a lunch line on the floor or blacktop to resemble a bowling lane. Select 2–3 children to stand at either end of the lane. These are the Mama Birds trying to feed the babies. Assign each Mama Bird a different-colored ball. Then have the rest of the children line up along the lunch line with a variety of different colored beanbags. These are the Lunchies trying to steal lunch. When a Mama Bird bowls her ball up or down the lane, the Lunchies throw their beanbags at the ball to knock it off course. To add challenge, set a rule that it only counts when someone hits a ball with a matching-colored beanbag. Switch roles each time a ball gets knocked out. (D 10–15 min.)

FOOD FIGHT. The baby birds are big and strong now and ready to leave the nest. Set up a running lane. Scatter several sturdy boxes or other similar barriers along the lane. Have the children line up along one side of the running lane. Give them balls and hoops to roll across the lane. Select a runner to start. The object of the game is for each runner to navigate the traffic of rolling balls, hoops, and other children to make it to the end of the lane. Standing on a box is a safe zone for the runner. *Note:* Starting the children all on 1 side requires them to chase after their own ball or hoop—great huff-and-puff play for all! Switch roles. (D 20–30 min.)

The Beanbaggles Juggle
Sequential Movement

The Beanbaggles are just learning how to play games, and there's one they'd really like to try. Can you show the Beanbaggles how to juggle?

EQUIPMENT
- Beanbags of varying colors and designs
- Basket
- Music
- Rope
- Plank
- Bucket
- Hoops
- Timer

KEY BENEFITS
- Rhythm
- Timing
- Body awareness
- Opposition movement
- Sequential movement

LANGUAGE FOCUS
side, front, back

CRITICAL SAFEGUARDS
When balancing on uneven structures or surfaces, ensure that children are supported and supervised at all times.

TEACHING GEMS
- Ensure that the beanbag fits snugly into the child's hand so she has a comfortable open grip around the center of it. Be sure to select beanbags that are firmly stuffed with beans.
- When children are using different parts of the body during play, reinforce the learning by verbalizing the name of that part (elbow, knee, and so on).

SARAH ALICE LEE

ON THE MOVE | **WATCH ME GROW** | **IN THE KNOW**

Snugglers

EXPLORING TEXTURES stimulates baby's sense of touch, sharpening an essential learning tool.

ROUND AND ROUND THE GARDEN. Lay baby on her back where she can see you. Play the traditional "Round and Round the Garden" fingerplay (see page 196) with her hands, feet, tummy, knees, and so forth. (D 2–3 min.)

THE BEANBAGGLES HANDSHAKE! Lay baby on her back where she can see you. Put a beanbag in each of baby's hands. Encourage her to squeeze and explore. Then hold baby's hands and clap the beanbags together. Next, place a beanbag under baby's knees and gently squeeze so she feels the texture. Repeat with the elbows and feet. (D 2–3 min.)

BEANBAGGLES DISAPPEARING ACT! Lay baby on her back where she can see you. Put a beanbag on your head and make funny faces. Then lean forward and drop it into your hand so she can't see it anymore. "Ta-da!" Continue play, encouraging her to reach and take the beanbag off your head. Try it on her head, too. (D 3–5 min.)

Squigglers

FLOOR TIME is more fun when you're down there with baby.

BEANBAGGLES SLEDDING. Lay baby on her tummy on a shiny floor. Skid beanbags along the floor across her field of vision. Then skid them toward and away from baby. Assist baby to try to skid them, too. (D 3–5 min.)

BEANBAGGLES OVERLOAD. Sit with baby on the floor with a pile of beanbags. Assist her to pick up the beanbags and put them in a basket. Fill it up as much as you can, then work with baby to tip it over and start again. (D 3–5 min.)

BEANBAGGLES TAXI. With baby on all fours, put a beanbag on her back. Now get on all fours with your own beanbag. Together, crawl toward a basket. When you "deliver" your beanbags, show them to baby and show her how to drop them into the basket. (R 3–5 times)

Scampers

EARLY LEFT AND RIGHT EXPERIENCES give the child a sense of how both sides of her body can work together.

BEANBAGGLES BOCCE. Sit down on the floor beside the child with a pile of beanbags. Choose a target and place 1 beanbag a few feet away from it. Show her how to skid or roll the beanbag toward the target. Assist her to play, encouraging her to use both hands separately and together. (D 3–5 min.)

BEANBAGGLES BACK AND FORTH. Sit on the floor in front of the child with a beanbag. Pass the beanbag to her and encourage her to pass it back. As you play, inch back a little at a time so she has to stretch to pass it to you. Drop it in between you to encourage her to reach. Toss it toward her. Encourage her to try to do what you do. Be sure to pass with both hands. (D 3–5 min.)

BEANBAGGLES BOP. With the child standing or sitting, put on music with a strong beat. Give her 1 beanbag and show her how to pass it from her right hand to her left to the beat of the music. Next, show her how to throw it in the air. Watch where it lands and go get it to play some more. See if you can get her to throw it toward you. (D 3–5 min.)

Stompers

BALANCE underpins coordination, both necessary components to moving reliably in sequential steps.

BEANBAGGLES CHARM SCHOOL. Lay out a rope on the floor. Place a beanbag on each child's head and encourage the children to walk the line, 1 at a time, without dropping the beanbag. Have them try walking forward, backward, and sideways. Then have them try it balancing 2, 3, or more beanbags at a time. For more challenge, try it on a slightly elevated plank. (R 3–5 times)

BEANBAGGLES BALANCE. This is best done barefoot. Have each child stand with both feet on a single beanbag. See how long children can keep their balance without falling off. Next, have them stand with their arms at their sides, with 1 eye shut, with both eyes shut, crouching, and so on. Mark their times on their PB charts (see page 28) so they can track their progress. (R 3–5 times each way)

BEANBAGGLES WALKING. This is best done barefoot. Lay out a line of different-colored beanbags. Encourage children to walk along the pathway without falling off. Next, encourage them to step only on a specific-colored beanbag. For added challenge, spread the beanbags a bit farther apart. (R 3–5 times)

Scooters

ONE STEP AT A TIME is the trick to all early learning and to the ability to build up to sequential movement—and thinking.

BEANBAGGLES GO A-FLYING. Lay out beanbags along a wide plank. One by one, encourage children to walk across the plank, kicking the beanbags off the plank as they go. Have them use the right foot to kick the beanbag to the left and the left foot to kick to the right. (R 3–5 times)

BEANBAGGLES GLOBETROTTERS. Show children how to pass a beanbag under their knee. Let them practice until this movement is fluid and reliable. Next, 1 child at a time, show them other passing tricks: under the arm, around the neck, and of course, all the way around the torso. (R 5–10 times) Once they've mastered 1 or more tricks, have them try doing the trick while walking on a wide plank.

UPSIDE-DOWN-AROUND BEANBAGGLE BALL. Give children 5 different-colored beanbags and have them stand a short distance from a bucket. Encourage them to shoot all 5 into the bucket. Next, keeping the distance the same, have them turn around, lean down, and shoot the beanbags through their legs. For added challenge, try two beanbags at once. (R 3–5 tries each)

Skedaddlers

SEQUENTIAL MOVEMENT PATTERNS work to develop important "superhighways" in the brain for complex movement and even more complex thinking and reasoning.

BEANBAGGLES TOSS. Lay out different-colored beanbags randomly along a wide plank. Alongside the plank, lay out matching-colored hoops. Have the children take turns crossing the plank as you (or the other children) call out a color. The child on the plank picks up that colored beanbag and tosses it into its matching hoop. The object is to clear the plank of all the beanbags. (R 3–5 times)

BEANBAGGLES KNEEBAGS. Give children 1 beanbag each and have them balance it on one knee. Once they've got their balance in order, have them flip it off the knee. Next, have them try bouncing it 1 or 2 times on their knee without dropping it. Then have them try it on the top of the foot. (D 10–15 min.)

THE BEANBAGGLES JUGGLE. In the tradition of classic Japanese Otedama (similar to jacks, using beanbags), line up 5 beanbags in front of children on the floor. Have children take turns playing. The object of the game is to always have 2 or more beanbags in the air at the same time. Have a child start by throwing 1 beanbag high in the air, and then try to throw the next beanbag up before the first hits the ground. The goal is for children to keep going as long as they can and keep track of how many they have airborne at a time so they can better their score next time. (D 10–15 min.)

Hopper Frog
Complex Coordinated Movement:
Learning to Skip

Hopper Frog skips across the pond. Gosh, he is hard to keep up with!

SARAH ALICE LEE

EQUIPMENT
- Soft toy
- Small, soft balls
- Parachute
- Blankets
- 3" plastic balls
- Adhesive dots
- Rope

KEY BENEFITS
- Skipping
- Midline development
- Balance
- Sophisticated movement

LANGUAGE FOCUS
forward, backward, on

CRITICAL SAFEGUARDS
When balancing on uneven structures or surfaces, ensure that children are supported and supervised at all times.

TEACHING GEMS
- Song lyrics on are on page 196.
- Hopping is a prerequisite for skipping.

- When children are free skipping, ensure that the toe lands first.
- Skipping is one of the most difficult locomotive skills for children to develop and master. Regular practice is necessary to master this skill, so take your time and feel free to go back and forth among the activities in this sequence to build skill and muscle memory.

ON THE MOVE

WATCH ME GROW

IN THE KNOW

 ### Snugglers
LEG AWARENESS. For a child, understanding that he has legs and that legs have power is one of the first steps on the road to moving on his own.

TADPOLE TANGO. Lay baby on his back on a flat surface and place a small soft toy between his knees. Gently squeeze his knees together. Keeping his knees and feet together, slowly raise them up, around, and back down. *Ribbit.* (D 2–3 min.)

TADPOLE OOPS! Sit baby in your lap facing away from you. Place a small soft ball between his ankles. Squeeze his ankles together, then move them apart, and watch the ball drop. Repeat between his knees. *Ribbit.* (D 2–3 min.)

MY FIRST BOING! Lay baby on his back and put your hands on the soles of his feet. Press gently down and feel him resist the pressure. Next, press a soft toy or foam ball on the soles. When you feel the resistance, let go of the toy and watch it fly! *Boing. Boing.* (D 3–5 min.)

 ### Squigglers
LOWER-BODY STRENGTH and control are quite literally the foundations for complex movement.

TADPOLE TURN. Lay out a parachute or blanket on the floor (the frog pond). Place baby on his back in the middle of the pond. Hold the edges of the parachute and slowly walk in a circle. Repeat with baby on his tummy. *Ribbit.* (D 2–3 min.)

TADPOLE ROCK AND ROLL. Roll up a blanket to act as your log. Lay it on top of the parachute (pond). Position baby on all fours over the log. Supporting him around the waist, rock him gently back and forth and side to side on the log. *Ribbit.* (D 2–3 min.)

MY FIRST FLY CATCHER. Lay out a parachute on the floor and scatter 3" plastic balls (the flies) on the top. Lay baby in the middle of the pond on his tummy. Wiggle the edges of the pond to scatter the balls and encourage baby to reach, chase, and catch his first flies. *Ribbit. Burp!* (D 3–5 min.)

Scampers

LET'S GET MOVING. Efficient and effective movement depends on coordinated action involving every part of the body and brain.

HOPPER FROG. Sit the child on your knee facing you. Give him a knee ride, gently bouncing up and down while singing the "Hopper Frog" song. *Ribbit.* Sing it again and bounce him from 1 knee to the other. *Ribbit. Ribbit.* (R 2–3 times)

BOING! BOING! With the child on all fours, lift him up by the waist a few inches off the ground and gently bounce him *(boing, boing)* up and down while singing the "Hopper Frog" song. (R 2–3 times)

OFF THE WALL. Clear away some floor space near a wall. Have the child sit down facing the wall, lie back, and put his feet up on the wall. Count, "Boing, boing, boing!" On the third *boing*, have him push himself backward. See how far he can slide! Mark his distance and try again. (R 5–10 times)

Stompers

JUMPING. Coordinating the body to leave the ground is a prerequisite to skipping.

MY FIRST LILY PAD. Have each child stand on a spot on the floor and jump to the beat as you sing the "Hopper Frog" song. Next, have children jump only when they hear a *boing*. (D 2–3 min.)

JUMPING LILY PADS! Press dots on floor about a foot apart, making sure they are securely affixed so they don't slip. These are the lily pads. Have a child crouch down on 1 lily pad to start. Sing the "Hopper Frog" song and have him do 2-footed jumps through all the lily pads by the end of the song, then crouch back down. Have children take turns jumping from lily pad to lily pad. For added challenge, increase the distance between lily pads. (R 2–3 times)

HOPPER FROG STUBBED HIS TOE. Lay dots on the floor as in "Jumping Lily Pads!" Have a child crouch down on 1 lily pad to start. Sing the "Hopper Frog" song while he hops on 1 foot through all the lily pads. Have children take turns hopping on 1 foot from lily pad to lily pad. For added challenge, increase the distance between lily pads. (R 2–3 times)

Scooters

HOMOLATERAL MOVEMENT. One-sided movement is a stepping stone to establishing deliberate coordinated movement of the whole body.

HOPPER FROG GOES FOR A SWIM. Have children lie on their tummies with arms still at their sides. To swim like a frog, have them bend their knees up and out to the side as high as they can, then back down with ankles together. Now have them repeat the movement, using their feet to slide themselves along the floor. Repeat with children lying on their backs. (D 2–3 min.)

THREE-LEGGED FROG HOP. Work with 1 child to demonstrate how to do a 3-legged hop: He stands and bends down to put his hands on the floor. Then he lifts up 1 leg, moves his hands forward, and hops his other foot forward. After everyone tries and has the hang of that, have children take 1 hand off the floor and move forward—hand and hop. Finally, have them stand and hop on 1 foot. (D 5–10 min.)

HOP TAG. Play your favorite tag rules, only have children hop instead of run. To increase the challenge, hop only on lily pads (see "Jumping Lily Pads"). (D 5–10 min.)

Skedaddlers

AUTOMATION LEADS TO SOPHISTICATION. When children's physical skills are easy, the game takes over.

HOPPER FROG HOP. Pair up 2 children. Have them face each other with their hands on one another's shoulders. Count, "Boing, boing, boing!" On the third *boing*, have them hop on 1 foot together. Next, have 1 child hop forward while the other hops backward. Repeat, going the other way. Just how far can Hopper Frog hop? (D 3–5 min.)

LEARNING TO SKIP. Start by asking children to hop once in place. Next, show them how to hop once and step forward with the raised foot. Repeat to help them build up their rhythm, then switch to the other foot. Now put the 2 together: hop-step, hop-step. Practice free-form skipping until children flow easily with the movement. For the rest of the day or even the whole week, skip everywhere you go to give children lots of practice time.

SKIP TO THE POND. Lay out a large rope in a circle. Pair up children. Have them hold hands and skip around the rope while you sing "Skip to the Pond." (1) "Skip, skip, skip to the pond": Children skip in pairs around the rope. (2) "I'll find another frog jumpier than you": Children separate from their partner, jumping around to find a new partner. (3) "Skip to the pond": Children skip in a circle with their new partner. (4) "Higher than you": Children lose their partner and jump as high as they can to find another partner. (5) "Skip to the pond": Children skip in a circle with their new partner. (D 10–15 min.)

My First Volleyball
Eye-Everything Coordination and Control

SARAH WHITING

There's something you need to know about volleyballs. They don't like touching the ground! Can you spot the volleyballs as they're flying through the air and help keep them from touching the ground?

EQUIPMENT
- Beach balls
- Scarf
- Feathers
- Soft balls
- Floor fan
- String
- Flyswatters
- Tennis paddle or wide lightweight plastic bat
- Rope or net
- Cones or chairs
- Hoops
- Laundry basket
- Volleyballs

KEY BENEFITS
- Eye-everything coordination
- Positioning
- Stability
- Eye tracking

LANGUAGE FOCUS
over, up, on

CRITICAL SAFEGUARDS
- Be very careful whenever you're using string that it does not wrap around the child's neck or any other part of the body.
- When you're using a fan, supervise children closely so children do not hurt their fingers or toes or knock over the fan.

TEACHING GEMS
Always keep a beach ball on hand for a simple game wherever you are. See "Play Ball! The Basics of Throwing, Bouncing, Catching, and Kicking" (pages 196–198) for ideas on teaching and developing children's ball skills.

ON THE MOVE	WATCH ME GROW	IN THE KNOW

Snugglers
THE EYES HAVE IT. Playing games with slow-moving objects is the beginning of eye fitness.

EYE AND SEEK. Lay baby on her back and get close to her (8"–12" away). Make eye contact while you talk and sing to her. Then put your hands over your own eyes for a few moments. Call out to baby, "Where am I?" Then quickly lift your hands and say, "Here I am." (R 3–5 times)

EYE AND PEEK. Lay baby on her tummy and lie down opposite her. Roll a beach ball between you. When the beach ball blocks her view of you, call out to her, "Where am I?" When it rolls past, say, "Here I am!" Be sure to give baby time to rest between rolls. (R 2–3 times)

EYE ON THE PRIZE. Tie a scarf onto a beach ball and hold it directly above baby's head or just out of reach. Gently wiggle and bounce the ball to encourage her to reach for it. Move it to her left and right slowly to encourage eye tracking. (D 2–3 min.)

Squigglers
EYES AND HANDS. As baby becomes more physically independent, eyes and hands begin to work together.

BALL-A-BOO. Draw baby's attention to a colorful beach ball, then drape a sheer scarf over it. Wiggle the beach ball and encourage her to find it by pulling off the scarf. (R 3 times)

FEATHER SHOWERS. With baby sitting or lying down, throw a bunch of feathers in the air and encourage her to reach or commando-crawl (belly-crawl) for them. (D 5 min.)

BABY BALL. Gather several soft balls and sit with baby on the floor. Gently bat the balls in her direction so they are coming toward her from the front and left and right sides. Encourage her to bat at them. (D 2–3 min.)

Scampers

EYE-EVERYTHING COORDINATION begins to develop when it's needed—when the child is beginning to move independently.

FEATHER CLAP. Sit with the child in your lap. Throw a few feathers in the air. Hold her hands and together clap the feathers as they fall. Encourage her to try clapping the feathers on her own. (D 2–3 min.)

FEATHER FEET. This is best done barefoot. Sit the child between your legs and hold her feet. Throw a few feathers in the air and clap her feet together as the feathers fall. Encourage the child to try clapping or kicking the feathers with her feet on her own. (D 2–3 min.)

FLYAWAY FEATHERS. Set up a fan off to the side and scatter a bunch of feathers around the floor. As the child approaches the feathers, turn on a fan to stir them up. Encourage her to chase the flyaway feathers! (D 3–5 min.)

Stompers

EYE-HAND COORDINATION. The eyes are the body's best partners for ensuring accuracy, often showing us the direction we need to move.

BATABILITY. Tie a beach ball to a piece of string and hang it from the ceiling or doorway. In pairs, give each child a flyswatter or lightweight bat and have them stand on either side of the ball. Encourage them to bat the ball to each other as many times as they can. (D 3–5 min.)

BATAGILITY. Lay out rope as a track to follow. Weave it around 3 cones or other obstacles to create a zigzag pattern. Give each child a flyswatter. Taking turns, encourage children to "putt" a beach ball along the rope, around the cones, and back again. (And don't worry about putting outside the lines. They'll eventually get the hang of it!) (D 3–5 min.)

AIRTIME. Bat a beach ball up in the air and, together with the children, don't let the ball touch the ground. Once children have the hang of it, challenge them to keep the beach ball up in the air by batting it with other parts of the body (such as their knees or elbows). (D 3–5 min.)

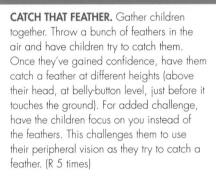 

Scooters

EYE-EVERYTHING CONTROL. To achieve automated, whole-body control, children have to learn how to simultaneously employ multiple tools in their physical toolkit.

CATCH THAT FEATHER. Gather children together. Throw a bunch of feathers in the air and have children try to catch them. Once they've gained confidence, have them catch a feather at different heights (above their head, at belly-button level, just before it touches the ground). For added challenge, have the children focus on you instead of the feathers. This challenges them to use their peripheral vision as they try to catch a feather. (R 5 times)

BALANCE THAT BALL. Give each child a flyswatter and place a small beach ball or feather on it. Have the children walk around the room while keeping the object balanced. Call out instructions, such as turn around, walk backward, and stop. Have the children try holding the flyswatter with both hands, then 1 hand a time. For added challenge, have them focus on you as they walk so that they're not watching their flyswatter. (R 5 times)

BOUNCE THAT BALL. Give each child a paddle or wide bat and balance a small beach ball on it. See how long the children can hold the ball steady. Next, show them how to *gently* bounce the ball on the end of the paddle. Encourage them to try bouncing the ball without letting it drop to the floor. When they have it mastered, scatter hoops along the floor and repeat the game, with children now trying to stay inside the hoop. (D 5–10 min.)

Skedaddlers

GETTING PHYSICALLY ORGANIZED. Moving the body to be at the right place at the right time requires control.

SCORE! Set up a goal using 2 cones or 2 chairs. Give each child a paddle or wide bat. Have them stand a few paces back and take turns batting a beach ball into the goal. Once they have confidence, change the starting point, moving it farther back to challenge their sense of distance, or off to the side to create different angles. (D 5–10 min.)

BUMPER BALL. Lay down a rope on the floor and pair up children (or form teams) on either side. As in volleyball, the object is to keep the ball in the air and bat it over the rope to the other team. Start by having the children use their hands. Once they have the idea, call out a different body part to use. For instance, have them use only their elbows, knees, feet, or bellies. Add extra beach balls for even more fun. (D 5–10 min.)

MY FIRST VOLLEYBALL. Repeat the "Bumper Ball" activity, only this time set up a tennis-style net or string a rope between 2 chairs waist high. As children master the game, raise the net until it is overhead and they're playing their first game of volleyball! (And remember, volleyballs don't like touching the ground!) (D 5–10 min.)

Finger Fun
Manipulative Play

Ten little fingers went out to play. When they got to the playground, they went every which way! Can you help teach 10 little fingers to work together? Because when we all work together, it's amazing what we can do.

EQUIPMENT

- Container for gloop
- Gloop (see recipe on page 198)
- Socks (variety of colors, textures, and sizes)
- Laundry basket
- Soft scarves
- Empty facial tissue box
- Nimble sticks (see page 49)
- Knucklebones (available at retail stores, or you can substitute anything that is small and flat on 2 sides, such as a flat stone, coin, or poker chip)
- Crinkles (crumpled balls of paper)

KEY BENEFITS

- Manipulation
- Dexterity
- Understanding force
- Fine-motor skills
- Eye-everything coordination

LANGUAGE FOCUS

up, in, on

CRITICAL SAFEGUARDS

- Ensure adult supervision at all times when creating and playing with gloop.
- Ensure there is a closed-lid container for knucklebones and that they are stored safely. Adult supervision is required at all times.
- Adult supervision is required at all times when playing with small parts with children under 3 or children who are still putting things in their mouths.

TEACHING GEMS

Song lyrics, rules for table football, and a recipe for gloop can be found on page 198.

ON THE MOVE   **WATCH ME GROW**   **IN THE KNOW**

Snugglers

FINGERPLAY. At first, babies don't realize their hands belong to them, so pay extra attention at playtime to give baby sensory experiences to awaken his awareness.

FIVE LITTLE FINGERS. Offer baby your finger to grasp. Slowly uncurl his fingers 1 at a time. Next, hold his hand palm up and very gently separate his fingers by putting your pinkie in between all of them. Repeat with both hands and feet. (D 2–3 min.)

BABY GRAND. As you sing baby's favorite song, hold his hand and gently manipulate his fingers as if he were tapping out the tune on piano keys. Play to the beat of the song. Try tapping his fingers on your face or kissing or blowing on each finger to the beat of the song. (D 2–3 min.)

FLAP AND CLAP. Hold baby's hands up and wave them in the air together while singing the classic song "If You're Happy and You Know It" (lyrics are on page 198). Clap baby's hands together on the beat. Try this with his legs and feet, too. (D 2–3 min.)

Squigglers

TACTILE PLAY builds the sense of touch along with muscle strength in the hands.

GLORIOUS GLOOP. Find a container and fill it with gloop. Sit on the floor where there's room to make a little mess and put baby between your legs. Assist him to put his hands into the gloop, squishing it through his fingers. Shake or clap hands to see the gloop fly. (D 5–10 min.) *Note:* Ensure adult supervision at all times.

SOCK BALLS. Tie socks of different sizes and colors together to make a variety of soft balls. Leave the ends loose for easy grasping. Explore the sock balls with baby. Put them in a laundry basket and then place the child in this "sock pit" for whole-body, sensory play. (D 5–10 min.)

THE VERY LONG SCARF. Tie several soft scarves together and tuck them into an empty facial tissue box, leaving 1 end sticking out slightly. Sit baby on the floor and show him how to pull on the scarf to make it come out. Work with him to continue pulling it all the way out. Next, show him how to put the scarf back in the box. (D 3–5 min.)

Scampers

FINGERPLAYS get the hands working together, and separately—preparing them for all the work and play to come.

SUNNY AND CLOUDY. Sing the "Sunny and Cloudy" song while you assist the child in this simple fingerplay: Open the fingers wide when it's sunny. Close the fingers into a fist when it's cloudy. Wave hello to Sunny, and clap Cloudy away! (R 2–3 times)

ITSY-BITSY'S DAY OUT. Sit the child in your lap or on the floor and introduce the "Itsy-Bitsy Spider" song and fingerplay. As you sing, show baby how to inch his fingers up the waterspout, wave the fingers down when it rains, and open his arms wide when the sun comes back out. Try this standing up so he engages with a whole-body experience. (D 2–3 min.)

SUNNY AND CLOUDY TAKE TURNS. Sit facing the child and sing the "Sunny and Cloudy" song. Hold up your hands and open them wide (Sunny). Encourage the child to mirror your movements on his own. High five! Close your hands into fists and encourage him to do the same (Cloudy). Fist bump! Open 1 hand, then the other. Close 1 hand, then the other. Try this standing, too. (D 2–3 min.)

 ## Stompers

EARLY MANIPULATIVE PLAY. From the youngest ages, children are learning to use their hands to manipulate objects. Objects with simple shapes provide enormous developmental benefit and fun when managed for optimal learning.

NIMBLE ROLLS. Have each child sit on the floor; put a nimble stick next to each. Show them how to roll the stick out to the side and back to their leg. Next, show them how to roll the stick forward and back. Repeat with both hands. (D 2–3 min.)

SUNNY AND CLOUDY DO THE NIMBLE. Have the children sit on the floor, each child holding the nimble stick vertically with both hands. Sing the "Sunny and Cloudy" song, rolling the stick between both hands to wave hello to Sunny. Tap the stick on the floor like a drumstick to "tap, tap, tap" Cloudy away! Repeat, holding the stick horizontally. (R 2–3 times)

EVERY WHICH WAY. Have the children sit on the floor; put a nimble stick on each side of them. Have them roll the sticks out away from their body and back with both hands at once. Then have them roll the sticks forward and back. Next, they repeat the activity using 1 hand at a time. Finally, have them roll in opposition: roll 1 stick forward while rolling the other stick to the back, then roll 1 stick out to the side while rolling the other back to the body. (D 3–5 min.)

 ## Scooters

MANIPULATIVE PLAY provides a platform for more complex controlled movement patterns that include dexterity, pressure, and force.

KNUCKLEBONES BOUNCE. Give each child 1 knucklebone (or a small flat stone, coin, or poker chip). Encourage children to explore it with their fingers to get a feel for its size and weight. Next, show them how to bounce it in their hand of choice, trying to keep it from falling. Now try it with the other hand. (R 5–10 tries)

KNUCKLEBONES PASS. Start with 1 knucklebone in each child's hand of choice. Have children pass it back and forth between their 2 hands, starting by clapping hands together and then gradually separating them so the knucklebone is "flying" between the hands. Next, have them put the knucklebone in 1 palm, then flip it over onto the back of the other hand and balance it there for a few seconds. (R 5–10 tries)

KNUCKLEBONES TWIST. Start with 1 knucklebone balanced on the back of each child's hand of choice. Show children how to flick it up in the air and catch it with their other hand. Next, starting with the knucklebone on the back of 1 hand, show them how to flick it in the air, twist the wrist, and catch it with the same hand. (R 5–10 tries)

Skedaddlers

FINGERS AS TOOLS. Nature's greatest gift to human ingenuity is the fingers—just look at what they can do! **Note:** These activities are trickier than they look, so take them in small steps and leave lots of time for practice.

POPPERS. Show children how to make the classic popper sound: (1) Put your index finger in your mouth and close your mouth around your finger. (2) Fill your cheeks with air so your cheeks stick out. (3) Push your finger against the inside of your cheek and pull it out. *Pop!* Let children give it a try and then repeat with the other hand and cheek. *Note:* This activity should be done with clean hands. (R 5 times)

SNAPPING. Teach children how to snap their fingers: Press the thumb and middle finger together very firmly. Then quickly slide and snap the fingers away from each other to create a snapping sound. Once children get the idea, have them try it with the other hand. (D 5–10 min.)

TABLE FOOTBALL. Get ready to play table football (see page 198) by showing the children how to flick! (1) Lock the second (index) finger underneath the thumb, forming a circle with the thumb and finger. (2) Firmly and quickly push the second finger against and past the tip of the thumb. Next, sit at a table and give each child a crinkle. Practice flicking the crinkle with no concern about aiming. Repeat with the other hand. Once the children have mastered the basics, create a goal for them to shoot at. And of course, once they have their aim down, pair them up and they're ready to play table football! (D 10–15 min.)

My First Rodeo
Learning to Change Direction

The rodeo's in town, so let's have a good old-fashioned hoedown—yeehaw!

EQUIPMENT
- Soft scarves
- Ribbons
- Mirror
- Stroller
- Hill (or pillows and gym mat)
- Cardboard tubes
- Board
- Small straight ladder
- Hats
- Rope
- High secure post
- Beanbags
- Frisbee
- Table
- Directional arrow
- Stickers

KEY BENEFITS
- Directionality
- Pacing
- Positioning
- Eye-everything coordination

LANGUAGE FOCUS
left, right, forward, back

CRITICAL SAFEGUARDS
- When carrying babies, ensure the floor is clear of things so you don't trip.
- Always supervise and then put away obstacles that a child could potentially fall on.

TEACHING GEMS
- If you don't have a hill, make one by stacking pillows and putting a gym mat or rug over the top.
- When facing children, remember to show the opposite direction to what you call so children see it correctly.

ON THE MOVE **WATCH ME GROW** **IN THE KNOW**

Snugglers

BODY CONTOURS. Discovering where one's body begins and ends is the starting point for learning that everything has a beginning and an ending.

TRAIL MAP. Give a 1-finger massage by "drawing" a continuous trail from the top of baby's head to her toes. Take different routes all over her body, but never take your finger off her skin. Talk about the sights you're seeing on the trail. "Oh, there's your knee!" (D 3–5 min.)

BANDANA WRAP. Wrap a soft scarf or ribbon around baby's tummy. Pull gently as the fabric unfurls around baby's body. Repeat around the arms and legs. (D 2–3 min.) *Note: Never wrap anything around a child's neck.*

GIDDYUP! Lean baby against you in front of a mirror so she can watch the fun. Use the tips of your fingers to "giddyup" around baby's body. Run your fingers up her arm and over to her nose. Then run down her chin and over to her fingers. Continue to change directions and talk about the sights you're seeing on the trail. Giddyup! (D 2–3 min.)

Squigglers

UNDERSTANDING 3-D. The world is a multidimensional place, and so even from the youngest ages, babies are already beginning to see and experience in 3-D.

LET'S RIDE. Even when baby is securely tucked in her stroller, she's learning about what movement feels like. During your walks, take time to explore movement—stroll fast and slow, stroll in circles, take sharp corners, zigzag, go uphill, go downhill. Talk about the direction you're taking. (R daily)

ON THE TRAIL. When you carry baby in your arms, you're giving her a preview of what independent movement will be like. Be deliberate in exploring different movement patterns: walk in circles, take sharp corners, zigzag, bob up and down, tilt and lean, and so on. (R daily)

TALL IN THE SADDLE. As baby can now hold herself upright independently, give her a view of the world from new heights. Carefully lift baby up on your shoulders and hold her securely around her waist. Move slowly and gently. As she becomes comfortable with the ride, add very gentle bouncing and turning. Giddyup! (D 2–3 min.)

Scampers

CHANGING TERRAIN. The world isn't flat. Simple props challenge children to discover and conquer variations in terrain.

PEEKABOO HILL. Take the child outside to a small mound or create a gentle incline (see page 169). Hide on the other side out of sight. As the child explores this new terrain, peek out and entice her to come find you. When the game is done, lay her down at the top of the incline and gently roll her back down. (D 5–10 min.)

MY FIRST RODEO. Lay several sturdy cardboard tubes together on the floor. Place a board on the top and lay the child on the board on her tummy. Hold onto the child's waist and slide the board forward and backward, rocking it gently. (D 3–5 min.)

CORRAL FENCE. Place a small ladder on its side on the floor and secure it so it doesn't tip. Place the child between the first rungs. Support her around the waist as she explores, crawling in and out of the rungs. (D 5–10 min.)

Stompers

TARGETING. In learning to aim and throw or kick, children are intuitively learning to make small adjustments in their use of speed, direction, and force.

HAT IN THE RING. Place several hats on the floor upside down (brims up). Circle the hats with rope and have the children stand outside the circle. Give the children lots of beanbags and tell them a target to shoot for. For instance, have them aim for the hat that is closest, the biggest hat, or the red hat. (D 3–5 min.)

HANG UP YOUR HAT. Set up a post in the middle of the room. Use the rope to create a circle around it and have the children stand outside the circle. Give 1 child a hat (cowboy hats work great for this, but any kind of hat will do), and have her aim and shoot to land her hat on top of the post. Allow several turns for each child. Next, have all the children aim and shoot at once to see if they can get more than 1 hat on the post together. Yeehaw! (R 5–10 times)

ROOTIN' TOOTIN' TOSS. Using a brimmed hat (such as a cowboy hat) or a Frisbee, show children how to throw sideways. Demonstrate the movement: bring your hand to your chest, pivot the wrist, and fling the hand forward. Then have children stand sideways next to a table and put 1 elbow on the table. Have them practice the motion by sliding their arm on the tabletop. Then show children how to hold a hat brim with their thumb on top and the other fingers underneath. Have them return to the table and practice flinging their hats across the tabletop. Practice with children as needed and then let them try it on their own until they're ready to "rootin' tootin' toss" without the table. (R 5–10 tries)

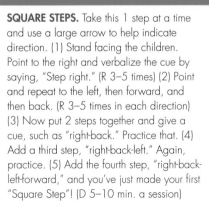

Scooters

PATTERNED MOVEMENTS. Physically experiencing patterns helps children internalize complex concepts through their senses, movement, and muscle memory.

SQUARE STEPS. Take this 1 step at a time and use a large arrow to help indicate direction. (1) Stand facing the children. Point to the right and verbalize the cue by saying, "Step right." (R 3–5 times) (2) Point and repeat to the left, then forward, and then back. (R 3–5 times in each direction) (3) Now put 2 steps together and give a cue, such as "right-back." Practice that. (4) Add a third step, "right-back-left." Again, practice. (5) Add the fourth step, "right-back-left-forward," and you've just made your first "Square Step"! (D 5–10 min. a session)

SHOULDER TO SHOULDER. Pair up the children and have them stand shoulder to shoulder facing in *opposite* directions from each other. Keeping their shoulders "glued" together, have them step forward and turn in a full circle back to their original position. Repeat several times, then have them circle around the other way by stepping backward. (D 5–10 min. per session)

SWING YOUR PARTNER. Form 2 lines with the children facing one another. Have them walk toward each other with right arms out. (Place a sticker on the right hand to make it easy for them to remember.) When they meet in the middle, have them hook arms and turn around 180 degrees, then unlock arms and return to their starting position. Repeat with left arms. Mix it up—have them turn 90 degrees to wind up on the other side, or turn around 2 times, then 3, 4, and 5. (D 10–15 min.)

Skedaddlers

OPPOSITE DIRECTIONS. Direction is about "my" orientation. Standing opposite helps children experience spatial orientation in new ways.

DO-SI-DO. Form 2 lines with the children facing one another. Have them walk toward each other, step to the right of their partner, and stop. (Children are now next to each other facing in different directions.) Now show them how to do-si-do: step forward, step to the right (behind your partner), then step back so they're now on the other side of their partner. Repeat until the children have mastered the move, then try it from the left. When they have it all under control, have them step backward to their original position after the do-si-do. (D 5–10 min.)

HOWDY, PARDNER. Have children stand in a circle with 1 child facing left, the next facing right, the next left, the next right, and so forth—in other words, each child is facing a partner. Tell them to hold out their right hands, shake hands, and then walk past the partner, letting go of right hands. To greet the next partner, have them hold out left hands and repeat the move. Keep going until you get all the way around the circle. Repeat going the other way. (D 5–10 min.)

HOEDOWN. Now put it all together! Put on some country music and call out the different dance steps children have learned. Be guided by the children. If they're struggling with a dance step, move on to another one. Keep the dance moving, even if children don't have it perfected. The point of a hoedown is high fun! (D 10–15 min.)

SARAH WHITING

Traffic Jam
Pacing: Changing Speed and Stopping

Traffic jams can be very sticky when drivers don't follow the rules of the road. Let's see if we can unstick this sticky traffic jam!

EQUIPMENT
- *Optional:* beach ball
- Beanbag
- Adhesive dots
- Hoop
- Rope
- Traffic-light cards (see Teaching GEMs)
- Tape or chalk
- Stop sign or flag
- *Optional:* gym mat
- Whistle

KEY BENEFITS
- Pacing and timing
- Role play
- Body rhythm
- Cooperation
- Body control

LANGUAGE FOCUS
stop, go, wait

CRITICAL SAFEGUARDS
When lifting young children into the air, be sure to bend your knees and tighten your abdomen to protect your back. Take a wide stance for stability.

TEACHING GEMS
• When moving a child incrementally, take regular stops along the way. Use the language of stop and go when the child is physically experiencing it.

• When children are working in pairs, help them vary their speed by putting a beach ball between their shoulders, hips, tummies, or knees.
• Make traffic-light cards to vary speed: green for go, yellow for slow, and red for stop.

ON THE MOVE **WATCH ME GROW** **IN THE KNOW**

 ## Snugglers
SENSATIONS OF MOVEMENT. Experiencing moving through space at speed gives baby his first experience of varying pace.

GLIDER. Hold the child close (at home, parents can do this skin-to-skin) against your chest, supported. Pretend you are ice-skating and glide around the room. Let your heartbeat provide the natural rhythm. Stop and start very gently. (D 2–5 min.)

HELICOPTER. Support baby under his chest and legs so that he is lying flat on his tummy in your arms. Hold him slightly away from your body with his feet toward you. Like a helicopter, keep him in this horizontal position and gently lower him down and hover over the floor. Slowly turn in circles. Then gently lift him back up. Repeat, only this time hold baby with his head toward you, fly the helicopter gently up overhead, and make eye contact. (D 2–5 min.)

JET PLANE. Hold baby in the same position as in the "Helicopter" activity. This time, bend your knees and lower him to the ground, ready for takeoff. Gently swoop him up from a horizontal to vertical position. Slowly turn in circles, then swoop back down low. *Zoom!* (D 2–5 min.)

Squigglers

START-STOP. Incremental moves give baby the opportunity to experience the difference between moving and being still.

DUMP TRUCK. Lay baby facing you in your arms. Support him under his back with one hand and wrap your other arm securely around his hips. For fun, put a beanbag on his tummy. In a ratchet-style movement (start-stop), tip his feet to the floor to "dump" his load, and slowly bring him back to horizontal. (D 2–3 min.)

FORKLIFT. Sit on the floor with baby in your lap facing away from you. Put his legs on your legs. Ratchet your right leg up in a start-stop motion—this lifts his leg, too. Alternate left and right. Supporting baby, roll back and lift both legs in the air. (D 2–5 min.)

AIRCRAFT CARRIER. Hold baby in your arms lying on his tummy with his head away from your body. Keep him slightly away from your body. Move quickly around the room on your approach to the "aircraft carrier" (couch, chair, or bed). Zoom in for a landing, stopping quickly. Now try a speedy takeoff and fly around the room again. (R 5 times)

Scampers

THRUST. The feeling of sudden thrust gives children the experience of speed and power.

DOCKING. Sit facing the child and hold him around the chest at arm's length. Count down to docking: 5, 4, 3, 2, 1—then quickly pull him close and give him a hug! (R 3–5 times)

BOBBING BLASTOFF. Assist the child into a crouching position on the floor. Holding him there, count down to blastoff, bobbing him slightly up and down: 5, 4, 3, 2, 1—blast-off! Hold him securely under the arms and gently lift him high in the air. *Whee!* Return to your launching pad for another liftoff. (R 3–5 times)

MOONWALKING. Put a few dots around the floor; these are your moon craters. In superslow motion, pick the child up under his arms and very slowly glide him up into the air and back down to a moon crater. Touch down and quickly bounce back up. Glide very slowly to the next crater and bounce right back up again. (D 2–3 min.)

Stompers

SPEED MANAGEMENT. Mastering deliberate control of their speed leads children to full body control.

YELLOW LIGHT. Have the children practice moving like different kinds of transportation (car, train, plane, bicycle, and so forth). When they're ready, hold up the yellow-light card and have them move as slowly as they possibly can. From time to time, hold up the red-light card and have them freeze in place. (D 5 min.)

GREEN LIGHT. Have the children practice moving like different kinds of transportation. When they're ready, hold up the green-light card and have them move as fast as they possibly can. From time to time (or whenever they're going too fast), hold up the red-light card and have them freeze in place. (D 5 min.)

BLINKING LIGHTS. Have children choose which kind of transport they want to be. Bring out your traffic lights. On green, have children go as fast as they can in any direction. On yellow, they go as slowly as possible. And on red, they stop and freeze in place. (D 10+ min.) For advanced play, have half of the room go fast on yellow and slow on green. (Everyone still stops on red.)

Scooters

SYNCHRONIZATION. Part of learning to work with others is finding a mutual rhythm and pace.

MERGING TRAFFIC. Lay a length of rope along the floor (10'–12') and have the children form 2 lines, 1 on each side of the rope, and standing shoulder to shoulder. When the light turns green (green-light card), the right lane merges into the left lane by stepping across the rope, each child moving in behind the child next to him. Repeat in the other direction. Then have the 2 lines walk forward. At the end of the rope, show them how to merge into 1 line by alternating right-left-right-left. Once they have the idea, pick up speed. (D 10–15 min.)

IT'S A CONVOY. Put down a hoop and have 1 child (the lead truck) stand inside it. Have the other children stand around him. Tell the lead truck to walk in circles inside the hoop. When he hears you toot the truck's horn, he selects another child to be a truck and form a convoy. Shoulder to shoulder, they hold hands and continue to circle around, with the lead truck staying inside the hoop and the other truck outside it. Continue turning in circles and adding trucks until all the children are marching shoulder to shoulder in a big circle (similar to the sweep of a second hand around a clock face). (D 3–5 min.)

CHOO-CHOO TRAIN. Select a child to be the train engine to lead the train. The engine decides the pace, and the others (the cars) have to keep up. Put red, yellow, and green traffic lights around the room or playground to signal where the engine needs to slow down or speed up. Invite the engine to go in any direction—in circles, under tunnels, jumping, hopping, and so on. At the end of each round, switch engines. Also, explore different ways to link the train cars, such as holding hands, linking arms, or standing side by side. (D 10–20 min.)

Skedaddlers

MANAGING DISORDER. Knowing when to speed up and when to slow down helps children develop full control of their bodies so they can stop and think.

TRAFFIC JAM. Create a roadway system on the floor with tape or on the pavement with chalk. Use this activity to have a general discussion of traffic rules. For instance, red means stop, green means go. When you're ready to play, have each child decide what kind of vehicle to be and pick a destination. As they play, they must follow the traffic rules you've discussed in order to get to their destination. From time to time, hold up a stop sign and introduce another traffic rule. For instance, add a speed bump (slow down!) by laying a rolled-up gym mat across the road. Add 1 new traffic rule each time you play. (D 10–15 min.)

OFFICER GO-AROUND. Repeat the "Traffic Jam" game, only this time Officer Go-Around is on duty! Assign 1 child to play the officer and give him a whistle and stop sign. Have the children take to the road. When Officer Go-Around signals for them to speed up, slow down, turn, or stop, they have to obey while still following all the other traffic rules. (D 10–15 min.)

COPS AND ROBBERS. Repeat the "Traffic Jam" game, but tell children that now a bad guy is on the loose and they have to catch him. And there's a catch: the bad guy doesn't have to follow any of the traffic rules! Choose someone or invite a volunteer to be the bad guy, and have children race and chase until someone tags him. But remember, good guys always follow the rules, even when the bad guys don't, so be sure all the other drivers continue to follow the rules! The tagger becomes the new bad guy, and the chase begins again. (D 10–15 min.)

Squish!
Understanding Pressure and Force

Play dough loves to squeeze and roll,
And stamp and stomp, and even bowl!
But play dough's special secret wish,
Is playing a game called "Squish! Squish! Squish!"

EQUIPMENT

- Soft blanket
- Soft squeaky toy
- Slime
- Play dough
- Tissue paper
- Shape-sorting toy

- Protective plastic sheet
- Sticks, leaves, flowers, blocks, or small toys
- Plastic cup
- 5 paper or cardboard circles, ranging from 1"–5" in diameter

KEY BENEFITS

- Pressure
- Force
- Eye-everything coordination

- Manipulative play
- Fine-motor development

LANGUAGE FOCUS

pull, push, roll

CRITICAL SAFEGUARDS

- Use nontoxic play dough and slime.
- Adult supervision is required at all times to ensure children do not put play dough or slime in their mouths.

TEACHING GEMS

To make homemade play dough, see the recipe on page 198.

ON THE MOVE	WATCH ME GROW	IN THE KNOW

Snugglers

WHY HUGGING WORKS. The sensation of enclosure not only makes baby feel safe and connected, it gives her early indicators of varying degrees of pressure and force.

GENTLE SQUEEZES. Lay baby on the floor, being sure she's warm and comfortable. Maintain eye contact. Gently squeeze down both sides of her body with your hands, then down 1 side at a time. (R 2 times)

PIZZA DOUGH ROLL. Lay baby on her back. Roll up a soft blanket like a rolling pin, lay it on her tummy, and gently unroll it, ensuring that it rolls out smoothly over her torso, arms, and legs. Roll it back up over her body. Turn baby over onto her tummy and repeat. (D 2–3 min.)

WHOOPEE CUSHION. Take a soft squeaky toy and gently press it against different parts of baby's body (arms, legs, tummy, feet). *Squeak!* Next, hold baby in your arms, put the toy between you, and give her a hug. *Squeak!* (D 2–3 min.)

Squigglers

TEXTURE PLAY. Exploring different textures shows little ones that not everything is the same.

MY FIRST SLIME. Hold baby in your lap and put some slime in the palm of her hand. Put your hand on top of hers and squish. Be sure to involve both hands. Take care that baby does not put her fingers in her mouth while playing with slime. (D 2–3 min.)

FOOTPRINTS IN THE DOUGH. Sit baby between your legs on the floor. Take a wad of play dough and press it firmly against her foot. Explore the impression you made together. Repeat with both feet and both hands. (D 2–3 min.)

KARATE KID. Have baby sit facing you. Hold up a piece of tissue paper in front of you so she can't see you. Be sure it's taut. Encourage her to poke holes in the paper to find you. This can also be done by holding up a flatly rolled piece of play dough for a different textural experience. (R 5 times)

Scampers

PLAYING WITH PRESSURE. Controlling the application of force begins with simple pushing and pulling activities.

SQUISH AND DESTROY! Place a wad of play dough within the child's reach and encourage her to grab it, smash it, squish it, squeeze it, pull it apart, and put it all back together again. (D 2–5 min.)

SQUISH AND PUSH. Clear out all the shapes from a shape-sorting toy, give the child a wad of play dough, and assist her to push the dough through the holes. But where did the dough go? Open the lid. Surprise! There it is! (D 3–5 min.)

SAUSAGE MAKING. Lay out a plastic sheet on the floor and sit with the child. Show her how to use her hands to roll play dough forward and backward into a sausage shape. (D 5 min.)

Stompers

CREATIVE PLAY. Children immerse themselves more deeply into play scenarios that they have a hand in creating for themselves.

LOOK AT MY GARDEN GROW. Have children gather materials to grow in their garden (sticks, leaves, flowers, blocks, small toys, and so on). Next, have them flatten out a wad of play dough to form the base, then "plant" their garden, pressing the objects firmly into the dough so that they stand upright. (D 5–10 min.)

SQUISH MOUNTAIN. Have or help children gather up all the well-used play dough and build a mountain as tall as they can. When they're through, tell them to stomp, squish, and squash the mountain as flat as they can! Talk about the transformation from tall to short, narrow to wide. (D 5 min.)

SQUISH BOWLING. Create 10 bowling pins out of play dough and set them up in a diamond shape at one end of the table or floor. Next, have each child make a bowling ball out of play dough. Challenge children to make their balls as round as they can. Next, children take turns bowling. Continue until all the pins are knocked over. (D 5 min.)

Scooters

EXPLORING VARIATIONS IN FORCE. Learning how much force to use fine-tunes muscle strength and control.

SQUISH-CANO. Give children plastic cups and play dough and have them fill the cups to the brim with play dough. Then have them use their thumbs to press down in the center and watch the dough ooze out over the sides of the cups like lava from a volcano. Try again, only this time, cut a small slit in the bottom of each cup and have children press until the dough squishes through the hole in the bottom. (D 5 min.)

SQUISH. Lay out 5 circles on the table increasing in diameter from approximately 1" to 5". Have the child roll up 5 play-dough balls to match the sizes of the circles. Next, have her squish each ball flat, starting with the smallest and continuing to the largest. Talk about how she needs to add more force—squish harder—as the balls get bigger. (D 5–10 min.)

LET'S STICK TOGETHER. Pair up children and give them a big wad of play dough. Call out a body part (such as elbow). They have to hold the wad of dough between them using only their elbows. Add another body part (such as knee). The children have to split the play dough in half and hold the dough between them using their elbows and knees. Continue with other body parts (legs, feet, arms, wrists, hands) until they are completely stuck together without dropping the dough. (D 5–10 min.)

Skedaddlers

PRECISION. Precise outcomes take coordinated, controlled refinements of movement while in motion.

SAUSAGE FACTORY. Explore different ways to roll the play dough into sausages. Start with the hands, then fists, elbows, knuckles, forearms, knees, and so forth. Encourage children to try to keep the sausages *evenly* rolled. Next, have them try rolling with the left hand and right elbow at the same time. (D 5–10 min.)

SAUSAGE SWITCH. Have or help each child break a wad of play dough in half. With the left hand, they roll the dough forward and backward on the table. At the same time, they use the right hand to roll it side to side. Encourage them to try to roll the sausages evenly. Switch sides and repeat. See how long and thin children can roll their sausages in this way. (D 5 min.)

MAKE A MAT. Have the children roll out different-colored play dough into strands of the same length. Working together, have them lay out 4 strands parallel to one another (vertically) and *carefully* weave the other 4 under and over (horizontally) to create a woven play-dough mat. Be sure not to break any of the strands, or you'll have to remove it and start again. *Note:* This provides hands-on practice in delicate movements while giving children an understanding of how materials behave (too thin and it will break, too thick and it will be hard to weave). Assist children as needed. (D 5–10 min.)

Trusty Yellow Rope
Dynamic Equilibrium: Stability in Motion

One day, the children arrived at school and found a great big surprise. Their whole classroom was empty except for 1 piece of yellow rope. Puzzled, they asked their teacher what they were going to do today. Teacher Wendy explained that Trusty Yellow Rope would show them. The children sat down along the rope and waited for the rope to start the lesson. The rope lay quiet on the floor. The children waited and waited. The rope waited and waited. For sure, this was going to be a very long and boring day.

Then Carter, tired of waiting, got up and tugged on the rope to see if it was awake. The rope wiggled. Next, Caitlin got up and tugged on the other end. The rope twisted. Jakie jumped over the rope. Max crawled under the rope. Kaleb walked along the rope. No matter what the children tried, Trusty Yellow Rope played along. They played all day, discovering all the tricks Trusty Yellow Rope had to teach! And when the day was done, everyone agreed that you can always trust Trusty for a day of fun and learning! (And Trusty had fun, too!)

SARAH ALICE LEE

EQUIPMENT
- Towel
- Baby toy
- Ball
- Toy vehicle
- Chair or table
- Ropes of different lengths (substitute masking tape or chalk if necessary)

KEY BENEFITS
- Temporal awareness
- Stability
- Locomotion

LANGUAGE FOCUS
wide, narrow, on, over

CRITICAL SAFEGUARDS
Adult supervision is required at all times when children are working with ropes.

TEACHING GEMS
- Directional activities require commentary with contextual language. Be sure to tell children often where they are (at the *wide* end of the rope, at the *narrow* end of the rope, jumping *over* the rope, walking *on* the rope).
- Automate 1 movement at a time. Complex activities require lots of practice, so repeat an activity as often as the child needs before moving to the next.
- Many of the rope tricks can be tried wherever there is a line, such as on a footpath, in the floor tiles, at a grass edge, or at the edge of the rug or carpet.

Snugglers

DYNAMIC EQUILIBRIUM. Whenever baby moves (or is moved), his brain is adjusting its understanding of the sensations of balance.

TOWEL ROLL. Gently lay baby on an open towel on his back. Lift both sides of the towel just off the ground and gently rock baby from side to side, smiling and keeping eye contact the whole time. Do this slowly so as not to stimulate the moro (startle) reflex. (D 2–3 min.)

TOWEL BALANCE. Fold a towel, then roll it up like a sausage. Lay baby on his tummy lengthwise on the towel and then gently rock him from side to side, supporting him around the hips. Now hold a toy in front of baby's eyes and encourage him to lift his head slightly to see the toy. (D 2–3 min.)

BABY AIRPLANE. Sit down and support baby under his chest and legs so that he is lying flat on his tummy in your arms. Hold him slightly away from your body with his feet toward you. Start gently, gliding baby back and forth by pulling your knees in and out. Next, lift your feet slowly and gently and tilt baby's head ever so slightly toward you. (D 2–3 min.)

Squigglers

MOTIVATING MOVEMENT. Instinctively, babies strive for independent movement from the start. Encourage that instinct with play that makes moving fun.

TUMMY TEASERS. Lay baby on the floor on his back or tummy. Dangle a ball on a rope in front of him. Move it to the left and right, encouraging him to twist and swivel his body to follow it. (D 2–3 min.)

3 OUT OF 4. With baby up on all fours, dangle a ball on a rope in front of him. Move it around him, encouraging him to touch it. This requires him to lift 1 hand up—the first step on the road to crawling. (D 2–3 min.)

I CRAWL, YOU CRAWL. Tie a ball on a rope to your own ankle. Crawl around the floor and encourage baby to follow you. Play keep-away for a few minutes, then allow him to catch you! (D 3–5 min.)

Scampers

DELIBERATE MOVEMENT. Simple challenges, like following a pathway, encourage children to sharpen their skills, even when they get off track.

TRACK CRAWLING. Lay 2 ropes on the floor to create a pathway. Encourage the child to crawl between the ropes. Create different patterns—straight, curved, zigzag. (D 3–5 min.)

ON TRACK. Lay a rope on the floor and encourage the child to crawl along it with 1 hand and leg on each side of the rope. Next, give him a toy vehicle and show him how it runs on the rope. Encourage him to crawl and keep the toy on track. (D 3–5 min.)

TRACK WALKING. Tie the ends of 2 ropes to a chair or table. Hold the other ends approximately waist high for the child and guide him to walk between the ropes from the chair or table to you, holding onto the ropes as he walks. Next, lay the ropes on the floor and repeat the game, having the child walk between them from the chair or table to you. (D 3–5 min.)

Stompers

NARROW AND WIDE. Experiencing the concepts of narrow and wide with their bodies gives children a physical understanding of early math concepts like *greater than* and *less than*.

RIVERBANKS. Lay out 2 ropes on the floor in a narrow *V* shape. Start the child at the pointed end and have him walk the "riverbanks," with 1 foot on each side as the banks get wider. Remind him to try not to fall in the river! Repeat in the other direction, from wide back to narrow. (R 2–3 times)

MONKEYS ON THE RIVERBANKS. Repeat the "Riverbanks" activity, but this time tell the child to walk like a monkey (see page 193). For extra challenge, have him try monkey walking the riverbanks backward! (R 2–3 times)

JUMP THE RIVER. Lay out 2 ropes on the floor in a narrow *V* shape. Starting at the pointed end of the V, encourage the child to jump over the river to the other side. Have him continue to move up the river, making the jump wider each time. Repeat, going from wide back to narrow. (R 1–2 times)

Scooters

MOVING TARGETS. A moving target is a great challenge for developing judgment, timing, balance, and control.

ROPE WAVES. Tie a long rope to a chair or table leg. Hold the end of the rope. Move the rope back and forth on the floor as the child tries to stomp on the rope with 1 foot or jump on it with 2 feet. Next, for solo or group play, have children line up and step or jump over the rope as it goes by. (D 2–3 min.)

WRIGGLE ROPE. Pull a rope along the floor, wriggling it back and forth like a snake as the children take turns trying to stomp or jump on it. Next, pair up the children and have them play the game with 1 wriggling the rope and the other stomping on it. For group play, have the children step or jump over the rope as it wriggles. Change speed as you go to keep the game unpredictable. (D 2–3 min.)

ROPE ROMP. Lay a rope on the floor and have children straddle the rope with 1 foot on either side of it. Start by having them turn in place, crossing their right foot over to the left and left over to the right. Next, encourage them to jump up and down with their feet on either side of the rope. Then, demonstrate how to jump and turn in midair, landing with 1 foot on either side of the rope. Have them see how many times in a row they can "rope romp"! (R 3–5 times)

Skedaddlers

MIDAIR MANEUVERS. Moving in midair, such as doing scissor jumps, takes time to master, but it signals highly sophisticated, whole-body control and concentration.

SCISSORS WARM-UP. Place a rope on the floor. Position the child facing the rope and tell him he is standing *behind* it. Have the child put 1 foot in front of the rope and keep the other behind it. Lift the child up over the rope. Have him practice a scissor-legs movement in midair, then put the child back down in his original position. Lift the child again and have him switch his legs and land. (R 3–5 times)

SCISSOR STEPS. Place a rope on the floor. Have the child place 1 foot in front of the rope and the other behind it and then leap up and switch his legs in midair. Watch to be sure the child is using only his legs and that his upper body remains facing forward. Stop after each leap. Next, work toward continuous movement—leaping and switching legs 2 times, then 3, then 4, increasing speed until his movement is fluid. (R 5–10 times)

SCISSORS FLYING. Warm up with "Scissor Steps." Next, have the child stand in the scissor position straddling the rope. Have him put 1 hand on his tummy, the other hand on his back. Give him a chance to practice switching hands from front to back. Then, put it all together in an opposite arm-leg movement (right arm on tummy with left leg forward, left hand on tummy with right leg forward). Encourage him to build up speed to create a smooth tempo for synchronized movement. (R 5–10 times)

Incredible Shrinking Target
Incrementalism: Adjusting Movements by Degrees

You have to be on your toes all the time, especially when you encounter the Incredible Shrinking Target! It's so smart, it knows how well you're doing, and just when you think you're right on target, it shrinks. Want to give it a try?

EQUIPMENT
- Music
- Baby toy
- Blanket
- Pillows
- Soft ball
- Apple
- Bowl with water
- Rope
- Chalk
- Sponge
- Hoops of varying sizes
- Beanbags
- Milk bottle
- Small chair
- Clothespins

KEY BENEFITS
- Self-organization
- Changing direction and changing plane
- Changing and judging speed
- Changing and judging force

LANGUAGE FOCUS
center, middle, between, forward, back, left, right

CRITICAL SAFEGUARDS
Never leave children unattended around water.

TEACHING GEMS
• When using equipment of different sizes, be sure to use words to remind children which hoop to aim for. "Aim for the large hoop." "Aim for the center hoop." Say it as they do it. Remember: Language + Experience = Understanding.
• Providing children with the physical experiences and opportunities to adapt their bodies through positioning, pacing, and pressure allows for increased accuracy, deliberation, and control of body movement.
• Provide visual cues for children to stand on and aim for, such as dots or lines on the floor, so children can mark their progress.

SARAH ALICE LEE

ON THE MOVE
WATCH ME GROW
IN THE KNOW

 ### Snugglers
TINY MOVES. Infants are just beginning to explore the world of movement. Go slowly so the brain has time to process the moves.

SLOW DANCE. Hold baby's feet and create a gentle and fluid repetitive pattern (up and down, in and out). Sing as you "dance" the feet to a very slow beat. Repeat, this time holding and dancing baby's hands. Try putting on music that has 60–80 beats per minute. (D 2–3 min.)

BABY ROBOT. Repeat the "Slow Dance" activity, only this time move very slowly, an inch at a time (think robotic movements). This gives baby a sense of moving in increments. (D 2–3 min.)

EYE-FLYING FUN. Lay baby on her back and hold a toy above her within her field of vision. Capture her attention, then very slowly fly it around in circles and dip it down toward baby. If she reaches for it, let her grab hold with her hands or her feet. (D 2–3 min.)

ON THE MOVE	WATCH ME GROW	IN THE KNOW

Squigglers
STEERING. Getting to where you want to go means learning how to steer yourself.

BABY-GO-ROUND. Lay baby on her tummy on a blanket with her favorite toy on a slippery surface. Holding 1 side of the blanket, gently and slowly turn in a circle, stopping and starting for fun. Change direction. As baby becomes more comfortable, change direction randomly. (D 1–2 min.)

PLAY-GO-ROUND. Lay baby on her tummy on the floor and kneel down next to her on her right side. Play and talk to her, encouraging her to turn toward you. Slowly make your way around to her left, stopping to play at different points along the way. Change the pace of your movements. Try this with baby lying on her back, too. (D 3–5 min.)

BABY STEERING. Create a short crawling path with pillows on either side and encourage baby to crawl through. Next, add a gentle curve to the path to encourage her to steer herself through, over, and under things. (D 3–5 min.)

Scampers
DYNAMIC TARGETING. As little ones learn to move, they must simultaneously learn to cope with a world that's in motion, too!

KIDDIE DODGEBALL. Put the child on all fours. Gently roll a soft ball to her as she crawls. Roll the ball in front of her, beside her, around her, toward her, and away from her, enticing her to chase it. (D 3–5 min.)

APPLE SNATCH. Float an apple in a bowl of water. Sit the child on your lap and show her how the apple bobs up and down. Encourage her to pick it up with 1 hand, then the other, then both hands. And remember, *never* leave a child unattended around water. (D 2–3 min.)

WRIGGLE AND STOMP. Once the child is steady on her feet, lay out a small piece of yellow rope and wriggle it. Encourage the child to try to step on the rope. If she succeeds, stop wriggling and cheer her success! (D 2–3 min.)

Stompers
ADJUSTMENTS. Fully realized body control requires the ability to adapt movements while in motion.

STOP THE MUSIC. To explore changing speeds, sing a song and encourage the child to dance with you. Sing slowly and slow down your movements. Sing fast and speed up. Stop singing and both of you freeze in place! Repeat several times, then mix up the order in which you speed up, slow down, and stop. (D 3–5 min.)

MY FIRST LINE DANCE. To explore changing direction, create several simple dance steps with the child. Be sure the choreography includes stepping forward and back, left and right. Repeat the dance several times until the child is familiar with the steps, then change the speed of the song from fast to slow. (D 3–5 min.)

STEP IT UP. To explore different-sized movements, repeat the dance steps you created for "My First Line Dance," only this time have the child exaggerate the movements, taking really big, long steps and then really small, short steps. For the finale, mix up the big and small steps. (D 3–5 min.)

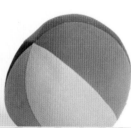

Scooters

LEARNING TO AIM is more than getting a child ready for sport. It's teaching her how to apply trial and error while measuring distance, direction, and force.

CLEAN THE BOARD. Draw a 3-ring target (the bull's-eye) on the wallboard. Give a child a wet sponge and have her step back several paces and shoot for the bull's-eye. The sponge will leave a wet spot. Examine where the sponge left its mark and talk about where it is in relation to the center of the bull's-eye. Let the child try again. Celebrate when she gets closer to the bull's-eye. Allow children to take a few turns each and continue rotating the play so everyone gets lots of tries. *Note:* If you don't have a board, you can play this on an outside surface, such as the building wall or a fence. (D 5–10 min.)

THROUGH THE HOOP. Hang a large hoop about 1' off the ground. Explore all the ways to move through the hoop without touching the sides. For instance: (1) Step through facing forward. (2) Step through facing backward. (3) Crawl through hands first. (4) Crawl through feetfirst. With a group, have them hold hands and go through the hoop without letting go. Now set up 3 different-sized hoops and try again. (D 2–3 min.)

SHOOT THE HOOP. Hang a large hoop. Give a child several beanbags and have her stand several paces back from the hoop. Show her how to aim and throw underhand. Repeat until she gains confidence, then have her step back 1 pace to increase challenge. Allow children to take a few turns each and continue rotating the play so everyone gets lots of tries. To change it up, hang the hoop at different heights. (R until children are confident at each distance)

Skedaddlers

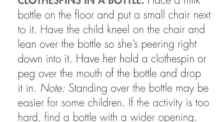

PRECISION MOVEMENTS require full control over the muscles for even the smallest changes in movement.

SHOOT THREE HOOPS. Hang 3 different-sized hoops next to one another. Give each child 3 beanbags and have children stand several paces back from the hoops. Begin at the largest hoop and have them shoot until they succeed. (Depending on the number of children, this can be done together or each can take their turn.) Then move to the next hoop. When children have been successful with all 3, go around to the other side, retrieve the beanbags, and shoot the hoops from that side. Next round, stand 1 pace back. (R 3–5 tries per hoop)

THE INCREDIBLE SHRINKING TARGET. Make a loop out of a piece of rope and put it on the floor. Give a child several beanbags and have her step back several paces. Have her throw the beanbags underhand into the loop. Once she's showing confidence, tighten the loop to make a smaller target. Continue to make the target smaller as she masters the activity. For group play, have the children stand around the loop. Once each has a try, tighten the loop for a smaller target. (R 3–5 tries)

CLOTHESPINS IN A BOTTLE. Place a milk bottle on the floor and put a small chair next to it. Have the child kneel on the chair and lean over the bottle so she's peering right down into it. Have her hold a clothespin or peg over the mouth of the bottle and drop it in. *Note:* Standing over the bottle may be easier for some children. If the activity is too hard, find a bottle with a wider opening. (R 3–5 tries per child)

49
CONTROL

Chicken Switch
Physical Problem Solving

Mama Cluck has a henhouse full of eggs to hatch. But they keep swapping nests! Can you help Mama Cluck keep track of her soon-to-be-hatchlings?

EQUIPMENT
- Textured small balls
- Buttons, sewing needle, and thread
- Baby socks
- Clear plastic container
- Warm water
- Baby-safe soap, shampoo, or bubble solution
- Beanbags
- Foam balls, pillows, and other soft materials
- 3" plastic balls
- Basket
- Cardboard box
- Plank (approximately 8" wide and 8'–10' long)
- Buckets of varying sizes
- Chair or low table
- Large spoon or spatula
- Hoops
- Feathers

KEY BENEFITS
- Positioning
- Pressure and force
- Strength and stamina
- Spatial awareness
- Problem solving

LANGUAGE FOCUS
through, inside, between

CRITICAL SAFEGUARDS
- Ensure children are supervised at all times when using small objects.
- Assist and support children when playing on inclines or uneven surfaces.

TEACHING GEMS
- To increase challenge, switch out small balls for the beanbags.
- Some children may not be able to cluck and move at the same time, so be prepared to cluck for them.

SARAH WHITING

ON THE MOVE   WATCH ME GROW   **IN THE KNOW**

Snugglers
THE BEGINNINGS OF BODY CONTROL. Body awareness is the starting point for all of baby's future physical capabilities, and it begins with his sense of touch.

THIS IS ME! As you sing baby his favorite song, massage and play with his right hand *only*. Sing the song again, playing only with his left hand. Tomorrow, focus on his feet. Each day, choose left and right parts of his body (elbows, knees, ears) and give them focused attention. (D 2–3 min.)

TEXTURE MASSAGE. Gather several textured small balls, such as a smooth plastic ball, foam ball, rubber ball, and pompom. Slowly but firmly massage baby's arms and chest with each ball. Next, massage his legs with each. Turn baby over and massage his back the same way. (D 3–5 min.)

BABY TAP DANCING. Sew buttons to the bottoms of baby's socks. Sit baby on your lap on a smooth floor. Assist baby to tap his toes on the floor. Put on some music and tap away! (D 2–3 min.)

Squigglers

CONTROL THROUGH STRENGTH. Little muscles build strength gradually over time, which leads to better and more refined control.

EGGBEATER. Fill a clear plastic container with warm water and baby-safe soap, shampoo, or bubble solution. Assist baby to play with the water, stirring and churning the water with your hands to create foam. Explore the foam—rub it in his hands, blow it up in the air and try to catch it, and so on. *Note:* Ensure that baby does not put soapy fingers in his mouth or eyes. (D 3–5 min.)

HUMPTY DUMPTY. Sit on the floor with baby straddling your knee facing you. Recite the "Humpty Dumpty" rhyme (see page 198). On "had a big fall," gently tip baby to the right. Watch to see him reach his hand out. Tip him until he touches the floor, then bring him back to center. Repeat in the other direction. Next, play again with baby facing away from you. (D 3–5 min.)

BEANBAG CRAWL. Create a pile of beanbags on the floor. Encourage baby to crawl over to the pile. When he begins to engage in the play, lay out a path of beanbags along the floor for him to follow. Try this with foam balls, pillows, and other soft materials that challenge his power to crawl. (D 5–10 min.)

Scampers

BALL PLAY. Early ball play provides simple ways for children to experience exerting control over their environment. See pages 196–198 for the basics of ball play with young children.

EGG SCRAMBLE. Scatter 3" plastic balls around the floor and go on an "egg" hunt with the child. To encourage crawling, show him how to return the eggs to a basket on the floor. Spill them out and start again. (D 5–10 min.)

MAIL-ORDER EGGS. Cut two 5" holes in a cardboard box. Encourage the child to "mail" 3" plastic balls in the box. Show the child what happens when you pick up the box and shake it. Dump the balls, chase them, and mail them again. (D 5–10 min.)

EGG MARBLES. Scatter 3" plastic balls around the floor. Show the child how to flick the balls around the floor. Press down on them and watch them pop. Bat at them, kick them, and so forth. Watch the balls knock into each other and scatter even more. Chase them down and play again. (D 5–10 min.)

Stompers

MANIPULATIVE SKILL. Managing the body while managing objects is a big advance toward total body control.

HIGH NEST. Place a basket of 3–5 beanbags on top of a gentle incline (a small mound or plank). Encourage the child to scamper up to the top, gather an "egg," and come back down. Support the child as he makes his way up and down. (R 3–5 times)

CLUCKETBALL. Set up large, medium, and small buckets on the floor. Have the child stand several paces back and shoot beanbags into the buckets. Have him cluck every time he scores! Next, raise the targets up off the floor onto a chair or low tabletop for a game of clucketball! (D 5–10 min.)

EGG RELAY. A classic game without the mess! Have the child hold a beanbag on a large spoon or spatula and race to the end of the play area without dropping it. With a group of children, line them up on either end of the play area and have them hand off the egg to the next player. (D 3–5 min.)

Scooters

AUTOMATICITY. As children master and automate physical capabilities, they are better able to listen carefully, follow instructions, and think on their feet.

EGGEVATOR. Have 2 children stand back to back; place a beanbag between them. Now have them squat down together, cluck, then stand back up without dropping the "egg." Next time, as they squat, have them flap like a chicken, too! (R 2–3 times)

EGG HUNT. Have each child select a different-colored ball and put it in a basket. Empty the basket on the floor and watch the "eggs" scatter. Each child has to chase and catch his egg. When he finds it, he must squat down, flap, and cluck like a chicken! Next time, children can chase the eggs while walking like chickens. (R 2–3 times)

EGG SNATCH. Mama Cluck has finally gotten all her eggs in one basket. But here comes the fox! Have each child select a different-colored ball and put it in a basket. Put the basket on the other side of the room. When you crow, "Cock-a-doodle-do!" all the children race to the basket, find their egg, and carry it to home base. For round 2, children carry the egg without using their hands. For round 3, they carry the egg without using their hands and while walking like chickens! Don't forget to cluck! (D 5–10 min.)

Skedaddlers

TRAFFIC. Group games challenge the body and brain to navigate both physical and intellectual "traffic"—to move while simultaneously thinking about the game's objective.

EGGS IN BASKETS. Lay out 1 hoop (the basket) for each child in the game and give each child a different-colored beanbag (the egg). When you crow, "Cock-a-doodle-do!" each child has to find an empty hoop and cluck when he drops his egg into it. If 2 eggs wind up in 1 basket, encourage children to work together to resolve the problem. Next round, have them hold the beanbag between their knees and walk like chickens! (R 3–5 times)

CHICKEN SWITCH. Play "Eggs in Baskets" again. This time, add multiple rooster crows. Each time you crow, "Cock-a-doodle-do!" the children have to retrieve their egg and put it into a different basket. Again, if 2 eggs wind up in the same basket, encourage them to resolve the problem themselves. For round 2, children walk like chickens (and don't forget to cluck!). (R 3–5 times)

FOX IN THE HENHOUSE. Play "Chicken Switch," only this time remove 1 hoop from the game (so you have one fewer hoop than the number of players). Play round 1. One child will have a homeless egg, but he's not out of the game: he becomes the fox! For round 2, everyone plays while the fox switches his egg for someone else's. On the next round, the player whose egg was switched becomes the fox. (R 3–5 times)

Mission: Possible
Synchronization

Mr. Gummer Upper is sticky-fingered, and he's really up to no good. Wait till you hear what he's planning now! He's after the Dynamo Diamond. We've got to stop him—can you help?

EQUIPMENT

- Music
- Pot lids
- Wooden spoon or stick
- Chair, bucket, and pot
- Quest Chest (see page 190)
- Chalk
- Blocks (in different colors)
- Ladder
- Chairs, ropes, and other materials for laser field
- Dynamo Diamond (object such as a large rock)
- Ropes

KEY BENEFITS

- Body rhythm
- Problem solving
- Body positioning
- Body awareness

LANGUAGE FOCUS

under, over, through

CRITICAL SAFEGUARDS

Adult supervision is needed at all times to complete the missions successfully.

TEACHING GEMS

Creating a ritual for starting this or any game gives the child time to mentally prepare for the activity and builds anticipation for the fun to come. For instance, each time you play Quest Chest, start with "The Quest Chest Creed" (see page 198).

ON THE MOVE	WATCH ME GROW	IN THE KNOW

 ## Snugglers

MODELING MOVEMENT. Using different dance steps helps baby internalize what it feels like to experience complex whole-body movement patterns.

BABY CHEEK TO CHEEK. Hold baby close against your body with your cheeks touching. Put on some slow (waltz) music and dance slowly and gently. Slowly turn around several times, then turn the other way. Hold baby up to your other cheek and repeat. (D 3–5 min.)

BABY TWIST AND TURN. Hold baby in your arms, supporting her in an upright position. Turn on some slow music and very slowly do the twist. Twist side to side, and twist down and up, too. Select another song with a slightly faster tempo and try it again. (D 3–5 min.)

BABY TANGO. Hold baby in your arms and do the tango: 3 steps forward, 1 to the left, 3 steps back, 1 to the right. Gently dip to the left, then to the right. End the dance with a grand dip—support baby's head and neck and slowly lower her so that her feet are above her head for a few moments. (D 3–5 min.)

| ON THE MOVE | WATCH ME GROW | IN THE KNOW |

Squigglers
BABY NAVIGATION. Movement is not only the road to independence, it is also baby's first experience with getting and staying in sync with her environment.

MOUNT HUG-ME. Lie on the ground next to baby. Supporting her at all times, pull her up on top of your chest for a great big hug. Next, guide and support her to climb back down to the floor by turning her so that she is reaching the floor feet first. As she gets the idea of transitioning from the floor to you and back to the floor, guide and support her to try to make the climb herself. (D 2–3 min.)

ROCKY MOUNTAIN HUGS. With baby on all fours, lie down in front of her and support her to put both hands up on your chest. Bring her all the way up on your chest for a big hug. Encourage her back to the all-fours position while she's still on your chest. Supporting her at the waist, bounce and rock gently to give her a sense of movement in the all-fours position. (D 2–3 min.)

MISSION: CRAWL. Once baby is crawling, create an obstacle course for her with your own body. Lie down and support her to crawl over your chest or down the length of your body. Get on all fours and encourage her to crawl under you. Place her on your leg and have her "straddle crawl" up your leg. Do these activities slowly and playfully so baby understands the game and starts to initiate other contact points between you. (D 3–5 min.)

Scampers
MUSIC AND MOVEMENT. Music provides a natural beat and rhythm that helps synchronize movement.

MISSION: BODY BEAT. Turn on some slow music and assist the child to make simple repetitive hand-body movements in time to the music (for example, have her pat her knees, clap her hands, or tap her tummy). Ensure these are done slowly so the child can feel and understand the pattern. Repeat, incorporating rattles or other sound-making toys. (D 2–3 min.)

MISSION: LOUD! Lay out a selection of pot lids and invite the child to choose 1 for each hand. Encourage her to bang them together to explore the sound. Sing her favorite song and have her bang to the beat. (D 2–3 min.)

MISSION: BANG! Have the child select a wooden spoon or stick. Together, explore the sounds of the environment. Bang your drumstick on the ground, a chair, a bucket, a pot. Move outside and discover sounds there. Sing the child's favorite song and encourage her to bang to the beat. (D 2–3 min.)

Stompers
ROLE PLAYING. Learning is easier when you're on a mission. Simple, playful objectives help children follow an idea from start to finish.

MISSION: QUEST CHEST. Select a quest (such as things that are blue, things that make noise, or small things). Have children go on a quest to fill their Quest Chest. When they're done, they can take the items out and explore what they all have in common. (D 3–5 min.)

MISSION: THE PACKAGE. Your mission: Deliver the package (but don't touch it!). Establish a start and finish line some distance apart (such as the length of the room). Use objects from the Quest Chest to move the chest from the start to the finish. Show the children the package and have them select whichever items they need from the Quest Chest to get the job done. Model what you want the child to do, then stand back and let them problem-solve to get the package delivered. (D 3–5 min.) Next time, have them try it solo, or as a team passing the package off from 1 teammate to the next.

MISSION: SHAPE SNOOPER. With chalk, draw 3 shapes in 3 different colors on the floor or pavement. Call out 1 shape at a time and have children take turns walking around it. Once children are gaining confidence, mix up the movements—for instance, walk the shape backward or sideways, on tippy-toe, or jumping with both feet. Next, try the game with 2 children at once. They must stay on the line and navigate "intersections" on their own. Add more shapes and more children for extended challenge. (D 3–5 min.)

Scooters

PHYSICAL PROBLEM SOLVING requires the body and brain to work in harmony.

MISSION: MAZE HAZE. Your mission: Get safely through the maze. Draw a maze on the pavement or floor, making sure the lines are different colors. Have each child follow 1 line at a time from beginning to end without stepping off the line. Next, have 4 children play at once, navigating "intersections" on their own without stepping off the line. (D 5–10 min.)

MISSION: DOUBLE-CROSS. Draw a new maze on the pavement or floor, all in the same color. Place different-colored blocks at the end of each line and call out a color for the child to find. Now play "Mission: Maze Haze." Midway through the game, swap the blocks around so the players have to find a new route. (D 5–10 min.)

MISSION: CLIMB THE LADDER. Despite all our best efforts, Mr. Gummer Upper stole the Dynamo Diamond from the mine. Let's go find him! Your mission: Use the ladder to get out of the mine. Lay a ladder on its side on the floor (so the rungs are vertical). Hold the ladder steady and have children crawl in and out of the rungs from 1 end of the ladder to the other. (D 3–5 min.)

 ## Skedaddlers

MAKE YOUR OWN PATH. When a child is in control of her whole body, she can use her body to solve problems.

MISSION: LASER FIELD. Set up a laser field (see instructions on page 198) and put the Dynamo Diamond at the end of the play area. Mr. Gummer Upper has hidden the diamond and laid a trap for us! Your mission: commando-crawl (belly-crawl) under all the lasers without touching them to get to the diamond, retrieve it, and bring it back the same way you came. Repeat, stepping over each laser (without touching it). Repeat again, this time alternating stepping under and over. (D 10–20 min.)

MISSION: SECRET CODE. Repeat "Mission: Laser Field," only this time remove 4 ropes to start. Give the child a secret code pattern for navigating the course (for example, under-over-over-under-under-over). Have the other children call out the secret code as each player navigates the course. (D 10–20 min.)

MISSION: FIND THE DIAMOND. Mr. Gummer Upper is at it again! He's taken the famous Dynamo Diamond and hidden it! String ropes across the room or hallway in different directions, like a spiderweb. The mission is for children to get through the web without touching any of the ropes, retrieve the diamond, and bring it back through the web. Add more ropes for added challenge. To make it a pairs challenge, have 2 children go through the web, passing off the diamond to each other on each step. (D 5–10 min.)

Additional Resources

//

Activity 2, Listening Mice

The Quest Chest

The Quest Chest can be as simple as a cardboard box or plastic pail, but it's even more fun if the child makes her own. Get out the arts and crafts supplies and encourage the child to make her own Quest Chest by drawing a picture or writing her name on 1 side of the container. Then, after each quest, have her add a souvenir from that quest by drawing more pictures or gluing on objects she's found. Keep the Quest Chest for this and other games in which collecting items is required.

Listening Mice

(sung to the tune of "Three Blind Mice")
Listening mice. Listening mice.
Turn on your ears. Turn on your ears.
To hear what nobody else can hear,
No matter how far, no matter how near.
When somebody's talking, you turn on your ears.
We're listening mice. Listening mice.

Activity 3, Different Drummers

I Hear Drummers

(sung to the tune of "Frère Jacques")
I hear drummers. I hear drummers.
Rum-a-tum-tum. Rum-a-tum-tum.
Rat-a-tat-a-pitter-pat. Rat-a-tat-a-pitter pat.
Here they come! Here they come!

Activity 10, Roll-Over Rover

Roll Over

(sung to the tune of "Ten in the Bed")
There were ten in the bed, and Rover said,
"Roll over! Roll over!"
So they all rolled over and one fell out!
Woof!
(Repeat for nine, eight, seven, and so forth.)

Activity 11, The Spinnagans

Spinnagans Go Round and Round

(sung to the tune of "London Bridge")
Spinnagans go round and round,
Round and round, round and round!
Spinnagans go round and round,
Let's get dizzy!

Alternative lyrics:
Spinnagans go front and back . . .
Spinnagans go side to side . . .

Activity 15, Tortoise and Hare: After the Race

Tortoise and Hare

(sung to the tune of "This Old Man")
Tortoise and Hare, off they go.
Hare goes fast, and Tortoise goes slow.
But they'll get there somehow in their special way,
Fast or slow, they're off today!

Tortoise moves slowwwwwwwww, careful he goes.
Step by step he tippy-toes.
But he'll get there somehow in his special way,
Slow and steady, he's off today.

Hare runs fast! Zooming past!
Out of breath—oh, can she last?
But she'll get there somehow in her special way
Fast and ready, she's off today.

Activity 17, Wiggle Where?

Can You Wiggle?

(sung to the tune of "Do Your Ears Hang Low?")
Can you wiggle over here? *(wiggle right)*
Can you wiggle over there? *(wiggle left)*
Can you wiggle really tall? *(wiggle high)*
Can you wiggle really small? *(wiggle low)*
Can you wiggle out ahead? *(wiggle front)*
Can you wiggle back instead? *(wiggle back)*
Can you wiggle everywhere? *(wiggle whole body)*

Instructions for Making "Me" Cards or Dice

Many of the activities call for picture cards or dice that you will need to make in advance. Take photographs as indicated; print the photos on cardstock or glue them to a six-sided cube, such as a tissue box. If possible, work with older children to create their own "me" cards or dice.

"Face" cards (for squigglers): Take photos of baby's eyes, ears, nose, mouth, cheek, and chin.

"Me" cards (for scampers, stompers, scooters, and skedaddlers): Photograph the child's head, shoulders or arms, hands, tummy, hips or legs, and feet.

"Me Too" cards (for stompers, scooters, and skedaddlers): Photograph the child's elbow, ankle, hip, neck, knee, and fingers. If you'd like, create additional "Me Too" cards with other parts of the body.

"Where" cards (for skedaddlers): Photograph the child holding a cardboard arrow in six different positions:

- Above his head, arrow pointing up

- Bending down, arrow pointing to his toes

- Hands holding arrow out in front of him, pointing toward camera

- Hands holding arrow behind his back, pointing away from camera
- Hand out to the left, arrow pointing left
- Hand out to the right, arrow pointing right

Kissing Menu

Kissing trails: Kiss baby up and down his arms and legs, across his tummy, and so on.
Blowing kisses: Kiss baby and blow gently.
Finger kisses: Kiss your finger and place the kiss on baby.
Tapping kisses: Kiss your finger and tap-tap-tap the kiss down baby's arms and legs, across his body, and so forth.
Butterfly kisses: Tickle your eyelashes on baby.
Smooches: Loudly kiss baby with a big *smooch* sound!
Poppers: Loudly kiss baby with a big *smooch* sound and a *pop*!
Raspberries: Create silly sounds (*pfft*) while kissing baby.

Activity 18, Getting to Know Me

Scrubbily-Bubbily-Tubbily

(sung to the tune of "Row, Row, Row Your Boat")
Wash, wash, wash my face,
Wash it nice and clean.
Scrubbily-bubbily-tubbily-too,
Look at how I gleam!

Dry, dry, dry my face,
Dry it really quick.
Scrubbily-bubbily-tubbily-too,
Drying lickety-split!

(Repeat with other body parts.)

Getting to Know Me

(additional lyrics for "Head, Shoulders, Knees, and Toes")
Head, shoulders, knees, and toes. Knees and toes.
Head, shoulders, knees, and toes. Knees and toes.
And eyes and ears and mouth and nose.
Head, shoulders, knees, and toes. Knees and toes.

Ankles, elbows, feet, and seat. Feet and seat.
Ankles, elbows, feet, and seat. Feet and seat.
And calves and hips and waist and cheeks.
Ankles, elbows, feet, and seat. Feet and seat.

Belly button, shins, and chin. Shins and chin.
Belly button, shins, and chin. Shins and chin.
And heels and thighs and a great big grin!
Belly button, shins, and chin. Shins and chin.

Activity 23, Game Day

Ring Around the Bull's-Eye

(sung to the tune of "Ring Around the Rosie")
Ring around the bull's-eye.
Ring around the bull's-eye.
Ready? Ready?
Let's jump to _____!

(Repeat with "Hop around the bull's-eye," "Skip . . . ," "Tiptoe . . . ," and so on.)

Checkerboard Diagram

Activity 24, Steposaur Steps

Behindadon Rhyme

Behindadon is oh so long,
She cannot find her tail.
Three spins to the left.
Three spins to the right.
"Oh look! My tail has scales!"

Activity 26, On the Road to Cartwheeling

Hickory Dickory Dock

Hickory dickory dock,
The mouse ran up the clock.
The clock struck one,
The mouse ran down.
Hickory dickory dock.

Activity 27, Grabbypillar

Grabbypillar Went Climbing

(sung to the tune of "The Bear Went Over the Mountain")
Grabbypillar went climbing,
Grabbypillar went climbing,
Grabbypillar went climbing,
With all one hundred legs.

With all one hundred legs.
With all one hundred legs.
Grabbypillar went climbing,
And that's a lot of legs!

Grabbypillar came back down,
Grabbypillar came back down,
Grabbypillar came back down,
With all one hundred legs.

With all one hundred legs.
With all one hundred legs.
Grabbypillar came back down,
And that's a lot of legs!

Grabbypillar Went Rolling

Grabbypillar went rolling,
Grabbypillar went rolling,
Grabbypillar went rolling,
With all one hundred legs.

With all one hundred legs.
With all one hundred legs.
Grabbypillar went rolling,
And that's a lot of legs!

The Grabby Twins Went Out to Play

The Grabby Twins went out to play,
The Grabby Twins went out to play,
The Grabby Twins went out to play,
And played one hundred games.

And played one hundred games.
And played one hundred games.
The Grabby Twins went out to play,
And that's a lot of games!

The Grabby Twins Went Up and Down

The Grabby Twins went up and down,
The Grabby Twins went up and down,
The Grabby Twins went up and down,
One hundred times a day.

One hundred times a day.
One hundred times a day.
The Grabby Twins went up and down,
And that's a long, long way!

Activity 28, Don't Drop Fidgety Fox

Ideas for "Don't Drop Fidgety Fox"

- One child gives another child a piggyback ride.
- Two children create a basket with their arms by crossing their arms over each other and holding on to each other's wrists. Fidgety Fox sits in the basket.
- The group circles around Fidgety Fox and carries her by the arms and legs.
- Fidgety Fox lies on a blanket, and the group lifts the blanket.
- Fidgety Fox stands on one child's toes, and that child walks.
- The children line up, and Fidgety Fox makes her way down the line, stepping on everyone's toes.
- The children lie down, and Fidgety Fox crawls over them.
- Be sure to let children invent their own ways (always standing by for safety, of course).

This Little Piggy

This little piggy went to market. *(wiggle big toe)*
This little piggy stayed home. *(wiggle second toe)*
This little piggy had roast beef. *(wiggle middle toe)*
This little piggy had none. *(wiggle fourth toe)*
And this little piggy cried, "Wee, wee, wee!" all the way home!
(wiggle pinky toe)

(If you wish, substitute a different animal, such as "this little mousy.")

Activity 29, Escape from the Zoo (also Activity 33)

There's More to Crawling and Walking Than Meets the Eye

Crawling and walking are considered major milestones in early childhood movement—and rightfully so.

Crawling and Walking

Crawling and walking assist development in a number of important ways:

ORIENTATION. When a child is first learning to crawl and walk, the shift from horizontal to vertical opens up new experiences in orientation and positioning.

MIDLINE DEVELOPMENT. Crawling and walking signal maturing physical coordination. Crawling in particular is an essential midline activity that grows and strengthens connections between the right and left hemispheres of the brain—which makes cognitive processing faster and richer.

MOTOR PLANNING. Placing one foot in front of the other means the ability to organize movements into specific patterns and, over time, to automate them.

STEERING AND NAVIGATION. Learning to modify movements (to change direction, speed, and force) starts in earnest when children begin to move for themselves. Not only does this help a child avoid bumping into things, but navigating the body is also the very beginning of critical reasoning and problem solving.

BODY AWARENESS. Crawling and walking build on the brain's growing understanding of the body as a whole unit with moving parts that act together *and* independently of one another.

SPATIAL AWARENESS. Likewise, the simple act of moving your body from here to there creates opportunities to develop a better understanding of space and how the whole body (and its parts) fit into the environment.

STRENGTH DEVELOPMENT. When the arm and leg muscles move into position to carry the body's weight, muscle development accelerates.

EYE DEVELOPMENT. The eyes are maturing right along with the body. During the crawling-to-walking period, focal distance increases and depth perception comes on board to help the child see where he's going.

FREEDOM TO EXPLORE. Perhaps most important of all, independent movement unlocks independent exploration.

All this is just what happens when children are crawling and walking in the traditional manner. Now imagine what happens when you show kids other ways to crawl and walk. What follows is a list of ideas you can apply to many of the Smart Steps activities to change them up, add challenge, or just for the fun of it!

A Couple of Definitions to Start

Here are a few shorthand terms you should know when working with these movements and all the Smart Steps activities.

OPPOSITION MOVEMENT, or to move *in opposition*, refers to opposite leg–opposite arm movement. For instance, in walking or marching, the human gait alternates right leg–left arm, left leg–right arm.

SAME-SIDED MOVEMENT alternates between the right side of the body (right arm and leg move together) and the left side of the body (left arm and leg move together).

ISOLATION MOVEMENT is moving with only one part or one side of the body while the rest of the body is still, such as hopping on one foot.

Fun Ways to Get from Here to There

TUMMY CRAWLING

COMMANDO CRAWLING. The child crawls on the tummy using opposition movement.

SEAL CRAWLING. The child crawls on the tummy using just the arms, while keeping the feet still. *Note:* If need be, tie a loose scarf around the feet to remind the child to keep his feet still.

FROG CRAWLING. The child crawls on the tummy, using just the hips, legs, and feet to push the body while keeping arms still at the sides.

WORM CRAWLING. The child crawls on the tummy, keeping arms at the sides and legs still, and rocks back and forth to wriggle forward.

ONE-ARMED COMMANDO. The child crawls on the tummy using the left arm and leg to propel the body while keeping the right side of the body still. (Repeat on the right side.)

CROCODILE COMMANDO. Same-sided crawl on the tummy.

ON ALL FOURS

TRADITIONAL CRAWLING. Crawl on all fours (hands and knees) using opposition movement.

MONKEY WALKING. Stand and put both hands on the floor (bottom in the air). Walk on the hands and feet in opposition.

BEAR WALKING. Stand and put both hands on the floor (bottom in the air). Walk same-sided on the hands and feet.

CROCODILE CRAWLING. Crawl same-sided on all fours.

CATERPILLAR CRAWLING. Stand and put both hands on the floor (bottom in the air). Walk the hands out away from the feet, then walk the feet back up to the hands.

BEETLE CRAWLING. Crawl on elbows and knees using opposition movement.

CRAB CRAWLING. Sit on the floor with the hands on the floor positioned under the shoulders. Push up onto the hands and feet (tummy facing up, parallel to the floor).

ON TWO FEET

TIPPY-TOES. Stand up on the toes and walk in opposition.

HEELIES. Stand up on the heels with the toes off the ground and walk in opposition.

TIPPY-HEELS. Walk in opposition with one foot in "Tippy-Toes" position and one in the "Heelies" position (see above).

HEEL-TOE WALKING. Walk in opposition by placing one foot in front of the other, putting the heel of the front foot right against the toe of the back foot.

ANKLE MEET ANKLE. Walk sideways, stepping the right leg out to the side and then bringing the left leg over to meet the right. Repeat in the other direction.

DO THE SHUFFLE. Shuffle the feet so they never leave the ground and walk in opposition.

DO THE SKATE. This is like "Do the Shuffle," but with long, skatelike strides in opposition.

PENGUIN WALKING. Put the heels together and point the toes outward. Keep the feet on the floor and waddle forward by rocking side to side.

PIGEON WALKING. Point toes together (pigeon-toed), keeping legs straight, and walk in opposition.

KNOCK-KNEED. Point the knees toward each other so they are touching and walk in opposition. (It may be easier to start children off with a soft toy or foam ball trapped between the knees, so they feel the need to keep the knees turned in.)

DUCK WALKING. Crouch down low with legs out to the side and the bottom between the legs. Walk in opposition. (Don't forget to quack!)

CROSS-WALKING. Walk in opposition, crossing one foot over the other. *Note:* This requires advanced midline development, so it may be difficult for early walkers to attempt.

And of course, don't forget to do all these moves backward, too!

Activity 30, Let's Go to Hopscotch Camp

Traditional Hopscotch Rules

Basic Rules

- Players must hop on one foot in each single space. They must jump on both feet in side-by-side spaces, one foot in each square.
- Players may not touch the lines. If you touch the lines, you lose your turn.
- Players must hop over any squares with markers in them. If you step on a square with a marker, you lose your turn.
- Players must pitch their markers within the squares. If the marker goes outside the lines, you lose your turn.

Game Play

To start, the player pitches her marker into the #1 square. She must hop over the #1 space and continue to hop along the game board in order: 2, 3, 4–5, 6, 7–8, 9, Home.

When she lands on the Home space, she must turn and return along the path: 9, 8–7, 6, 5–4, 3, 2. If there are other markers on the board during her turn, she must hop over those spaces.

On her return, when the player reaches the #2 space, she must stop and, while balancing on one foot, lean over and pick up her marker. With her marker in hand, she may then hop on space #1 and off the board.

On the next round, the player must pitch her marker to the next space on the board.

The first player to complete nine rounds successfully wins.

Simplified Hopscotch

For children who are just getting comfortable with hopping, here are a few quick ways to make hopscotch more accessible to them:

- Shorten the board to a 5- or 7-step game.
- Offer children the option to hop up the board on one foot and jump two-footed on the return trip.
- Loosen the restrictions for stepping on the lines. If part of a child's foot lands in the square, that counts, and she can continue.
- Loosen the restrictions for hopping over spaces with markers. If children need to, they may jump two-footed over those spaces.
- Balance can be an issue when picking up a marker. If need be, allow the child to stand on two feet to pick up her marker.
- Restrict the number of players to two per game.

Activity 32, Pop Go the Bubbles

Homemade Bubble Recipe

- 1 tablespoon sugar
- 3 tablespoons boiling water
- 9 tablespoons liquid detergent
- 1 teaspoon glycerin

Stir sugar and water together until sugar is dissolved. Add remaining ingredients. Cover and store for three days before using.

Activity 33, Crawlimals

Moving Songs

(all sung to the tune of "The Old Grey Mare")

Note: For these songs, we've kept the lyrics very simple and repetitive for young children, which allows you to improvise as you see fit. For instance, use the child's favorite animal or pet, and change the gender as needed.

Inchy Inchworm: Up and Down

Inchy inchworm, he crawls up and down a lot,
Up and down a lot,
Up and down a lot.
Inchy inchworm, he crawls up and down a lot,
And that's how he gets there.

Chirpy Bluebird: In and Out

Chirpy bluebird, she flies in and out a lot,
In and out a lot,
In and out a lot.
Chirpy bluebird, she flies in and out a lot,
And that's how she gets there.

Funny Little Monkey: Tangled Up

(crossed-over legs and arms)

Funny little monkey, he gets tangled up a lot,
Tangled up a lot,
Tangled up a lot.
Funny little monkey, he gets tangled up a lot,
And that's how he gets there.

Little Green Frog: Out and Back

(out to the side and back to the center)

Little green frog, she jumps out and back a lot,
Out and back a lot,
Out and back a lot.
Little green frog, she jumps out and back a lot,
And that's how she gets there.

Little Chickadee: Side to Side

Little chickadee, he steps side to side a lot,
Side to side a lot,
Side to side a lot.
Little chickadee, he steps side to side a lot,
And that's how he gets there.

Little Grey Hare: Front and Back

Little grey hare, she hops front and back a lot,
Front and back a lot,
Front and back a lot.
Little grey hare, she hops front and back a lot,
And that's how she gets there.

Big Old Bear: To the Right

Big old bear, he walks to the right a lot,
To the right a lot.
To the right a lot.
Big old bear, he walks to the right a lot,
And that's how he gets there.

Big Old Whale: To the Left

Big old whale, she swims to the left a lot,
To the left a lot,
To the left a lot.
Big old whale, she swims to the left a lot,
And that's how she gets there.

Silly Little Puppy: Round and Round

Silly little puppy, he moves round and round a lot,
Round and round a lot,
Round and round a lot.
Silly little puppy, he moves round and round a lot,
And that's how he gets there.

Bold Little Mole: Down and Under

Bold little mole, she digs down and under a lot,
Down and under a lot,
Down and under a lot.
Bold little mole, she digs down and under a lot,
And that's how she gets there.

Baby Elephant: Slow

Baby elephant, he goes very slow a lot,
Goes very slow a lot,
Goes very slow a lot.
Baby elephant, he goes very slow a lot,
And that's how he gets there.

Speedy Little Pony: Fast

Speedy little pony, she runs really fast a lot,
Runs really fast a lot,
Runs really fast a lot.
Speedy little pony, she runs really fast a lot,
And that's how she gets there.

Silly Little Spider: Stops and Goes

Silly little spider, he stops and goes a lot,
Stops and goes a lot,
Stops and goes a lot.
The silly little spider, he stops and goes a lot,
And that's how he gets there.

Playful Little Kitty: Left and Right

Playful little kitty, she runs left and right a lot,
Left and right a lot,
Left and right a lot.
Playful little kitty, she runs left and right a lot,
And that's how she gets there.

Animal Parade: All Sorts of Ways

The animal parade, it moves in all sorts of ways,
In all sorts of ways,
In all sorts of ways.
The animal parade, it moves in all sorts of ways,
So, how do you get there?

Activity 35, Crocodile Flop

Crocodile Flop Songs (Coordination Activity 35)
(sung to the tune of "Here We Go Round the Mulberry Bush")

Flopping Crocs (moderate tempo)

Crocodiles flopping in the sun,
In the sun. Oh, what fun!
Crocodiles flopping in the sun.
Look! Here comes the rain!

Dancing Crocs (fast tempo)

Crocodiles dancing in the rain,
In the rain. They entertain!
Crocodiles dancing in the rain.
Look! Here comes the snow!

Tromping Crocs (slow/stop tempo)

Crocodiles tromping in the snow,
In the snow. Ohhhh, soooo sloooow.
Crocodiles stompppppping in the snooooow.
Look! They're crocsicles!

Crocodiles Left and Right

Crocodiles flopping left and right,
Left and right. What a sight!
Crocodiles flopping left and right.
Listen to them roar!

Activity 38, Put Your Tap Shoes On

The Quackities
(all sung to the tune of "This Old Man")

Quackity Tap

Quackity tap,
Quackity tap,
Duckie dancing
Tippity tap.

Put your tap shoes on,
And tap a tap or two.
Quackity tap,
I'm dancing with you!

Quackity Flap

Quackity flap,
Quackity flap,
Duckie twirling,
Flippity flap.

Put your tap shoes on,
And flap a tap or two.
Quackity flap,
I'm twirling with you!

Quackity Snap

Quackity snap,
Quackity snap,
Duckie waddling,
Snippity snap.

Put your tap shoes on,
And snap a tap or two.
Quackity snap,
I'm waddling with you.

Quackity Clap

Quackity clap,
Quackity clap,
Duckie cheering,
Clippity clap.

Put your tap shoes on,
And clap a tap or two.
Quackity clap,
I'm cheering for you.

Quackity Nap

Quackity nap,
Quackity nap,
Duckie snoozing,
Nippity nap.

Put your PJs on,
And nap a tap or two.
Quackity nap,
I'm sleepy, too.

Five Little Ducks

Five little ducks went out one day,
Over the hills and far away.
Mother Duck said, "Quack, quack, quack, quack,"
But only four little ducks came back.

Four little ducks went out one day,
Over the hills and far away.
Mother Duck said, "Quack, quack, quack, quack,"
But only three little ducks came back.

Three little ducks went out one day,
Over the hills and far away.
Mother Duck said, "Quack, quack, quack, quack,"
But only two little ducks came back.

Two little ducks went out one day,
Over the hills and far away.
Mother Duck said, "Quack, quack, quack, quack,"
But only one little duck came back.

One little duck went out one day,
Over the hills and far away.
Mother Duck said, "Quack, quack, quack, quack,"
But none of the five little ducks came back.

Sad mother duck went out one day,
Over the hills and far away.
Mother Duck said "Quack, quack, quack, quack,"
And all of the five little ducks came back.

Activity 40, The Beanbaggles Juggle

Round and Round the Garden

Round and round the garden (*make circles with your fingertips on baby's skin*)
Went the teddy bear.
One step, two step, (*walk your fingers*)
Tickle under there! (*tickle gently*)

Activity 41: Hopper Frog

Hopper Frog

(*sung to the tune of "John Jacob Jingleheimer Schmidt"*)

Boing, boing, boing! There goes Hopper Frog!
Hard to keep up with him!
Wherever Hopper goes, he's up on all his toes.
When he goes boing, boing, boing, the fun begins!
Ribbit.

Skip to the Pond

(*sung to the tune of "Skip to My Lou"*)

Skip, skip, skip to the pond.
Skip, skip, skip to the pond.
Skip, skip, skip to the pond.
Skip to the pond this morning!

I'll find another frog jumpier than you!
I'll find another frog jumpier than you!
I'll find another frog jumpier than you!
Skip to the pond this morning!

Skip, skip, skip to the pond.
Skip, skip, skip to the pond.
Skip, skip, skip to the pond.
Skip to the pond this morning!

I can jump higher, higher than you!
I can jump higher, higher than you!
I can jump higher, higher than you!
Skip to the pond this morning!

Skip, skip, skip to the pond.
Skip, skip, skip to the pond.
Skip, skip, skip to the pond.
Skip to the pond this morning!

Activity 42, My First Volleyball (also Activity 49)

Play Ball! The Basics of Throwing, Bouncing, Catching, and Kicking

Perhaps the most perfect toy ever invented is the red rubber ball. It yields to pretty much anything a child wants to play. And it's jam-packed with kinetic value. For instance:

PROPRIOCEPTION. When a ball is coming at you, it's a real-life lesson in how objects move through space. (And maybe a lesson in how to duck, too!)

SPATIAL AWARENESS. When the ball is moving and the child is moving, too, the brain is learning valuable concepts in the areas of perceptual judgment, estimation, and prediction. The brain is simultaneously calculating speed, direction, and distance.

TIMING. Simply bouncing a ball gives children an immediate and tangible experience with rhythm and timing.

EYE FITNESS. Tracking a moving object such as a bouncing ball not only is great preparation for future ball-playing skills, but also builds muscles in the eye for smooth eye tracking.

EYE-EVERYTHING COORDINATION. Depending on the game, the hands, feet, arms, legs, and even the head can be involved in getting the ball to where you want it to go. And, of course, the eyes are directing all that action.

MANIPULATION. Learning to bat a ball is a great first experience in working with tools to achieve your aim.

POWER. Chasing after a ball is great motor motivation.

CONTROL. A rolling ball is one of life's first lessons in unpredictability. Learning to control the ball's dynamics fine-tunes muscle adaptation and control.

How to Teach Basic Ball Skills

Learning to play ball is a step-by-step process. Developing ball-playing skills can start very early and continue all through life.

When introducing the idea of ball play, start with beach balls or balloons in balloon bags (if appropriate—many settings do not allow balloons for children under age five) instead of balls. Beach balls and balloons move slowly, which makes it easier for young eyes, hands, and feet to keep up.

And when focusing on introducing new skills, do not bring in ideas of distance or targets. Focus on the foundations. And continually narrate and affirm what the child is doing right as a way of reinforcing her movements, regardless of what happens to the ball. For instance, "I like how you keep your hands up ready to catch."

Play often and practice without the ball and then with the ball. This will help her develop the familiarity and muscle memory needed to one day automate her ball-playing skills.

Following are guidelines for basic ball-handling skills. Little ones will know what feels right to them. Always follow their lead. Technique will come with maturity (and midlines). For now, the most important thing is to enjoy the play.

ROLLING. Have the child stand with her feet apart. Show her how to bend down and reach her hands between her feet to touch the ground behind her. Then, like digging sand in the sandbox, have her pull her hands forward together along the ground and come back to standing. Practice that a few times without the ball and then try it with the ball. Go slow at first so she memorizes the sensation of the movement and reliably releases the ball so that it rolls along the ground. Pay less attention to distance at first. Once the child has mastered the movement, then move on to build up speed and thrust. And when she's ready, reverse the movement, rolling backward between her legs.

UNDERHAND TOSS. Repeat the rolling steps, but this time have the child bring the ball through the legs and up off the ground before releasing it, so the ball flies in the air.

BOWLING. Have the child choose which hand she wants to bowl with. For this example, we'll choose the right. Have her stand with her left foot forward and right foot back, with the knees bent. Before introducing the ball, show her how to swing her arm straight back, then forward in one smooth motion. Practice the move several times so she has the feel for it. Next, with the child maintaining the same stance, introduce the ball. Have her hold it underneath with one hand. (That may take practice, too.) Have her swing the ball back and forward, letting it roll off her fingertips.

OVERHAND THROW. To throw like the big kids do, you need strong arms! Start by having the child turn her body sideways from the target. (If she's right-handed, her left foot is toward the target.) Now, have her raise her arms to shoulder height and bend her elbows so that her hands are pointing to the sky (90-degree angle at the elbow), and then make a fist. These are "strongman arms." Next, have her point with the nonthrowing hand to the target and then move the throwing hand past the ear, straightening out to meet the pointing hand. Practice this move, repeating the sequence: "Make a strongman, point, and throw." Once she's comfortable with this three-step sequence, introduce the ball. Again, each time she tries, repeat the movement sequence verbally so she feels, hears, and sees the process.

BASIC BOUNCING. Have the child stand with feet apart, holding the ball in front of her with both hands. Have her drop the ball and try to catch it on the rebound. Even if she happens to catch it on the first try, practice this for quite a while to be sure she's developing her reaction time to the bounce.

ADVANCED BOUNCING. Sit with the child and the ball on the floor. Show her how to pat on top of the ball with both hands. Pat, pat, pat. Keep the rhythm even as she pats, using a song or nursery rhyme to establish the beat. Then, stand and repeat the basic bouncing steps. Once she's all warmed up, have her try to pat the ball back down. This will take lots of practice, of course, but half the fun for her will be chasing the ball. And once she does get the hang of it, start to count the bounces for her: 1, 2, 3. Keep track of her personal best so she's always encouraged to do more the next time.

Once the two-handed bounce is mastered, repeat all the steps with one hand, then the other.

LEARNING TO CATCH. Start by having the child hold both hands out like a plate, with the elbows tucked into the tummy (the "catch-ready" position). Place the ball in her arms and have her hug it. Do this several times. Now, with her in catch-ready position, tell her you're going to toss the ball to her. Before you do, have her show you how she's going to hug the ball. Then, gently toss the ball to her.

INTRODUCTION TO KICKING. Have the child stand holding onto a support for balance. Show her how to lift her knee and swing her foot back behind her, then swing it forward. Do this slowly at first, building up speed and thrust. Practice until she feels comfortable with the movement. Next, try it without holding on for support. This will help her feel for balance as well as feel the kicking movement. When the child is steady, she's ready.

Put a ball in front of her approximately 12" away from her kicking foot, and let her kick! Have her practice kicking from a stationary position until she shows signs of eye-foot consistency.

LEARNING TO BAT. Have the child hold her arms out to the side at shoulder height, then slowly flap the arms across the body and back out over and over again. Next, give the child a flyswatter or plastic spoon for each hand and have her repeat the flapping movement. Now, hang a beach ball from the ceiling. Using the same flapping movement, have the child try to bat the beach ball.

Activity 43, Finger Fun

Sunny and Cloudy
(sung to the tune of "Short'nin' Bread")
Sunny and Cloudy
Sunny and Cloudy
Wave, wave, wave
To Sunny today.

Cloudy and Sunny
Cloudy and Sunny
Clap, clap, clap
That Cloudy away.

Itsy-Bitsy Spider
The itsy-bitsy spider
Climbed up the waterspout.

Down came the rain
And washed the spider out.

Out came the sun
And dried up all the rain,

And the itsy-bitsy spider
Climbed up the spout again.

If You're Happy and You Know It
If you're happy and you know it, clap your hands.
If you're happy and you know it, clap your hands.
If you're happy and you know it,
Then your face will surely show it.
If you're happy and you know it, clap your hands.

Table Football
- Crinkle up a small piece of paper into a tight ball.
- Put goals, such as paper cups, on either end of the table.
- Each player sits at either end of the table and takes turns trying to flick the football into the goal.

How to Make Gloop
Mix together:
- 2 cups corn starch
- 1 cup water
- Child-safe food coloring (optional)

Activity 46, Squish!

Play Dough Recipe
- 3 teaspoons cream of tartar
- 6 cups boiling water
- 1½ cups salt
- Child-safe food coloring of your choice
- 6 teaspoons cooking oil
- 6 cups flour

Mix the first five ingredients together until the salt is dissolved. Add the flour and mix until there are no lumps. Let it cool. Knead it to make it smooth.

Note: To make more than one color, divide the recipe in half or in thirds and make each batch a different color. Store dough in an airtight container.

Activity 49, Chicken Switch

Humpty Dumpty
Humpty Dumpty sat on a wall.
Humpty Dumpty had a great fall.
All the king's horses and all the king's men
Couldn't put Humpty together again.

Activity 50, Mission: Possible

The Quest Chest Creed
We're on a quest
To fill our chest
With treasures you will never guess
From north and south
And east and west.
We will find the most
AMAZINGEST _____!

Setting Up a Laser Field
Take lengths of rope, string, or yarn and secure them to the walls and sturdy furniture, crossing them in random directions to create a spiderweb effect. Make sure the "lasers" are about 12"–18" off the ground so children can crawl under or step over them. *Note:* Making a laser field is a really fun activity to do with the children as well, so include them in the project if you can.

Glossary

asensory: lacking sensory input

auditory discrimination: the ability to hear the difference between sounds

auditory figure ground: the ability to focus on a sound while shutting out other sounds

auditory sequencing: the ability to hear patterns in sound, as in music or poetry

automaticity: the ability to do something automatically, without having to think about it. In young children, automaticity emerges through repetition.

belly crawling: lying on tummy, pulling oneself along the ground

bilateral movement: mirrored movement. When one side of the body moves, the other side or part mirrors that movement. For instance, young babies reach for things with both hands.

body mapping: having a visual image of what you look like

commando crawling: lying on tummy, pulling oneself along the ground

cross-lateral movement: movement that crosses the midlines, such as reaching across your body with your right hand to touch your left shoulder

directionality: understanding directional words, such as *over, in front of, behind, left, right, up, down, top,* and *bottom,* in many different contexts. Directionality aids young children in understanding the nuances of language, such as in the phrases *the top of the page, the top of your head,* and *the top of the table.*

dynamic equilibrium: the ability to maintain balance while moving

dynamic orientation: the ability to maintain orientation or the direction you are facing while moving

eye tracking: the ability for the eye muscles to move in any direction smoothly, including up and down, in and out, left and right, in a circle, and so on

homolateral movement: moving one side of the body while the other side remains still, such as scooting on a scooter, hopping, and handwriting

individualize down: to simplify by taking away a component of the movement, such as stepping down from a balance beam and balancing along a line on the ground

individualize up: to add challenge by adding another (more complex) component to the movement being carried out, such as walking along a plank while balancing a beanbag on your head

lateral movement: movement that uses an opposite arm–opposite leg motion, such as walking, running, or marching. This requires the child knowing the body has two sides and that each side can operate independently.

locomotion: the act of moving the body from one place to another

midlines: three imaginary lines that divide the body into halves, including left and right, front and back, and top and bottom. Integrating midlines allows independent body part movement to occur, which unlocks the ability to achieve complex, coordinated movement patterns and high-performance skills.

moro or startle reflex: serves as a baby's alarm bell. When baby is startled, the body goes stiff; the arms, legs, and fingers spread; and the eyes open wide. This reaction usually lasts for a few seconds, then baby relaxes again.

motor overflow: an unconscious movement of one body part while another part of the body is moving deliberately, such as the mouth moving or the tongue sticking out while a child is learning to write

motory: obstacle or challenge course

object permanence: understanding that what is out of sight still exists even though it can't be seen

opposition movement: movement that requires parts of the body to move in opposition to each other, such as left arm–right leg followed by right arm–left leg when walking

parachute reflex: to maintain sitting balance, a baby will spread the legs wide to create a wide base and instinctively use the arms to avoid falling sideways

perpetual-focus learning (PFL): focusing on one concept, such as learning left and right, and using it in a variety of different ways throughout a given period of time

physicalities: key ingredients of the Kinetic Scale, which provides the road map to a well-balanced physical diet. The six physicalities are the senses, balance, intuition, power, coordination, and control.

pincer grip: grasping an object by squeezing it with the pointer finger and the thumb

proprioception (intuition): the body's internal sense that determines position in relation to other things, gravity, and how much force or effort to exert on an object to achieve a desired result

push-away reflex: involuntary pushing reflex on the bottom of the feet. When a baby's feet are touched, baby will push back against the touch.

seriation: the arrangement of a collection of things into a specific order or sequence, such as from smallest to biggest

six Ds: methods for adjusting an activity according to a child's current abilities, including dynamics, distance, direction, duality, duration, and difficulty

sound discrimination: the ability to hear the differences between sounds

synchronization: moving at the same time as another person

temporal awareness: sense of judging distance, speed, and timing, as in catching or kicking balls

vestibular system: the brain's internal sense of balance, which underpins all independent movement. Movements such as rolling and slow spinning encourage vestibular development.

visual discrimination: the ability to visually detect differences in things seen, such as shape, pattern, and color

Additional Reading

//

Bulluss J., and P. Coles. *Smart Start with P.M.P.: A Perceptual Motor Program Manual*. Mordialloc, Victoria: Smart Starters, 2007.

Cheatum, B.A., and A.A. Hammond. *Physical Activities for Improving Children's Learning and Behavior*. Champaign, IL: Human Kinetics, 2000.

Connell, G., and C. McCarthy. *A Moving Child Is a Learning Child: How the Body Teaches the Brain to Think (Birth to Age 7)*. Minneapolis: Free Spirit Publishing, 2014.

Copple, C., and S. Bredekamp, eds. *Developmentally Appropriate Practice in Early Childhood Programs Serving Children Birth Through Age 8*. Washington, DC: National Association for the Education of Young Children, 2010.

DeBenedet, A.T., and L.J. Cohen. *The Art of Roughhousing*. Philadelphia, PA: Quirk Books, 2010.

Hannaford, C. *Smart Moves: Why Learning Is Not All in Your Head*. Salt Lake City, UT: Great River Books, 2007.

Sunderland, M. *The Science of Parenting*. New York: DK Publishing, 2016.

White, J. *Every Child a Mover: A Practical Guide to Providing Young Children with the Physical Opportunities They Need*. London, England: The British Association for Early Childhood Education, 2015.

Index

About the Authors

Gill Connell is a globally recognized presenter and child development authority, specializing in the foundations of learning through movement and play. She provides developmental expertise to parents, preschools, schools, and companies such as Hasbro, Inc., based on her more than 30 years in preschool and primary education. She is the former national director of Gymbaroo Preschool Activity Centers and the founder of Moving Smart, Ltd. (movingsmart. co.nz), which offers resources, tools, trainings, and workshops. She coauthored the books *A Moving Child Is a Learning Child: How the Body Teaches the Brain to Think* and *Moving to Learn: An Essential Guide for All Parents, Carers and Educators*. Gill lives in New Zealand, and travels regularly to the United States.

Wendy Pirie, M.H.Sc., is a consultant in preschool movement and the director of TimberNook New Zealand, which offers camps where children grow and learn through active, creative outdoor experiences. She has a special interest in the growth and development of the child through the relationship between the body and the brain. She is also passionate about empowering parents and educators to play with and engage children. Wendy lives in New Zealand with her husband and three sons.

Cheryl McCarthy is a former vice president of intellectual property development for Hasbro, Inc. She is a 30-year veteran of the world of children's play, specializing in young children's storytelling and entertainment. As executive producer, she managed the creative development of properties such as My Little Pony, Candy Land, Mr. Potato Head, and many other beloved children's icons. She is currently the creative director at Moving Smart, Ltd. Cheryl is the coauthor of *A Moving Child Is a Learning Child: How the Body Teaches the Brain to Think*. She lives in Massachusetts.

More Early Childhood Educator Resources
from Free Spirit Publishing

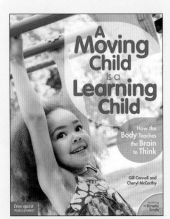

A Moving Child Is a Learning Child
How the Body Teaches the Brain to Think (Birth to Age 7)

For teachers, caregivers, clinicians, special education practitioners, and parents of children ages 0–7. 336 pp., full color, photos, paperback, 7¼" x 9¼"

The Thinking Teacher
A Framework for Intentional Teaching in the Early Childhood Classroom

For early childhood teachers and providers, instructional coaches, directors, administrators. 216 pp., paperback, 7" x 9"

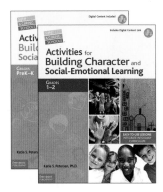

Activites for Building Character and Social-Emotional Learning
Grades PreK-K

For educators, grades preK–K. 160 pp., paperback, 8½" x 11"

Grades 1–2
For educators, grades 1–2 208 pp., paperback, 8½" x 11"

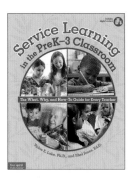

Service Learning in the PreK–3 Classroom
The What, Why, and How-To Guide for Every Teacher

For educators, grades preK–3. 224 pp., paperback, 8½" x 11"

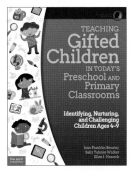

Teaching Gifted Children in Today's Preschool and Primary Classrooms
Identifying, Nurturing, and Challenging Children Ages 4–9

For educators, grades preK–3. 248 pp., paperback, 8½" x 11"

Interested in purchasing multiple quantities and receiving volume discounts?
Contact edsales@freespirit.com or call 1.800.735.7323 and ask for Education Sales.

Many Free Spirit authors are available for speaking engagements, workshops, and keynotes.
Contact speakers@freespirit.com or call 1.800.735.7323.

For pricing information, to place an order, or to request a free catalog, contact:

Free Spirit Publishing Inc.
6325 Sandburg Road • Suite 100 • Minneapolis, MN 55427-3674
toll-free 800.735.7323 • local 612.338.2068 • fax 612.337.5050
help4kids@freespirit.com • www.freespirit.com